THE BLOCK MANAGER

THE BLOCK MANAGER

*A True Story of Love in the
Midst of Japanese American Internment Camps*

Judy Mundle

Open Books Press
Bloomington, Indiana

Published by Open Books Press, USA

www.OpenBooksPress.com
info@OpenBooksPress.com

An imprint of Pen & Publish, Inc.
www.PenandPublish.com
Bloomington, Indiana
(314) 827-6567

Paperback ISBN: 978-1-941799-66-6
Hardcover ISBN: 978-1-941799-67-3
e-book ISBN: 978-1-941799-68-0

Library of Congress Control Number: 2018965387

Printed on acid-free paper.

Cover concept by Tim Day

Contents

Acknowledgments

Since there were many family and friends identified in this book, I have changed everyone's name to maintain anonymity of all parties. The story you are about to read is true.

Thank you to the many family members and friends who shared their valuable insight and kept my battery charged on my journey of writing this memoir. I am forever indebted to you.

It is with a most humble heart that I dedicate this book to my eternal friend Janet. We became acquainted when I found myself working in a small office, sitting at a desk next to hers. Ours was an unlikely friendship, considering she was thirty-five years my senior. Janet taught me how to prepare Japanese dishes and to make her famous sour cream chocolate chip cake. We rode to work together. I was mesmerized when she spoke about World War II, and I can still recall the moment when she first shared her story of being assigned the job of block manager at an internment camp in America. All I could say was, "Are you kidding me?"

It's now forty years later. Our friendship has flourished over the years as we have shared life's joys and sorrows together. Words can scarcely express the admiration and affection in my heart for Janet. I could never have a higher honor in my life than her trust in me to share her soul with me. To me, Janet's story is one for the ages.

Judy Mundle
St. Louis, Missouri

PART 1

GAMAN

Prologue

Ray was eager to show off the latest addition to his favorite Japanese garden. As he explained how he'd picked up the large boulders from the side of the interstate, lugged them into his truck, and then arranged them perfectly in place, I smiled at him. He was proud of the spectacular Japanese garden he created for Mr. Busch.

"Mr. Busch told me how much he liked my garden, and I told him the whole country likes his beer." His grin filled his face as he spoke.

I continued smiling, but I could only think of the irony of the moment. "Does Mr. Busch know you grew up with gardeners tending to your family gardens at your estate in Japan?"

"Oh no, I never mention that."

"Ray, you have worked hard to build such a successful business. Who would have thought twenty-five years ago that you would ever be allowed to return to America?"

We walked together through the rest of the garden as I pondered the moment. It was 1986. We lived a comfortable, quiet, simple life as middle-class Americans in St. Louis. Ray was creating Japanese-style gardens for members of the August Busch family, the American beer icons. However, during the twenty years from the onset of World War II to 1961, our lives had been anything but ordinary.

My husband and I met in the most unlikely way, when I was assigned to be his block manager in a Japanese internment camp mandated by the United States, after Pearl Harbor changed our lives forever.

Chapter 1
Welcome to Internment Camp, 1942

The process was strikingly orderly, considering we Japanese were following orders to pile all our worldly possessions into suitcases and prepare to be jailed indefinitely. No one barged into our homes or handcuffed us to take us away, as had happened to the Jewish people in Europe, although we had been shunned and chastised like the Jews since Pearl Harbor. The government simply notified all the West Coast Japanese when and where we would be moved to so-called assembly centers.

I don't know of anyone in Stockton, California—my hometown—who refused. Many people were fiercely angry; all were scared. Four to five thousand Japanese lived in Stockton then, and we shared the same fate at the hands of the US government: on May 10, 1942, we forfeited our homes, jobs, private lives, beloved pets, worldly goods beyond what we could carry, and all freedoms guaranteed by the Constitution of our country. Everyone I knew or knew of did as instructed by the authorities.

An outsider watching us enter our confinement would have seen fear, sorrow, apprehension, anger, resignation, and patience in our eyes—but also peace and calm. I was proud of my people. It was part of our culture to be obedient, a tradition from ancient times, and many of us Japanese Americans coped with the government-mandated internment by clinging to peace and calmness.

As we were about to enter prison, I was not bitter. Through the years of confinement, I was not bitter, and to this day, I am not bitter. It was wartime, and I accepted my fate. And so, the Wartime Civilian

Control Administration (WCCA) took control of my life in May of 1942.

I was twenty-two when my family joined the line to enter the internment camp. We stood together, patiently waiting, as the line progressed slowly. Mom told us to hold on to our bags and not let them get dirty. Five-year-old Tom couldn't hold the weight of even a bag packed as lightly as possible, so big brother Will carried Tom's bag along with his own two heavy bags.

When it was our turn to register with the authorities, Pop asked me to help, since I was much more comfortable with English than he was. I spelled out the names of all ten Hayashis, and the lady put a checkmark by each of our names on her prepared list. Before she gave us instructions for finding our new home in the internment camp, she repeated each of our names. Then she politely looked up at me.

"Miss Hayashi, your family may proceed on. Would you please step to the side? Our superintendent, Mr. Ben Richardson, would like to speak to you."

"Is something wrong?" I asked.

"No. You will understand shortly. Please wait back here. You will be able to join your family later."

The other woman seated at the desk turned to me. "The Hayashi family has been assigned to block four. As a family of ten, you will have two rooms, number five and number six. You'll find a pile of beds down the next pathway along the barracks to the left. Take one for each member of your family. Then go to your mess hall and get a mattress from the stack to put on each bed. There are separate barracks for the ladies' and men's restrooms and showers. You'll eat all your meals in the mess hall at eight a.m., noon, and five p.m. Leave your bags here so they can be inspected. We're working as fast as possible, but we're backed up now, so you'll just have to leave them here. You can come back later and reclaim them after they've been checked, and you'll be given more instructions as needed in the mess hall. Next, please."

Pop didn't want to walk away with the family and leave me behind.

"Move on," said the woman at the desk. "She'll join you shortly."

My family begrudgingly moved on as instructed. I knew my parents did not trust anyone at that moment. How could they? *Why* would they? No one trusted them—that was certain. I'm sure they were just as terrified and confused as I was about what the officials could possibly want with me.

I tried to be brave as I stood where I was told, but I was petrified.

The bureaucrats, wearing their WCCA badges, processed us with no expression of emotion or empathy. They weren't rude. They weren't kind. They were just doing as instructed by the chain of command, from President Roosevelt and General DeWitt to the WCCA to the clerk at the desk. I wondered if it occurred to any of them what they were really doing to us or bothered them that they were participating in this mass incarceration of innocent people. Did they really believe we were a threat that must be dealt with or—as they told us—that we must be isolated for our own protection?

The whole scene was surreal. On these same fairgrounds, I had sold origami and other trinkets we made at the Women's Club. I'd walked around with my friends during the fair, an annual event in our community. My family had come here to see the fireworks on July 4. The irony of this struck me as I stood quietly where I'd been told. Independence Day, and now imprisonment day—both taking place at the same spot.

I told myself to remember *gaman*—patience with dignity.

Then Mr. Richardson, a tall, slender man with a pointy nose, approached me. He wore a shiny badge.

"Miss Hayashi," he said. "I understand you are fluent in Japanese and English."

"Yes, I am," I said.

"You have been assigned the job of block manager. Please follow me."

Off I went, following the strange man.

Job? Block manager? What was he talking about? He led me into a room with chairs around its walls. Several Japanese men were already seated when we walked in. Mr. Richardson told me to take a seat, and I did. I was scared out of my mind. Why was I singled out from the rest of my family? What was going on? Mr. Richardson left the room. No one said anything. I waited for what seemed like an hour until another Japanese man was escorted into the room and told to sit down with the rest of us.

This time, the man in charge stayed in the room, which now contained nine Japanese men and me. He began to speak.

"My name is Mr. Ben Richardson. Please call me Ben, if you like. I am the superintendent of the Stockton Assembly Center. Congratulations—you have been identified as bilingual in English and Japanese and also as a trustworthy Japanese person. You will be paid eleven dollars per month by the government to serve as block managers at this camp. As block managers, you will be responsible for each resident in your block. Every day at ten p.m., you will complete a bed check to make sure each person is present in his or her assigned room. If any of your residents have any grievances, you will report these to the office. If any of your residents are not in their rooms as assigned or are otherwise not compliant with the rules of this camp, you will report them to the superintendent in the office. Also, if there are disagreements, you need to attempt to intervene and diffuse the situation. If that is not possible, you need to contact the office for assistance."

One man raised his hand. "Excuse me—do I have to take this job as block manager? I would prefer not to."

The man in charge didn't react aggressively; he simply stated he'd been given the names of the people selected to be block managers and that ten more would arrive tomorrow, completing the group.

"I'm sorry, sir," said Mr. Richardson, "but you are not permitted to decline this job. Each of you will play a vital role in the safety and security of everyone at Stockton Assembly Center."

The man nodded.

"Report back here tomorrow at two o'clock when the rest of the block managers have been checked in," Mr. Richardson continued. "You will be given your lists and further instructions."

As we left the building, none of the ten newly anointed block managers said anything to each other. I was the only woman. I also may have been the youngest block manager, but I'm not sure about that. I needed to find my way to block four to find my family.

I looked around at the county fairgrounds, now home. I detected a distinct foul odor that I couldn't identify, and I wanted to hold my nose. When I looked back toward where I'd entered, I noticed the towers built at intervals around the outside of the racetrack, just inside freshly installed barbed-wire fencing. The soldiers and their massive machine guns stood in the towers, looking in at the camp. The mere sight of those soldiers glaring with suspicion at the Japanese milling around, doing what they could to sort out their lives, sent chills up and down my body.

We hadn't been sent away for our own protection; we hadn't been brought to so-called assembly centers: we'd been sent to prison. We were now prisoners.

And now, I was being forced to assist in the management of my friends, neighbors, and other fellow Japanese.

But I couldn't allow these thoughts to overcome me.

Think of gaman, *patience with dignity*, I told myself, *and carry on.*

PART 2
SUSPICION

Chapter 2

The FBI Investigates West Coast Japanese of Stockton, California, 1937–1941

Our eventual removal to the internment camp had become inevitable several years before conflict with Japan erupted. The Office of Naval Intelligence began spying on Japanese American communities in Hawaii in the 1930s and put together a "special list of those who would be the first to be placed in concentration camps in the event of trouble." In 1939, President Roosevelt ordered the Military Intelligence Division and the FBI to put together a Custodial Detention Index, which resulted in extensive interviewing of Japanese on the West Coast. The Munson Report was delivered to President Roosevelt in November of 1941 after all the interviewing was completed. The report's conclusion was that the interviews had found "a remarkable, even extraordinary degree of loyalty among this generally suspect ethnic group."

The Stockton public schools were crowded. Because I had completed all the required credits, I graduated high school a semester early, in December of 1937, just a few weeks before I turned eighteen. The Stockton schools were integrated, and my class had 344 students, who were approximately 86 percent Caucasian, 11 percent Japanese, and 3 percent Chinese, along with one Korean boy. Other California cities at this time, including San Francisco, had segregated schools, with "Orientals" separated out in grade school. I experienced no prejudice; our high school offered activities and clubs for all. One of my best friends, Marie, was Caucasian. We'd had several classes together and studied together, and I often helped her with her homework because her father expected only straight As on her report card.

At this time, we Japanese in America were either *Nisei*—born in America and thus American citizens—or *Issei*—born in Japan and part of the first generation to immigrate to the United States. I was a *Nisei*; my parents were both *Issei*. The laws of the time prevented them from ever gaining US citizenship or from owning land. A few years after Mom arrived in the United States, no more Japanese were even allowed to immigrate to America. But my parents and the other *Issei* who made it to America before the ban was implemented persevered, worked long and hard on farms, established successful businesses, and worked in trades, despite the restrictions on them. My parents and the other *Issei* I knew were law-abiding, honest people and good parents, and yet, they were prevented from gaining citizenship in the country they now called home.

The generational differences between our *Issei* and *Nisei* were pronounced: generally, the *Issei* lived according to their native Japanese culture, while the *Nisei* adopted more of the American culture. Sometimes, the American-born *Nisei* children would argue with their *Issei* parents, who defended their homeland of Japan. We *Nisei* hadn't experienced the way our parents had grown up—bowing to everyone of higher status or accepting marriages arranged by parents, although we sometimes feared we'd be subject to arranged marriages, too. Our parents were used to the highly male-oriented Japanese culture, which dated to ancient times. I and my fellow *Nisei* were Americans; America was all we knew.

Everyone heard stories about the Imperial Japanese Army's conquests across Asia. In December of 1937, we heard horrific stories of Japan conquering Nanking, China: the Chinese soldiers who surrendered were all murdered and many forced to dig their own graves to be buried alive. Pop had moved to America to escape being drafted, and he wanted to support Japan, but he was troubled about its military aggression. For me, I dreamed of seeing the beautiful land of my ancestors—the magical gardens, cherry tree blossoms, and ancient Buddhist shrines, but I was terrified by the newspapers' unfathomable stories of torture inflicted by the Imperial Japanese Army.

After completing my public-school education in 1937, I completed another year of study at my Buddhist temple, mastering the written and oral Japanese I had studied since age six. Most of the *Nisei* students who started after school study with me had long before given up the difficult study of Japanese. I was asked to deliver the Japanese school-commencement speech, and luckily, the speech was prewritten, so all I had to do was memorize it. Most of the speech thanked the teachers, the students, and the community for their support. I'll never forget the massive crowd gathered on the steps and in rows of chairs beyond the temple as I walked up to deliver my speech.

After both of my graduations, I had several jobs, at a diner-style restaurant, a laundromat, and selling tickets at the Star Theater. We were a poor family, living off Pop's foreman's salary at Mr. Zuckerman's farm, so I gave my paychecks to Mom. She did her best to make sure we had what we needed. Often, she sacrificed clothes and shoes for herself to provide for us. When I began sewing school, she used some of the funds I'd earned to pay my tuition. This continuing-education class allowed me to make clothes for my siblings—as well as more fashionable clothes for myself than Mom sewed for me.

When I turned twenty in 1940, my social life revolved primarily around the Buddhist temple, where Women's Club meetings were held and Sunday services took place. The Women's Club spent hours preparing origami crafts to sell at the county fair and planning convention trips to other cities in California for competitions in dancing, public speaking, art, and music. I was always our club's contestant in the oratory competition. We bunked together in hotel rooms when we attended these conventions, which were always a thrill for us. The conventions culminated in a banquet on the last night, for which we dressed in our finest. I even wore high-heeled shoes and shiny red lipstick.

Mom needed help—she was caring for both a newborn and an active two-year-old. My siblings were still in school, making me the most available to help with my little brothers. With babies came diapers we made from the same cotton roll we girls used each month. It was hard work using our old washboard to scrub out the stains by hand. If I wasn't careful, I scraped my fingers, and *yazoo*! Did that hurt! Luckily, Tom was fully toilet trained before he was two, leaving only Ed still wearing diapers.

My parents devoted their lives to earning a living and taking care of their eight children, all born in America with the assistance of a midwife. Born in 1920, I was the eldest at twenty. My sister Christine came along quickly in 1922, followed by Marian in 1924. Then I got my first brother, Will, in 1926, and another sister, Loretta in 1927. My last sister, Fran, came along soon after Loretta. What a surprise it was when Mom had another son, Tom, ten years later and he got a playmate, Ed, in 1939 when Mom was forty-two. For this time in history, my parents were fortunate that all their children were born healthy and all lived to adulthood.

It was fun to sew little outfits for my brothers. Mom managed to get some new fabric for me to use on her pedal-pushing sewing machine, which wasn't as functional as the machines at the sewing school, but I managed. She thanked me often for helping her out, which made me feel good. Pleasing Mom and Pop was more important to me than worrying about me—yet I wondered what I was going to do with my own life. I graduated from sewing school, as I had from Stockton High School and the Stockton Buddhist Japanese School, at the top of my class. My parents, who spoke and wrote Japanese, knew only limited English—although Mom took several English classes and Pop picked up English from us and the farm where he worked. Because of this, they needed me more than ever, since I was both the firstborn child and fully educated.

I was quite content to stay at home. Because it was too expensive to live on our own, all the kids of my generation lived with our parents until we got married. To the extent I could, it was my duty to help support my family. I went shopping; washed diapers, dresses, and underwear; ironed the clean clothes; cooked; scrubbed the floors; did dishes; took care of my little brothers; and sewed new clothes for my brothers and sisters. Whatever Mom needed me to do, I did. Pop worked hard on the farm, and we looked forward to seeing him on the weekends, though it was often just for one day, sometimes if we were lucky he had two days off. We kids were especially excited about the better meals Mom cooked when Pop was home.

At this time, war raged in Europe. The 1940 Summer Olympics were cancelled. Although the United States was officially staying neutral, President Roosevelt took several actions that indicated he wanted to be prepared if America went to war, such as asking for $900 million to build fifty thousand airplanes. France had been overtaken by Germany. Hitler was bombing England. It seemed that only England could stop Hitler, but many wondered if England was up to this challenge; Prime Minister Churchill told the British people to "prepare for hard and heavy tidings." Meanwhile, Japan marched across Asia and now controlled most of China, Korea, and parts of Indochina. Americans, however, still remembered WWI and wanted no part of another European war. So, the summer of 1940 started out similar to other summers in Stockton, except that everyone talked about the war in Europe. However, our day-to-day lives weren't changed by the chaos in Europe, Asia, and Africa. Pop would say what a great country America was and how happy he was to be living in a free country, despite the fact that US law prevented all Chinese and Japanese immigrants from owning land or becoming US citizens.

My friendship with my neighbor Grace Yamaguchi distracted me a bit from the nervous talk. Grace was about nine years older than I was, but we were friends. She lived alone. Her father owned a Japanese bank and provided for her monthly rent, so she only had to work a part-time job. I felt sorry for her because she seemed lonely; I suspected her tendency to be opinionated might hurt her attempts at building friendships. Her commentary didn't bother me; I tried to get along with everyone. She asked me to go on vacation with her to the beach and offered to pay the expenses. Since I had never seen a beach, I was thrilled at the chance, though I didn't know how to swim. Mom was scared for me to go to the ocean, but she knew she could trust me, and wanted me to have fun. Typical of Mom, she found the money for me to buy a swimsuit. Grace and I went twice that summer. I loved running through the waves and feeling the powerful surging of the ocean.

I read the news to Pop in September of 1940 when Germany, Italy, and Japan signed the Tripartite Pact. Were these countries now working together to take over the world? The news worried Pop, although he already knew most of it from talk on the farm. Will was sixteen—not eligible to be drafted—but Pop was clearly worried about what the future held for his son.

Christmas of 1940 brought another modern convenience to the Hayashi family: a refrigerator. This was Pop's biggest investment of his life. No more ice blocks to be delivered or water trays to empty. The refrigerator stood just four feet tall but could hold much more food than we were used to. Pop was proud once again to bring this new ultimate convenience to his family, and we were all thrilled too. Mom recalled her years living on Bacon Island, when there was no way to preserve fresh meat or milk. Then, she'd thought it was wonderful to get an ice box when we first came to town. Now, she owned a refrigerator. She and I couldn't wait to walk to the Green Frog Supermarket the next day to buy enough food to fill our new refrigerator.

On January 12, 1941, I turned twenty-one. We celebrated my birthday with a typical family party; Mom prepared a tasty round-steak dinner and baked me a cake. She and Pop always made sure we received gifts on our birthday, no matter how inexpensive or minimal they had to be.

Throughout the spring of 1941, Will constructed a little shed in our backyard to use as a science laboratory. He was curious about anything related to science. A professor from College of the Pacific in Stockton came to the high school to perform a demonstration and to talk to students about attending his college when they graduated. Most families, including ours, couldn't afford tuition, but Mom and Pop may have tried to send Will if they could have. He brought home chemicals his teacher shared with him, and he worked in his homemade laboratory as often as possible. He built a working darkroom and was quite proud of the pictures he shot and developed. If we couldn't find Will, we all knew the mad scientist was back in his laboratory.

One sunny Sunday afternoon, after we'd returned home from classes and services at the Buddhist temple, Will dashed out to his laboratory without taking off his Sunday suit—not unusual. Suddenly, we heard a resounding *boom*. The house shook. We ran out the back door toward Will's shed as he ran toward us. He wasn't hurt, but his Sunday suit was ruined—covered with debris and ripped in many places. Mom and Pop were simply relieved he wasn't seriously hurt, and didn't scold him for not changing out of his Sunday clothes. Will was flustered and vowed to be more careful.

The following weekend, there was a knock at the door. Two men in dark suits pulled out their badges and asked to speak to Mr. Hayashi. Marian found Pop and told him he must come quickly. The men were from the FBI. They began asking questions about the explosion and laboratory in our backyard, and Pop asked me to translate the questions he couldn't understand. The men asked Pop and me to come with them, so I explained to Mom what was happening, and we climbed into their unmarked car. As we left, several men, wearing white suits that covered them from head to toe, walked into the backyard toward the remnants of Will's laboratory.

We arrived at a plain building in town with a sign stating "United States of America" on the door. The men invited us in and directed us to a room at the end of the corridor. Several other men joined us. My heart was pounding and body quivering. Were we all in big trouble? I was scared. The man in charge must have realized how petrified I was. As big and intimidating as he appeared, he talked with a smooth and gentle demeanor. He thanked Pop and me for coming and explained they needed information. Then he asked us to relax and offered us a drink of water or Coke. As they asked Pop questions, I translated each into Japanese for him, and then I translated his answers back for the FBI.

As we spoke, one of the men took detailed notes. They wanted to know if Will was making gunpowder and why there was a laboratory in our backyard. Pop explained that his son loved science and the backyard laboratory was his hobby—nothing more.

The man in charge stood up and said, "The world needs more scientists like this one!"

Pop and I laughed nervously.

He directed his men to take us home. Before we left, the men shook Pop's hand and thanked him for his assistance, and the man who had asked most of the questions told me how much he appreciated my excellent translation.

Pop and I returned home to find the family huddled together and wondering where the authorities had taken us. Will felt terrible for causing trouble and embarrassment to our family. And though the men had been generally kind to us, the event was still traumatic; my heart didn't return to its regular beat for a few more hours.

Life returned to normal for our family, except for one more visit from the men in white suits. This time, they took everything left of the Will Hayashi laboratory and even dismantled his little hut. No evidence of it remained; it was gone but not forgotten. Will was sad, but he understood it was his fault for having the accident, although no one had been hurt and it could have been much worse.

Our quiet, unassuming family was briefly the talk of the town. Party lines were full of discussion about the backyard laboratory and explosion and the trip to the FBI for Sei and Janet Hayashi. Soon, everyone knew it had all been about Will and his chemistry laboratory. I'm sure people wondered if my family was in big trouble with the law; everyone knew tensions between Japan and the United States were increasing.

Toward the week's end, two men from the FBI appeared at our door again, but this time they came calling for me. I recognized one of the men from the FBI's previous visit; he asked if I would come back down to their office. I told Mom I needed to go with the men again, and she looked puzzled; she didn't understand. I assured her I would be fine and told her not to worry, but this time, I was going alone.

I left with the men in dark suits for my second trip to the FBI's office that week, again anxious but, this time, more curious than scared. I kept thinking to myself, *What more information could they possibly need about my little brother Will?* Most of the same men were in the room when I arrived. The large man in charge explained that Will had been making gunpowder in his laboratory and had produced enough supply to blow up the whole block. He'd been lucky his explosion hadn't ignited his entire stockpile.

I wasn't expecting this. Once again, I explained that Will meant no harm to anyone. He was just my little brother who loved science; he was playing the mad scientist using the chemicals he managed to get from school and a few Pop bought for him. They accepted my explanation about my brother and thanked me again before driving me home. I could have given my brother a hard time for causing me the humiliation of being questioned by the FBI, but since Will was so hard on himself for causing the explosion in the first place, I assured him everything would be fine. That was the end of that—I thought.

Marian and Christine both graduated in 1941 from Stockton High School. Because of our move from the country into Stockton, Christine had been held back at school, so she and Marian had walked to and from school together. They'd both attended Japanese classes at the temple before it proved too much for them to keep up. After graduation, they set out to find jobs in Stockton.

That summer, we heard about horrendous ghettos in Germany and Poland, but we didn't find out until later that Hitler was systematically exterminating the Jewish people and used his first gas chamber to eliminate his own people with mental and physical disabilities. We heard that President Roosevelt had been warned about new, unimaginably destructive weaponry being researched by German and English scientists, and he signed an executive order establishing the Office of Scientific Research and Development, which eventually produced the Manhattan Project and atomic weaponry. While these things were happening, I read whatever I could about the war raging in Europe, but I also felt safe and secure living in Stockton.

Then the dark-suited men once again appeared at our door. I'd thought the incident of Will's laboratory was resolved, and we had moved on with our lives; when Loretta called me to the door, I was quite surprised. One of the men said they were sorry to disturb me but asked if I would please come with them. He explained this visit had nothing to do with the accident in our backyard, but the FBI needed me to assist with translation. I accepted his explanation, then told Mom I was leaving once again with men from the FBI.

When we arrived at the same office in the same building, where the same men were in the room, another man also sat at the table. I recognized him as Mr. Saiki from our temple. I knew he owned some Japanese businesses in Stockton; to me, he was considerably prosperous. I was told anything I heard or saw in the FBI office was to remain strictly confidential, and I promised I would honor their command and not even tell my own family.

I quickly realized the interrogators were anxious about the Japanese in our community and elsewhere in California. They explained that the US government was concerned about the loyalty of the *Issei*, many of whom lived on the West Coast without the ability to ever become naturalized citizens, as was the law. The men wanted to know if the Japanese community leaders were loyal to the United States or Japan. One of the seated agents took the lead in questioning Mr. Saiki.

"Do you consider yourself loyal to Japan?" said the FBI agent matter-of-factly.

Mr. Saiki said, "I will always be proud of my Japanese heritage, but I am not happy with how aggressive Japan has become in recent years."

"Do you correspond with family and friends in Japan?"

"Yes, I do receive letters from relatives in Japan on occasion."

"Do the letters ever talk about the possibility of America and Japan going to war?"

Mr. Saiki looked surprised. "Oh no, my correspondence is strictly about family news."

"Would you assist Japan in any way if you were asked?"

Mr. Saiki appeared slightly offended. "Of course not. I consider myself to be an American citizen, even though I'm not. I am very happy to be living and working in America."

"Have you ever been asked to gather information about America for the benefit of Japan?"

"Absolutely not," said Mr. Saiki sternly.

"Are you aware of anyone in Stockton who might be inclined to provide assistance to Japan?"

"No."

"Are you aware of anyone in Stockton who has been asked to provide assistance to Japan?"

"No!"

"I understand you are an officer of the Stockton Buddhist Temple Men's Club. What is discussed at your meetings?"

Mr. Saiki paused briefly. "We discuss our finances, what events are upcoming, who will be in charge of organizing the events, who will be assisting with the events, and general operations of the club."

"Do you ever discuss politics at your meetings?"

Mr. Saiki again seemed frustrated. "Never!"

"Mr. Saiki, what will happen to your remains when you pass away?"

Mr. Saiki looked quizzical and slightly offended. I discussed the question with him and explained to the FBI that his intention was to be cremated and buried here in America.

"Thank you for your time, Mr. Saiki. We may need to ask you additional questions at another date, but that is all for today. Agent Johnson will take you home."

Mr. Saiki nodded, and everyone stood to exit the room.

The dark-suited men were once again polite and promptly took me home, thanked me, and reminded me to keep everything confidential. At dinner that evening, my family peppered me with questions. The more I told them I could not say anything about what had happened, the more curious they were. Under no circumstances would I reveal anything. I'd given my word.

The FBI asked me to translate maybe a dozen more times. The setup was the same, except each time, a different Japanese man of prominence in our community sat at the table. Twice I arrived and waited for the person who would be questioned that day. I could see much in the eyes of the Japanese who were brought in—anger, hurt, disgust, surprise, disappointment, and disbelief. The men, obedient Japanese who respected authority, complied with the questions, despite their obvious feelings of betrayal that the government suspected them of disloyalty. They were all good people who worked hard at their professions and businesses in the Stockton area. I wondered what these men could possibly be doing that might endanger the United States. How could Stockton contain anything worth spying on? Some of the men actually spoke English quite well; I think the FBI brought me in just in case translation was needed.

After multiple trips to the FBI, my family finally quit asking me questions. They understood I wouldn't say anything, and they also knew no one harmed me.

While it wasn't pleasant to be translating for the FBI, the agents treated me with the utmost respect and courtesy. I was never paid for my service, nor did it even occur to me to ask to be paid; somehow, I thought I was helping. It was obvious these FBI men were alarmed about the Japanese in our area who were not American citizens, particularly the *Issei*, who were criticized for not assimilating into the community, for keeping to themselves. I could tell Americans found this behavior suspicious, but I knew this was more due to the language barrier and to the *Issei*'s desire to pass their cultural traditions on to their *Nisei* children than to a dislike for Caucasians. All Japanese I knew were practicing Buddhists, so they learned the same Judeo-Christian values taught by Christianity itself: Do not lie. Do not harm others. Honor your mother and father. Do not cheat. Return the kindness of others with a token of gratitude. The *Issei* and *Nisei* of Stockton were good people, as far as I knew; although we had our fair share of status climbers and gossips. I knew the FBI agents were doing their job to protect America, and so I hoped to do my part by reassuring them that the *Issei* in Stockton posed absolutely no threat to national security.

We'd begun the summer of 1941 thinking the last weekend of May would be the beginning of a fun summer—after we'd put the disaster of Will's laboratory behind us—but, on that weekend, FDR had proclaimed an "unlimited national emergency." The news from Europe was troubling; I followed the developments closely in the *Stockton Record*. Germany invaded Yugoslavia and Greece. All German and Italian assets in the United States were frozen. German and Italian consulates in America were ordered to close and all staffers instructed to leave America by July 10. Italy declared war on the Soviet Union in June. On July 26, all Japanese assets in the United States were also frozen. By October, Germany had sent a million troops into the Soviet Union to overtake Moscow. The German soldiers were not prepared for the cold weather, and by Thanksgiving, they were freezing. Hitler would not retreat, condemning thousands to die of exposure. By December, the Soviets had pushed the Germans back hundreds of miles, but the war raged on as Germany forged ahead with reinforcements and began occupying sections of the Soviet Bloc. It was terrifying to read about the progression of the war in Europe.

News increased of growing trouble with my ancestral homeland. Japan seemed intent on taking over all the Asian countries, which it considered subject to the Empire of Japan. I learned in school about Japan's success in invading Korea, much of China, parts of Russia, and Indochina in recent decades. This aggression had stirred up the United States' apprehension, so the US government had restricted trade of fuel oil with Japan. Only a few obstacles stood in the way of Japan's total domination of Asia: the military presence of the United States in the Philippines, the United Kingdom's presence in Hong Kong and Malaysia, and, until 1940, the Dutch presence in the oil-rich Dutch East Indies. In May 1940, Germany had conquered the Netherlands and the Dutch East Indies, which, as part of the pact between Germany, Italy, and Japan, had been put under the control of Japan—a step forward in Emperor Hirohito's master plan to rule all Asia.

While the United Kingdom was tied up fighting Hitler, Japan schemed to get the United States out of Asia at all costs. On January 27, 1941, the US ambassador to Japan reported to the State Department that he'd heard a rumor Japan could launch a surprise attack on Pearl Harbor. Through 1941, the paper reported continuing tense negotiations between Japan and the United States. On November 20, Japan made its final offer to withdraw its occupying forces and not launch further attacks in Asia, if the United States lifted all sanctions and stopped aiding China. The US reply sent on November 26 stipulated Japan must evacuate from the China region without conditions and enter into nonaggression pacts with the three Pacific powers. Further, on November 26, the US ambassador sent a second warning by cable from Tokyo to the secretary of state stating Japan may strike suddenly and unexpectedly. On December 1, Emperor Hirohito authorized an attack on the United States, hoping a devastating blow would force the United States to yield to Japan's demands. The United States had cracked the Japanese secret diplomatic code, and on November 18, the message was "*Higashi no kaze ame*," meaning east wind, rain. East wind was the United States, and rain meant a diplomatic break—war. On December 2, a coded message was sent to the Japanese convoy launched days earlier in anticipation of the attack: "Climb Mount Nitaka"—execute the plan, and attack Pearl Harbor. I, like the rest of America, learned all of this much later and couldn't have imagined Japan was secretly planning a massive surprise attack.

Chapter 3
Pearl Harbor

As an American, I was shocked and overwhelmed with sadness when the news arrived that Japan was striking the American forces at Pearl Harbor. All I could think was that it just couldn't be true. Japan sending hundreds of bombers to Hawaii, ships full of men sinking in the harbor? I was overcome with shock and grief.

While defenseless sailors and airmen, asleep in their bunks, were awakening to sirens blaring and nowhere to escape, we Hayashis went to the temple, as we did every Sunday, and returned home for lunch. I headed off to my job at the theater for the afternoon, thinking there would no doubt be a large crowd for the matinee show. Then the manager came out from the theater to my little sales kiosk and told me America was under attack by Japan. I wiggled and squirmed all afternoon and into early evening, trapped in my circular sales booth, as more and more people confirmed what he'd said.

When it was finally time to leave, I ran home the entire six blocks from the theater.

"Did you hear what's happened?" Christine asked. "Are the bombers coming to California next? Where can we hide? We have no basement!"

Pop spoke quickly and decisively. "Don't panic. California is a long way from Hawaii. We are safe. Japan would never bomb here—many Japanese live in California. My ride to the farm will be here soon; I will be home next Saturday. Don't worry—America will always be safe."

Almost as soon as he said it, the truck pulled up, and Pop left his eight children and wife to return to his livelihood. Pop was visibly upset about the news of Pearl Harbor, but he kept his family calm as the crisis unfolded.

All night, we listened to the radio for every sliver of information. We heard about the message blasted over the loudspeakers of the aircraft carriers and on shore: "Air raid Pearl Harbor. This is not a drill." The American men were asleep and caught off guard; the guns on the ships were unmanned. We didn't hear the final tally of damage that Japan had wreaked on the United States until weeks later: 2,403 Americans killed, 1,178 Americans wounded, 188 airplanes on the ground destroyed, 8 navy battleships damaged, and 4 battleships sunk.

Even Tom and Ed understood the seriousness of that night; I held Ed on my knees, and Mom cradled Tom on hers, and neither made a peep. They stayed up late with the rest of us—Mom wouldn't leave the radio even long enough to put them to bed. Finally, Mom said we must get our rest, and we quietly slipped into bed.

As soon as morning light came, our radio was back on: President Roosevelt would be giving a speech soon. Mom sent Will, Loretta, and Fran off to school. Christine worked at a restaurant, and Marian was still looking for a job after her recent graduation, but at that moment, we were home together. Our radio crackled at times; we turned up the volume so we wouldn't miss a word. At 10:30 a.m. California time, President Roosevelt spoke to a joint session of Congress, to all Americans listening on radios, and all others to the farthest corners of the world. "Yesterday, December 7, 1941, a date which will live in infamy—the United States of America was suddenly and deliberately attacked by naval and air forces of the Empire of Japan . . . since the unprovoked and dastardly attack by Japan on Sunday, December 7, 1941, a state of war has existed between the United States and the Japanese empire."

Congress followed up the president's speech and declared war on Japan within the hour. The United States was now at war with the country of my parents' birth, my ancestors' homeland. I was terribly scared for America, thinking of the boys I knew from my schools who might be leaving for war. I was scared my own brother might have to go to war, since he was less than a year from his eighteenth birthday. War meant that everything I knew of my normal routine of life would soon change.

That afternoon, I walked briskly to the theater and was promptly greeted by Charlie, the manager. Mondays were normally a light day.

"Hello, Janet. It's good to see you today," Charlie said without emotion.

"Thank you, Charlie. It's good to be back at work."

Charlie looked concerned. "Janet, I'm going to keep an eye on you tonight—there could be trouble."

"What kind of trouble? Here at the theater?"

"Janet," Charlie continued, "you need to understand that people are incensed with all Japanese because of the Pearl Harbor attack. I'm concerned someone could take their anger out on you."

I was puzzled. "Angry at me?" I said softly.

Charlie walked away, and I sat down in my booth, thinking, *How could anyone be mad at me? I am an American, just like other Americans. I just happen to be Japanese.*

I quickly understood. Passersby said, "Damn Japs," and other hurtful words when they saw me. If there had been a hole in the floor underneath my chair in the ticket booth, I would have crawled into it. I said as little as possible all evening.

When it was time for me to go home, the manager told me he would be advertising in the paper the next day to find my replacement. I could work another day or two until he hired someone, he said, but I would be expected to train my replacement. The person would need to be honest, reliable, able to make correct change—and most importantly, *not* Japanese.

I knew this wasn't personal—the manager added how pleased he was with my work in the ticket booth—yet I was crushed. Life hadn't dealt me such a rejection before, certainly not one of this magnitude which was completely out of my control.

I scurried home as quickly as I could, never looking up. I was trembling when I ran in the house and into Mom's arms. As I explained everything to her, I began to process what had transpired. I'd lost my job at the theater because I was Japanese. That was it—no one in Stockton would now hire a Japanese person. Somehow people thought we were complicit with the Japanese across the world. Did they not understand we were just as angry as everyone else in America?

"You must not say anything back to anyone who insults you, no matter what is said," Mom told me. I assured her I understood.

After I settled down, Mom sat down with Christine, Marian, and me. She looked directly at us as she spoke. "I've been talking with the neighbors, and they all have been saying we must always remember *gaman*."

Marian replied with a shaky voice, "Mom, I'm scared. What happens if someone yells at me or curses at me or—"

Mom interrupted her. "We must hunker down at home and only go out when absolutely necessary. Tom and Ed must be kept in the backyard. Will, Loretta, and Fran will continue to go to school unless we hear of trouble there. It's obvious we're not safe on the streets of Stockton at this time." She paused. "How lucky we are that Pop can continue to work on the farm. We have already heard stories of Japanese men in Stockton fired the day after Pearl Harbor."

As if a lever had been pulled, Stockton no longer resembled the city I grew up in and loved. I soon learned there were leaders in our community, state, and government who believed people of Japanese heritage living in the West Coast and Hawaii were not loyal to America. There was no basis for this opinion, as there were no acts of espionage, but still, we were considered part of the evil Empire of Japan and labelled "Yellow Peril." Possibly these feelings had been a part of Stockton all along and I was simply unaware of it; perhaps only a few people felt this way. Prior to December 7, 1941, I had never felt ill will directed toward me for being Japanese, but after Pearl Harbor, everything changed. Our home became a bunker for us; we suddenly felt like unwelcomed outsiders in our own city. Since I was six years old, when I'd first encountered bullies, I'd tried to avoid them if possible; now it seemed like they were everywhere in Stockton.

I knew I couldn't talk long on the telephone—anyone on our party line could be listening at any time—yet I couldn't wait to talk to some of my friends. I got through to the lines of Dorothy and Gladys from the Japanese club; they'd heard many of the same stories I had. Dorothy said she'd heard Andy, a bully from way back in our childhood, stole some candy from the five-and-ten store. He told the Japanese cashier he didn't owe anything to a Jap and just walked out. The cashier was too scared to say anything. We remembered what Andy was like, so this story wasn't surprising to us. And though we talked only briefly, I felt comforted knowing we were all in this together. We were coping as best we could with the contempt our community now held for us.

After the phone rang several times, I was relieved to hear Marie answer her phone.

"Hi, Marie—it's Janet. It's good to hear your voice. How are your piano lessons going?"

There was a long pause on the other end.

"Janet, I'm sorry to tell you this, but my father has told me we can no longer be friends. He said Japanese are not welcome in America and Stockton anymore. All Japanese need to go back to Japan."

I choked back tears and softly said, "I understand." I put the receiver down with a clunk.

As I put my head in my hands, I was so ashamed. I wished I wasn't Japanese.

The whole world thinks I'm terrible, and I'm not welcome in America anymore, I thought.

When strangers taunted, stared at, or insulted me, it was easy to dismiss, but being rejected by my friend of many years hurt to the core. Many times through our school years, I'd helped Marie with her papers and homework. It all meant nothing now. I felt empty and lonely—disgraced, discarded, rejected, helpless. I wanted to escape to my bed and leave the world behind. How could I carry on with my life?

I awakened early the next morning. Before I arose, I thought about the events of the day before and my conversation with Marie. I needed to be strong for Mom; she was anxious about her family in Japan and what would become of us in Stockton. As was the routine, Pop only came home one day a week, so Mom was in charge of the home, which meant keeping all eight children calm and safe. I knew my Japanese friends and I were all in the same situation. We couldn't do anything to change the feelings of the people who decided all Japanese were to blame for the attack on Pearl Harbor. We could only avoid contact with the outside world and, when we ventured out, say nothing, no matter what was said to us.

I worked at the theater for two more days before my replacement arrived. She was a friendly Caucasian girl, embarrassed, I think, because she knew why I was being terminated. I carefully explained everything she needed to do to take over my job. I didn't blame her;

this was the new norm. Once she was comfortable with her new responsibilities, I made the six-block walk home for the last time. I walked slowly, unlike the days of and after Pearl Harbor; I needed time to myself to reflect about the whirlwind of the last several days.

In the days following, the radio told the news of Germany and their Axis partners declaring war on America. The United States returned the favor. This would not and could not be a happy Christmas in 1941. War engulfed the civilized world. Only America could save the world from Axis domination. The US Navy and Marines graduated their academy seniors a semester early and immediately made these men officers prepared for war.

Soon we heard news from the fight overseas. Japan's assault on the Pacific region continued with a defeat of the Americans on Wake Island. As Christmas Day neared, the military leaders of the United States and United Kingdom met in Washington to strategize their war plans. Winston Churchill spoke to a joint session of Congress the day after Christmas, the first British prime minister ever given this honor.

As the end of 1941 arrived, I marveled at how the world order had changed in one short month. I read the newspapers, carefully sharing all the news with my parents. The Rose Bowl was moved across the country, to the Duke University campus in Durham, North Carolina, because the president feared Japan could attack again on American soil. Oregon State's team roster included one Japanese player; he was not allowed to make the trip with his team. The new prejudice had even influenced college sports.

Chapter 4

Living as Despicables

Mom and I settled into a routine for grocery shopping. She carefully prepared a list, so we wouldn't waste any time or money; off we trekked down the street pulling our small cart. We dared not look at anyone we encountered. If we made eye contact with someone, we risked an insult, a curse word, or worse. I was pleased Mom trusted me enough to take me on these journeys out of our safe house. Each week, she and I went about our business with great caution. Our world had shrunk to a few blocks—we dared not venture farther.

One day, I noticed the eyes of the young cashier at Green Frog. She looked at us softly; her eyes watered as she observed our anxiety. I could tell she understood the predicament in which Pearl Harbor had placed us Japanese and how Mom, I, and all our Japanese neighbors ventured out of our homes as if walking on eggshells. Her face showed a depth of compassion I will never forget. It was odd how some locals were cruel, while others showed kindness.

Then, more shocking news hit the newspapers.

On January 14, 1942, just two days after my twenty-second birthday, President Roosevelt signed Proclamation 2537, which required all Italian, German, and Japanese residents living in the United States to register with the Department of Justice. Each would be given what was called a Certificate of Identification for Aliens of Enemy Nationality. This included the *Issei* and even the *Nisei*, who were American citizens. Bank accounts of those registered could or would be frozen. "Exclusion zones" would be established, and anyone registered under this proclamation would not be allowed to enter those locations, which included all ports, water-treatment plants, military bases, and even areas of California where there was a high risk for brush fires.

On that same day, the Canadian government passed a law dictating that all male Japanese ages eighteen to forty-five would be removed from their homes and taken to camps in Alberta. The article I read said that the government feared the Japanese living in Canada because the officials didn't know whose side they were on. It seemed Canada wanted to avoid all risk of these men spying or causing trouble, so they arrested them and took them away. Pop and Mom listened intently as I read and translated this news for them, although they didn't know anyone in Canada. I wondered if America would do what Canada had done and take away men of that age range. Pop was in his fifties, and Will was seventeen, so maybe our family would be spared if America followed Canada's path. At least we didn't have to worry about our bank accounts being seized—we didn't have any—but I knew Pop was most worried about Will, who was approaching the universal conscription age.

The United States' countless factories were in full war-production mode. Rations were announced, the first pertaining to tires; because we didn't own a car, this wasn't a problem for my family. We heard of lots of open jobs in our area, some to replace Japanese who were fired, others related to the war-building effort. I read these advertisements in the newspaper, but I knew it wasn't safe for me to work anywhere—and that no one would hire me even if I were qualified.

One day, Dorothy rang me up on the party line as I was sewing a new pair of trousers for growing Tom. She was short of breath as she spoke, obviously quite agitated.

"Janet, have you seen any Chinese in Stockton lately?"

"No, Dorothy, I haven't—Mom and I went to the store yesterday, but otherwise, I haven't left our house in days. What's wrong?"

"I was walking Rascal when I saw a couple of Chinese guys who went to Stockton High—I don't know their names, but I'm pretty sure they were a year or two ahead of us. They were wearing buttons that said, 'I am Chinese'!"

"Wow—really?"

"When I got home, I told Mom about it—she said she'd heard that someone is passing the buttons out by city hall so the Chinese won't be confused with us. Can you believe it? It's like we have leprosy or something. What a bunch of jerks. They must be so proud out there in town, walking around with their stinkin' buttons."

I was hurt by this news too, but I knew I needed to console Dorothy. "Dorothy, I understand you're upset, but how are the Chinese and their buttons any different from strangers hollering 'damn Japs' at us? We've both lived through that insult. We just have to look away and not let them bug us. You know we can't change anything."

"I know you're right, Janet. Maybe it's just one more thing we have to deal with. But I just want to sit down and cry. Everyone hates us."

"Not everyone—we have each other, and we always will. Dorothy, let the Chinese wear their buttons. We have no control over what's happening in Stockton, and we have to make sure we don't stir up any trouble until this is all over."

"Thanks, Janet. I'll see you at our club meeting on Tuesday, if we have one."

It seemed there was no end to the prejudice and hatred consuming Stockton; every day seemed to bring a new story. And beyond Stockton, countries were at war, and the world was full of race hatred.

Canada expanded its first segregation order to include "all male persons of Japanese origin." The choice for these men? Return to Japan, or go to the camps. This latest development was extremely alarming. How would these men be treated in the camps? It was a relief that we were safe in America; I felt anxious but wouldn't allow myself to think the same thing could happen here. Most of us had been born in America—the American authorities would never take US citizens away to camps, would they? I was keenly aware of the Executive Order, because it set up exclusion zones and required the Japanese to register—was FDR preparing to do what Canada was doing with Japanese men? If Pop was sent away from us, I worried how we would survive. We barely got by on his farm paycheck. The more I pondered this, the more anxiety I felt deep in my soul.

Going to the temple for services or club meetings were the only times I left the house, besides helping Mom with groceries; we walked as a family for Sunday service, feeling safe in our large group. It was consoling to see my friends. At the temple that Sunday, we listened to Reverend Toufuku preach on love, peace, and tolerance—a most timely message—and we talked about what had happened in Canada. Everyone feared what happened there could happen in America as well.

Despite our concern, we decided there were too many local Japanese to be sent to camps. And besides, why would anyone think we would cause any trouble? I thought the same, but the more we talked, the more I thought about my visits with the FBI, who were suspicious of the *Issei* living in Stockton. My friends didn't know any specifics about my assistance in interrogating prominent Japanese—I hadn't told anyone—but rumors abounded that I had made trips to the FBI. My family knew I'd spoken with the FBI but knew no details. I assumed the interrogated men also said nothing. It seemed everyone was keeping to themselves and staying home as much as possible, as my family did, especially after many lost their jobs following Pearl Harbor.

Occasionally, after we'd been together in our house too long, arguments and tension sprang up in my family. My sisters complained about what the other did, used, or borrowed. Ed and Tom were now three and five and full of energy. We wouldn't let them out of our sight, but we could no longer take them on long walks to wear them out or visit the jungle gym in the schoolyard; they were allowed to play only in our backyard. Mom kept order in our house but understood we were confined in our apartment, which we'd thought was so big when we first moved in. Pop was home a day or so each weekend. My siblings often played board or card games, and when there were no chores for me to do, I read and reread books, although finding a quiet place to read was a challenge. I missed the chop suey and sesame chicken dinners we occasionally enjoyed at the local Chinese restaurant. I wondered what the future would bring— we couldn't live secluded in our apartment indefinitely. I also noticed Mom and Pop no longer defended Japan like they used to; after all, it was Japan's fault we were in this predicament.

On February 20, the phone rang, and Mom answered. She listened, then replied in Japanese. "Thanks—we will put on the radio right away."

She asked me to turn up the radio so we could hear over the static. The announcer was preparing to read an executive order President Roosevelt had signed the day before. I knew Mom wouldn't understand much of the fancy wording of the presidential proclamation; her English was still quite limited.

After reading the official order, the announcer explained that the government was setting up restrictive military zones in America. Military commanders were given the authority to take steps deemed advisable to exclude persons from military zones and must provide transportation, food, shelter, and other accommodations as may be necessary. The announcer also said that the British had just surrendered Singapore to the Japanese; even Princess Elizabeth, the future queen of England, had registered for war service.

Mom and I looked at each other and didn't say a word. The announcer's voice was somber. What did this mean? I felt a strong suspicion of what the order was saying, but after a few moments, I tried to reassure Mom that there'd been no specific mention of Japanese people and the military zones. My assurance did nothing to allay her fears. She nervously wrung out her washrag several times without paying attention to what she was doing, then vigorously dried the dishes she'd just washed. For a moment, I felt like I was the mom in the room, assuring her that this new order was just more of the same, that we just needed to continue our new way of life, and hopefully the war would be short.

When Pop came home, he asked us all to gather in the kitchen. Even with Pop's limited English skills, he had learned from Mr. Zuckerman and others what was happening. The president's order decreed that we were to relocate because we were enemy aliens living in a military zone.

Pop looked at us all. "We have nowhere to go. If we get on a train and leave, I don't know where we could go or where we would live, but most importantly, I don't know how I could find a job. No one would hire a Japanese man for farm work; I am lucky to still have this job with Mr. Zuckerman. Our family must remain in Stockton. We have no choice in this matter."

I couldn't understand why FDR had signed this proclamation, but the *Stockton Record* soon clarified the meaning of the president's new order. According to the paper, if you were Japanese and lived in California, Oregon, Washington, or Hawaii, you could be living in a military zone, and you should leave immediately if you could, or else the government would force you out. As the reality of this message sank in, I no longer felt America would keep me safe, as Pop had promised. Suddenly, there was no safe foundation in my life; it was like a perpetual earthquake was shaking the ground.

After the president's strong words, a few families from the temple moved away; they had family elsewhere in America. In total, about five thousand West Coast Japanese moved voluntarily. How lucky for those people who had friends or relatives living in safe areas far from the West Coast. For the rest of us, there were no options except to stay despite being despised, feared, rejected, and now considered enemy aliens and threatened by the president with forced relocation.

General DeWitt, commander of the West Coast, became a familiar name in the news. He disdained us Japanese, and he issued his own proclamation, Public Proclamation No. 1, on March 2, 1942, which followed up on the president's directive. DeWitt set up military areas in California, Washington, Oregon, and Arizona, and within the military areas, he established zones. Stockton was part of Military Area 1. All Japanese, German, and Italian aliens living in the military zones were required to notify the government if they moved. On March 11, General DeWitt established the Wartime Civil Control Administration, or WCCA, to provide for the evacuation of all persons of Japanese ancestry from West Coast military zones. The WCCA headquarters was opened in San Francisco, followed by forty-eight field offices and ninety-seven short-term civil control stations. The bureaucracy was established and immediately began searching for existing facilities that could be quickly transformed into internment camps. One week later, on March 18, the Wartime Relocation Authority, or WRA, was formed with the mission of establishing long-term facilities in remote locations for housing the interred Japanese after they were removed by the WCCA.

With the official notices coming from the White House and Pacific Command, I understood that my family and I were in great peril. America was at war with our people, and we couldn't blend in with the world. The feeling of all-encompassing fear and the worry of what would happen next crept into my mind. I tried to hide my anxiety from my family, understanding that we were all in this together, and I often thought of Mom and how she kept us safe, well fed, and cared for. She seemed so helpless in our current situation. I tried to be her cheerleader when I helped out at home and reassured her we were good citizens of Stockton, which she already knew; if we had to leave for a little while, it would all work out fine. I'm not sure she believed this.

One night, around eleven, there was a tap at our door. Christine and I were still awake, sitting on the couch, reading books. I often read before bed if I wasn't too tired; usually I reread a favorite old book, since we couldn't visit the library.

We answered the door, and standing outside was Mrs. Biavati and her son, Federico, our old neighbors from across the hall in the apartment building where we'd lived back in 1928. The Biavati family and the Hayashi family spoke different native languages, but we'd been good friends and had helped each other out many times through the difficult Depression years. I invited them in and dashed to get Mom, who was in bed but not asleep. She jumped up quickly and threw on a sweater to greet our guests. The women embraced. Both spoke limited English but had communicated just the same over the years and had forged a warm and caring friendship which endured even now.

The two visitors each carried a big bag. Inside each bag were two big pots filled with Mrs. Biavati's homemade spaghetti. She said to Mom, "I know these are extraordinary times for you. We served a large gathering today, and I wanted you to have these leftovers. I remember how the kids loved our spaghetti. It's not much, but I thought it might help out a bit."

Mom and I were touched by Mrs. Biavati's gift, more than we could express to her.

We went to the kitchen and transferred the spaghetti from the Biavatis' pots into our pots. Then we all sat down at the kitchen table, and Federico and I translated between Japanese, Italian, and English. The two mothers talked primarily about their children, as they often did; they'd helped each other raise their small children, and now those children were growing up. This visit from our old friends seemed so normal, aside from the fact that Mrs. Biavati and her son were forced to call on their Japanese friends late at night so as to not be seen associating with us. We understood the risk the Biavatis had taken by coming to our home; they, like us, were regular folks caught up in the furor that consumed our community and country.

Stockton had a large population of Italians along with us Japanese, and now Italy and Japan were partners against the Allies in the war. Luckily for the Biavatis and the other Italians in Stockton, I never heard talk of herding them up and incarcerating them.

The Biavatis' visit made me feel, for a brief time, accepted as a normal American who happened to live in Stockton, California, in 1942. It was a profound moment, monumental in its simplicity, that touched the deepest part of my soul. Our thank-yous and goodbyes were gut wrenching for both families; we sadly watched them walk away into the dead of night. I never saw any of the Biavati family again, but I will forever remember them in my heart.

One afternoon days later, Mom ventured out alone after asking me to watch the boys. She looked like she was on a mission. I was hoping for something delicious for dinner, but when she returned, I realized she'd gone to Stockton Dry Goods. She pulled out a big, heavy roll of gray-green canvas and carried it into the kitchen.

Mom and I had talked about seeing more and more soldiers in their uniforms, machine guns in hand, roaming the streets of Stockton. We were told the soldiers were dispatched to Stockton to keep the Japanese people safe, because the vitriol toward the Japanese could quickly escalate beyond the verbal taunts and slurs and turn into violence. Then Mom had noticed something I did not: occasionally, a soldier carried a big duffel bag. Since it seemed likely we would be forced to leave Stockton soon, observant Mom and her brilliant mind cooked up a clever brainstorm: we could make our own bags, similar to the soldiers', that would hold much more than our few small cardboard-style suitcases.

"Janet, our day is coming when we will be forced to pack up everything and leave Stockton," Mom said, looking determined. "We need to prepare for what is coming. Please take this canvas and make ten duffel bags like the ones the soldiers carry, one for everyone in our family. I know you have no pattern, but I'm sure you can figure it out with your sewing skills. I have every confidence you can make them as big and strong as the ones carried by the soldiers. The authorities will surely not object to bags similar to the ones they use."

I smiled and shook my head. "Mom, are you ever clever to think of these bags and plan ahead. Maybe—hopefully—we won't need them. But just in case, of course I will start right away."

I was lucky to have such a caring and compassionate mom. Once again, she was a step ahead of others in thinking about her family. She encouraged me to do my best on this project, to prepare as much as possible. Everything else was out of our control; we didn't know where we would be taken, how long we would stay there, or how we would be treated. It was good therapy for me to have a big project to work on for my family. It kept me occupied.

Making duffel bags was not as easy as it looked. It took me several days to create a master pattern to work from; the bag needed to be expandable and sturdy. Sewing was another obstacle, since the material was too thick and heavy to place in Mom's old sewing machine and required hand stitching. My hands ached after pushing the needle through the heavy canvas, and it required quite a lot of time to complete each bag. Attaching handles was another challenge; they needed double thickness and stitching so they wouldn't tear under the duress of a heavy load. Once I had the pattern figured out, I made duffel bags one after the other and felt proud after completing each one. Mom thanked me over and over again, so pleased with the Hayashis' ten new duffel bags.

The uncertainty about our future escalated quickly. We listened on the radio as General DeWitt's Civilian Exclusion Order No. 1 was announced on March 24. Everyone of Japanese ancestry, even those who were only one-sixteenth Japanese, must leave Bainbridge Island in Washington and report to the Wartime Civil Control Administration to be placed in a camp. Each person had six days to report to the administration before noon on March 30 or else face criminal penalties.

This made it official; Japanese Americans were now considered criminals.

I was glad I had our duffel bags ready. I wondered when the government orders would come to Stockton; it felt as though I was in the middle of a waiting game. On one hand, I comprehended the government was preparing to force me to leave my home, life, and city for somewhere else. On the other, I tried to convince myself that Stockton was mainly a farming area, far from the coast (eighty-three miles east of San Francisco), surely no threat to national security. Maybe we would be spared.

Government officials stated on the radio that they were issuing the exclusion orders to protect Japanese citizens. Japanese would be put in camps, where there would be no danger of violence. The outrage from the public over Pearl Harbor necessitated keeping the Japanese safe for now, said the government. I was left with an odd feeling as these executive orders and proclamations appeared in 1942. Somehow it seemed the commentary that the Japanese needed to be protected was an attempt to placate all of us. We were living a secluded life and feeling ill at ease in our own community. I wondered how people could become so angry that they would attack innocent Japanese in America who had nothing to do with the emperor's insane decision, made thousands of miles away in Japan. Soon enough it would become clear to me what the US government was really thinking.

Pop complied with the order to register our family as persons of Japanese ancestry living in Stockton. He didn't ask me to accompany him to translate, so it must have been a simple process. I found out later that officials with the Census Bureau had illegally provided the confidential census reports to other government agencies, so registration was just for confirmation of data they already possessed.

We saw plenty of Help Wanted notices in the paper and posted around town. The most common notices advertised for construction jobs, yet we understood that Japanese need not apply. Rumors started about a project at the San Joaquin County Fairgrounds. Some said the government was building barracks for soldiers to be stationed in Stockton. A group of my friends from the temple decided to walk to the fairgrounds to see what was going on, and when they returned, they told of buildings going up on the infield inside the horse track and towers being built around the track's perimeter, with barbed wire on the outside. Were they setting up a new prison?

"Of course it's a prison," said my friend Herbert, "and we will be the prisoners sooner than we can imagine."

I was shocked. We would never be prisoners—we'd done nothing wrong! The government just wanted to protect us—right?

As April arrived, I heard of civilian exclusion orders being issued, but none near Stockton. However, I knew I needed to expect that Stockton would receive one soon and to psychologically accept what appeared to be unfolding: the US government was constructing a prison in the San Joaquin County Fairgrounds and would soon force me to enter it. It was one thing to understand what was now inevitable but quite another to consider leaving the security of my home, family, familiar surroundings, and community. Despite my attempts to remain calm, I was grieving my loss of control over my life and starting to panic with the uncertainty of what was next. Somehow, I managed to carry on without revealing my personal anguish. Each of us coped in our own way as we contemplated the enormous change about to forcibly take over our lives.

Chapter 5

Preparing for Internment

It never occurred to me I shouldn't tell my sewing teacher about making duffel bags when I saw her at the temple. Mrs. Oshita was proud of her former student for this accomplishment, and what happened next was both unexpected and overwhelming. She told a few people about my handmade duffel bags, and soon, it seemed all the Japanese of Stockton had heard about my bags and wanted them for themselves.

One call came from Mrs. Morimoto, who asked if she could purchase material and drop it off at our home so I could make bags for her family. Of course! But before I completed her bag, I was hearing from friends, neighbors, and people I'd never met. People were asking my mom, sisters, and brother Will if I would make bags for them. Knowing we would all soon be forced to leave our homes, everyone was panicked to some degree. I'm sure no one intended to overwhelm me, but that was the result.

I quickly realized I must limit my bag making to one per family, although I didn't know if I could accomplish even that goal. People told me how desperate they were because they couldn't possibly fit enough in their little hard-back suitcases; some begged and pleaded for me to make their bags. I did my best to be fair and help as many as I could.

Material started arriving at our door, often left in a bag with a name on it. Some people brought lighter-weight fabric I was able to sew on Mom's machine. Mom had always taught me to be charitable no matter how poor we were; however, during the next few weeks, she was not pleased about people taking advantage of my kindness. She wanted to assist me, but her sewing experience was limited to sewing basic dresses and clothes for her family, and she didn't have time to spare. She could only tell me how proud she was of my hard work helping so many others.

The pressure was intense: I had to get as many bags ready for as many families as possible, and to do so, I worked late into the night, night after night. At one point, I dropped a needle in my shoe and cut my foot. I felt the weight of the world on me. With the arduous and tedious work, my hands ached, cracked, and even bled. With little rest and the feverish pace of the work, I became completely exhausted. Late one night, as everyone slept and I sewed, I found myself in the bathroom throwing up. It was just too much. I wanted to tell everyone to go away, but I was obsessed with helping as many people as I physically could. They were all counting on me, and I desperately did not want to let anyone down.

In April of 1942, as I worked feverishly on making duffel bags, we learned Japan was victorious in a battle for control of the Philippines. Japan captured as many as sixty thousand prisoners of war who were both native Filipino and American. Years later, we learned how these POWs were made to march sixty miles in the heat without food and water. If a prisoner collapsed, that person was bayoneted or beheaded. It is estimated twenty thousand prisoners perished along the Bataan Death March.

President Roosevelt had said that December 7 was "a date which will live in infamy" for America, but exactly five months later, FDR and his chain of command proclaimed a day that would live in infamy for me, my family, and all the Japanese living in Stockton: the day our imprisonment was ordered.

On May 7, 1942, General DeWitt issued Civilian Exclusion Order No. 53, which encompassed the entire city of Stockton. The fancy proclamations of the president and his general now turned to stark reality. Posters of the order were hung up almost instantly all over Stockton.

My hometown was being evacuated of all Japanese.

Almost as soon as the notices were posted, the phone started ringing. My friends with pet dogs and cats were panicking. No pets would be allowed in the camp. My family never owned pets, but many of my friends dearly loved their dogs and cats. Pets were family members; I understood that. I hoped to have a pet someday, but Mom said we didn't have the room and she didn't need another mouth to feed. Because of that, I was spared the agony of leaving behind a beloved member of my family.

My friends were frantically calling Caucasian friends to see if any would take care of their beloved pets. When my friend Kimi called to ask if I knew anyone who would take her dog, Buster, she was sobbing. She was an only child, so Buster was her best friend. She walked him, groomed him, fed him, and pampered him any way she could; when I often saw Kimi walking Buster, we would talk while Buster sat and patiently waited. I knew she was scheming to run away with Buster, but unfortunately, this was not *The Wizard of Oz*. Kimi would have to leave her best friend behind in six days. Her only hope was to find someone who would keep Buster and take good care of him until, hopefully, we were released and reunited with our pets left behind.

My heart ached for Kimi and Dorothy, who adored Buster and Rascal and many others too. I felt useless: I no longer had any Caucasian friends I could ask to care for my friends' precious pets. It seemed many Caucasians didn't want to risk even associating with Japanese, as that might make them targets for the authorities. If any Japanese couldn't find new homes for their pets, they didn't trust the authorities to take them to the pound, as they might just be put down straight away. It seemed they decided their only recourse was to leave as much food as possible, knowing that when that was gone, the dogs and cats would have to fend for themselves on the streets.

As it was, I was at the end of my own rope sewing the last duffel bags. Mom had planned more thoroughly than many other Japanese matriarchs; her anticipation and my hard work resulted in duffel bags ready to go. The notice said we could take only what we could carry and that "no personal items and no household goods will be shipped to the assembly center." We'd expected this, but the notice's other requirements were surprising:

Evacuees must carry with them on departure for the assembly center, the following property:

> (a) Bedding and linens (no mattress) for each member of the family;
> (b) Toilet articles for each member of the family;

(c) Extra clothing for each member of the family;

(d) Sufficient knives, forks, spoons, plates, bowls, and cups for each member of the family;

(e) Essential personal effects for each member of the family.

The list contained items we hadn't expected we'd need to bring; all of it had to fit in our duffel bags and perhaps an extra cardboard suitcase each. We were each required to carry our own bag; I wondered how much Ed and Tom could carry at three and five years old.

Pop arrived home from the Zuckerman farm on Friday, May 8, but not for a long weekend: Mr. Zuckerman had driven him home for the last time. As Pop waved goodbye to his employer of nearly fourteen years, neither knew they would never see each other again. The two men spoke different languages, but their long relationship yielded mutual respect. Mr. Zuckerman appreciated having a foreman who worked hard, was honest, and took great care of his farm, and Pop, who had moved our family to Stockton for the job with Mr. Zuckerman, had earned enough to rent an apartment and feed and clothe us.

I knew where we were headed, since my friends had seen the workers readying the San Joaquin County Fairgrounds. Because of the hysteria and urgency, the builders had abandoned customary construction practices in favor of quickly erected barracks ready for habitation. Trees were cut down, and their green wood was processed immediately for use by the WCCA. Giant rolls of black tar paper were acquired to form exteriors. Concrete was poured on uneven surfaces and in shallow layers. Preparation work to convert the livestock barn into barracks was minimal. Durability, quality, and craftsmanship were sacrificed for expediency. Since these facilities were for the Japs, it didn't matter how the accommodations were thrown together or if they would fall apart in short order. So it was with the Stockton Assembly Center.

I remembered my American history class. The United States had been established based on freedoms outlined in the Declaration of Independence over 150 years prior. These freedoms, the Constitution, and America's rule of law set the United States apart from any other country, and among other things, they prohibited detaining anyone without probable cause. But now, that protection had been revoked for anyone of Japanese descent who happened to live on the West Coast.

Two days before we left, there was a knock at our door. Marian answered. A small round Caucasian man and a larger bulky man stood outside.

"Hello, ma'am—is your mother or father home? "

"Sure. Please wait one minute, and I'll get them."

Marian called Pop to the door.

"Hello. What can I do for you?" Pop asked in his broken English.

"Well, we know you Japs are leaving in a couple of days. I'll give you ten dollars for your refrigerator."

Bam! Just like that! A kick in the gut would have felt better. This was one of the lowest moments in Pop's life. He'd saved for months to collect over two hundred dollars for a refrigerator. His accomplishment had brought such joy to his wife and family. Now, these men had insulted him by both calling him a Jap and hustling him. However, he didn't curse or slam the door in the men's faces. Though I knew he'd been hurt to the core, he was polite. It was the only way he ever treated people, no matter what they did or said. He told the men to come back later.

I heard Mom and Pop talking about the men preying on the vulnerable. There was no respect or civility left. Pop had known we were going to be forced to leave but hadn't considered the implications of this or what would become of our household possessions. Mom suggested they get what they could for the refrigerator, since most items would be stolen if left behind. Pop realized she was right. He summoned all his strength and swallowed his pride, though the man who had asked for the refrigerator deserved no kindness or respect of any kind. Reality had just hit Pop between the eyes; somehow he felt like a failure because he couldn't protect his family's most valuable possession. Yet Pop did have the most valuable possession of all: his family. I know that thinking about his family gave him the strength to carry on.

The lowlife deadbeats returned, and Pop managed to negotiate a price of twelve dollars for his prized refrigerator. The burly man retrieved gloves from his back pocket, and the two men marched into our kitchen. They placed the modest contents of the refrigerator on the table, then hoisted up the refrigerator, with the big brute carrying the lower half. Out the door they pranced, carrying some of our pride along with our precious appliance. We stood quietly and watched; Tom and Ed held my hands tightly, understanding something bad had just happened.

Just like that, it was over. This event was further evidence of the unfortunate truth that has surfaced over and over again throughout the ages: hard times often bring out the immoral and unscrupulous individuals who prey on the helpless. In a few short years, I would witness this again.

As I sewed the last of the duffel bags for other families, Mom planned what to take in our own precious bags, now neatly stacked in the corner of the living room. Then she and Pop sat all eight of us down for a family meeting. They told us to remember *gaman*, patience with dignity. We were proud Japanese Buddhists who, now more than ever, honored the commands of Lord Buddha. We were repulsed with Emperor Hirohito, who considered himself to be a proud leader of the Shinto Buddhist faith, and his imperial military generals' choice to enact ruthless aggression and create war. We could never forget the United States hadn't wanted war; it was Japan's massacre at Pearl Harbor that necessitated America's military response. But still, Pop said there was nothing to be ashamed of, since none of us had done anything wrong.

"Follow the rules the government has now demanded of us," he said, "and in the end, it will all work out fine. We have no choice, so carry on with *gaman*. Lord Buddha will be with us always."

Then Pop's eyes twinkled, and I noticed a smirk on his face when he looked at each of us. He said he was looking forward to a paid vacation courtesy of the US government. For many years now, he'd worked long, hard, hot days of toil, on Mr. Zuckerman's farm, before that on his little plot of rented land on Bacon Island, and even back before that on the sugarcane farms of Hawaii, where he'd slaved for years. He spoke slowly and with great passion as he thought about his adult life and his years of hard labor. Pop was now fifty-six years old, and I wondered how many more years he could continue farming. His parents had both passed away in their early sixties.

"I am tired," he said. "I am going to relax as long as I can. After this is all over, I will likely be back on the farm in a few months. Mr. Zuckerman told me he couldn't guarantee my foreman's job when

I returned but that I would always be welcome to return as a farm-hand, no matter when."

Mom looked at us, and her eyes teared up. She loved her family so much; we were lucky to have a mom who would do anything for us. She looked directly at each one of us and told us that all she cared about was that our family would all be together, even during our imprisonment.

"They can take us away and shame us for something we weren't associated with, but we know who we are inside, and that is what matters," she said. "We will never allow the government to change our hearts. We are now and will forever be good people."

Mom and Pop continued to prepare us for life as it was about to unfold.

Mom asked me to go visit my friend next door, Grace, because she lived alone in her apartment. The WCCA had offered to store items for evacuees but would not guarantee their safety, so, rather than trusting this agency with our property, Mom wanted to know if there was any room in Grace's apartment for some of our leftover belongings. Grace understood my sincerity and was very accommodating. Grace had already prepaid her rent through the end of the year, and the landlord had promised to safeguard the contents of her apartment. So, the complete dismantling of our home was settled: the refrigerator had been "legally stolen," the bags would soon be packed, the beds and couch would be left behind, and everything else would go to Grace's home. It was a relief for Mom and Pop to leave all remaining Hayashi possessions in Grace's apartment, where they would be safe until our return.

Mom planned what to take with us, basing her decisions on the little information provided by the WCCA. She decided it was important to take all photos, records, and papers pertaining to our family, so she gave me the birth certificates to place in my bag and packed family photos in hers and Pop's bags. Since we didn't know how or if we'd be able to wash clothes, Mom thought it would be helpful to take dark-colored dresses, since they wouldn't show dirt. We'd sewn these dresses for my sisters before I'd started working on duffel bags; I'd never worn pants in my twenty-two years. We would also each take an overcoat, a raincoat, and sturdy leather button-down shoes. We stuffed dishes and sets of single bedsheets in each bag. There was no room for pillows, so we decided we could make them when we arrived. The exclusion order hadn't explained anything about meals, and Mom didn't know whether we would do our own cooking, so she packed some pots and pans. When we finished packing, our duffel bags—and even our pillowcases we used as extra bags—were bulging to capacity with every precious and essential item we thought we'd need in an internment camp.

At 10:00 a.m. on May 10, our family of ten, carrying our bulging duffel bags, pillowcases, and some smaller cardboard suitcases, walked from our apartment on Lafayette Street to the National Guard Armory building on North California Street.

We didn't know at that moment none of us would ever live again in Stockton. The WCCA employees were typical bureaucrats following the rules and procedures established to ensure the relocation went smoothly. I assumed these people were accustomed to the process, since Stockton was the fifty-third exclusion order. Of the total Japanese moved to the camps, about eighty thousand were *Nisei* and therefore US citizens, as I was. The remaining thirty-seven thousand to forty thousand had been born in Japan but had lived for years or decades in America, precluded from becoming citizens.

Our bags were checked for legible name and address labels, and we were each given a name tag to wear. We got in line and waited for the next truck to arrive to drive us the short distance to the assembly center. The workers indicated that we would receive more instructions upon arrival at the assembly center. Among us Japanese, there was no small talk. No one smiled. All we could hear were instructions given by people in uniforms wearing official badges.

After a relatively short wait, a large construction vehicle arrived, one evidently used to haul dirt. We climbed into the back. The floor was filthy. We squeezed together, which helped us keep our balance while we held tightly to the last of what we owned in the world. With gas rationing in effect, officials didn't want to waste any gas with extra trips back and forth. It was a short, bumpy ride to the San Joaquin County Fairgrounds, now named an assembly center but truthfully a concentration camp. We were like sheep loaded for a journey to the shearer. We were scared, cautious, and suspicious of the people directing us. What would happen next? We complied with the orders given to us.

I knew almost everyone in the truck bed. Some were neighbors we knew well; others I recognized from temple. As a large family, we knew at least one person from most of the families of our community. On a normal day, we would have said hello and chatted when we saw each other; that day, we exchanged no pleasantries. We spoke only to answer the bureaucrats' questions.

The truck passed the newly constructed barbed-wire fence, crossed the racetrack surrounding the fairgrounds, and stopped abruptly. We lunged forward, each of us falling against the person in front of us, then quickly regained our balance while the front-seat passenger hopped out and opened the back gate. The man pushed a large block of wood to the truck for us to use as a step and offered his hand to each of us as we jumped off the back of the truck. He took my bag and extended his free hand to help me leap down, and I appreciated his smile and assistance. A weak smile was all I could offer back to him.

The first thing I saw when I disembarked was a tower next to the truck. Standing in the tower was a guard holding a machine gun. I looked around and saw more towers on the perimeter, each manned with an armed soldier. The county fairground was now the county jail.

We were directed to stand in a lengthy queue. All ten Hayashis stood together, waiting our turn to move into our new home, just miles from our real home yet a world away. When we reached the registration desk, I wrote down the names of all my family members, and almost immediately, I was asked to step to the side and informed I'd been chosen to serve as a bilingual block manager in the assembly center.

And my life in the internment camp began.

PART 3

LIFE AS A BLOCK MANAGER

Chapter 6
Block Manager Training, Stockton Assembly Center

When I left the room where Mr. Ben Richardson had given me and the other selected Japanese information about our new jobs as block managers and instructions to meet there again at two o'clock the next day, I immediately searched for block four, where my family would be waiting for me.

The pathways between the barracks were all dirt packed. Tall weeds seemed to crowd everywhere else; surely a real military base wouldn't be covered with weeds. Barracks number four was easy to locate, and my heart lightened when I was reunited with my family after our brief but stressful separation. My block manager duties encompassed several nearby barracks and a horse barn.

While I'd been gone, my family had placed our heavy bags in our rooms and found the huge pile of metal-frame beds stacked and tangled together. Will and Pop had carried one bed from the top of the pile down the pathway and around the corner to our barracks; then Marian, Christine, Loretta, and Fran had helped them carry more beds until they had one for each of us, while Mom watched Tom and Ed. Then they repeated the whole process with the army mattresses.

Each room was approximately twenty by twenty feet. Mom and my sisters carefully arranged five beds in each of the two side-by-side rooms, which would be our home for who knew how long. Then they made up the beds with the sheet sets we'd brought, after security had cleared our bags and returned them to us. Mom, Pop, Will, Tom, and Ed lived in room number five; Christine, Marian, Loretta, Fran, and I took room number six. Besides our beds, our rooms contained no other furniture, so we couldn't unpack our bags. Mom insisted we leave our bags on the ends of our beds, rather than on the floor, to keep them clean; we were all short—Mom wasn't even five feet tall—so there was plenty of room on the military-length metal beds to hold our bags and us while we slept.

After we set up the rooms, Marian and Loretta did some exploring. They found the barracks with restrooms and showers.

"You won't believe what they look like," they said.

When they showed me, I understood what they meant.

The room held lines of toilets and sinks and rows of showerheads protruding from the walls, with no privacy—none. My mouth gaped open. I'd only taken a glance, because a lady was using the toilet; I felt like I'd walked in on her. At least the constructors had built separate facilities for men and women.

Next, Marian and Loretta showed me our mess hall, one of many scattered across the camp. Some mattresses were still stacked up in the corner for the remaining people expected to arrive the next day.

We returned to our rooms and sat down on the beds for a few minutes. Each room had only an outside door, so we had to walk outdoors to go between our two Hayashi rooms. The walls extended only partway up to the ceiling; our own assigned rooms afforded no real privacy, either. There was no private space anywhere in the camp.

Suddenly, I heard a chorus of hellos. I looked up to see three young men smiling broadly over the wall from the next-door room.

"We're neighbors; this is going to be fun!" one exclaimed.

Marian knew one of the boys. "What are you doing?" she said.

"Oh, we heard your voices, and we realized the bed was next to the wall, so we wanted to say hello. I'm Richard; this is Henry, and this is George."

"It's nice to meet you, Henry and George."

Marian already knew Richard, and she introduced the rest of us to our over-the-partition guests. They seemed to think it was great to live next to a room filled with five young ladies. Marian told Richard and his brothers it was nice to see them again, but next time, could they please say hi through the door?

They laughed together. "Okay. See you soon."

While we were annoyed at the boys next door for peeking over at us, we couldn't help but chuckle. It was a lighter moment in an otherwise intensely stressful day. In all, over four thousand Japanese had been crammed into the newly constructed barracks on the San Joaquin County Fairgrounds. If misery loves company, there was plenty to go around.

Mom came to the girls' room and told us to find our dishes, chopsticks, and silverware packed carefully in each of our bags, since it was almost time for dinner. We were all hungry; we'd eaten only a small breakfast that morning, to clean up the remaining bits of food at home, and during our journey from our apartment to the armory to the assembly center and finally to our new "homes," we hadn't been served lunch by our new captors.

We left our rooms and stopped at the ladies' and men's restrooms, where we waited patiently in line and swallowed our embarrassment to use the facilities communal style, and wash up before dinner. There were no alternatives to the scantily built government bathrooms. We then walked to the mess hall, seeing friends and acquaintances heading to the same destination. For the first time in that long day, we all seemed to have the courage to speak.

"So nice to see you—where is your room?"

Evidently, our room assignments were allocated according to our addresses, so our old neighbors were now our new neighbors in our new residences. In the mess hall, we were assigned seating at wooden picnic tables, just like ones I'd used for picnics in the park; our family of ten received two tables.

We got in line for food. I saw green beans in one big square container with a large slotted spoon, white rice in a similar container, and then the main course in a long pan, perfect slices placed neatly one slice atop the other—*Spam!*

My stomach was growling, so I took a portion of Spam on my plate, even though I'd never liked it whenever Mom bought some. There were pineapple slices in the pan, so I took one of those, too.

I didn't say anything about the dinner menu, but of course, Fran said, "*Ewwww!* I'm not eating that disgusting meat."

"Me either," Tom agreed.

Mom calmly replied, "It is up to you, but you may get hungry before breakfast if you don't eat the Spam now."

I was hungry, so the Spam went down pretty well with the pineapple slice. I think Fran and Tom only ate the rice. Someone shouted from the kitchen that we could have more until it was all gone, and with that announcement, many people went back for seconds. As I ate my first meal in the assembly center; little did I know how many thousand more meals I would eat courtesy of the US government.

We were instructed to turn in our dirty dishes, chopsticks, and silverware after we first scraped off the plates. Then we left the dining hall and walked back to our rooms in the barracks. It was close to the summer solstice, so the days were long, but when darkness arrived at the Stockton Assembly Center, everything turned black. There was no electricity in our rooms or outside them, so we had nothing more to do other than go to bed. But without any lights, how could anyone find the way to use the restroom or take a shower?

The shower would have to wait till the next day, and Mom concluded we'd just have to relieve ourselves by our rooms to be safe. What if we got lost trying to find the bathrooms or returning from them? What if a soldier thought we were trying to escape? We older girls knew how to squat to potty from our early years living in the country. This was the Japanese way—there was no toilet seat. Mom instructed us to walk away several steps so no one would walk into any remnant the next day. That's how we relieved ourselves that night and most nights inside the confines of Stockton Assembly Center.

Eventually, I learned that others also stayed at "home" in lieu of trekking to the bathrooms when night fell over the camp. It wasn't something to be proud of or embarrassed by, since it was a necessity in the situation, but also it wasn't anything to discuss.

That night, we all took some of our clothes out of our bags and stuffed them into pillowcases. I put my head down and pulled the sheet up over me. Marian was to my left, and Christine was by my feet. We five sisters fit tightly in our room, but we'd slept in close quarters all our life, so this wasn't new. With the room partitions only rising partway to the ceiling, we could easily hear all conversations in the nearby rooms. Most people were quiet and respectful, but there was one family arguing about who was sleeping where. I just lay awake quietly until they fell silent. Once I was a fully functioning block manager, I would be expected to get up and speak to the rude family.

That night, it was difficult to sleep on my army mattress and bed frame. So much had happened in that one day, my head was swimming. Leaving home, arriving at the camp, checking in, setting up our rooms with only beds, eating in a mess hall, learning about my new job as a block manager—all this was rolling around in my head. I was glad to be past these events, but I hoped we'd be allowed to go home in a few months. Until then, I was relieved my family was safe and sound together in the US internment camp.

The next morning, as instructed, we lined up in the mess hall for breakfast at eight. We each took a clean plate from the stack; the plates each family had brought were mixed together. Someone tried to retrieve his own plate from near the bottom of the stack, but the man in the kitchen barked that he should just take the next one. Breakfast was scrambled eggs with leftover Spam. Once again, anyone who wanted seconds was welcome to eat anything left over after everyone was served.

Before we'd finished eating, Superintendent Ben walked to the front of the chow line. He instructed us all to stay in our seats and listen to his important announcements, and the room grew quiet as he spoke.

He began by stressing the importance of staying away from the barbed-wire fence and the track area, because if we approached them, it might seem like we were attempting to escape, and he didn't want harm to come to anyone. I think we'd all understood this without being told—we were terrified of the soldiers and their machine guns. Next, he discussed how the camp would be operated: jobs were available to the "residents," for which the government would pay a modest wage.

"Would anyone like to work in the kitchen?" he asked. "Would anyone like to work in the hospital? Are there any nurses or doctors here? Please come to the office and let us know if you are interested in these jobs."

Ben Richardson scanned the room and told us we would find out later in the day who was assigned to be the block manager in each block. That person would be responsible for bed checks every night at ten.

"If you have a complaint," he said, "tell your block manger, who will report it to the superintendent. If anyone does not follow the rules, the block manager will report them to the superintendent."

The more he talked, the more I felt my face flush; only my family knew I'd been pegged for this assignment. Why me? I didn't want any part of this responsibility. Would anyone think I'd asked to be a block manager? Maybe I would get lucky and someone else would ask to manage our block, so I wouldn't have to.

Finally, the man finished his announcements. I couldn't wait to exit the mess hall.

Back in my room, I dropped onto my bed. I didn't cry, but I felt like I wanted to. Too much was being expected of me. Soon, Mom came into the room all smiles; she didn't realize how anxious I was about assuming my soon-to-be-new role. Still, she made me smile with her excitement: she now knew with certainty we wouldn't need our pots and pans, because all meals would be provided by the government. While she regretted wasting so much precious space bringing along something unnecessary, she was thrilled someone else would be cooking for our family of ten. I realized Pop and Mom were both on a holiday of sorts from the hard work of their daily lives, and both were ready to be relieved of the responsibilities of working on the farm and in the kitchen. Mom's joy lightened my mood.

Mom and my sisters checked out the laundry and ironing rooms. The laundry room contained several big sinks and washboards, but everyone needed to provide their own soap. The irons and ironing tables were ready to go, but Mom said, laughing, that the tables were too tall for her, so her daughters could take care of the ironing. We girls had always taken turns ironing at home, but Mom said that I was the one who got the wrinkles out the best. My sisters agreed, wearing big smiles.

After lunch at 1:40 p.m., I walked to the office barracks close to the entrance of the assembly center, where I'd been told to return to receive further instructions regarding my job as block manager. I wanted to be early, and I was the first person to arrive, so I sat alone in the room until the other block managers started to gather during the next twenty minutes. All twenty of us were seated by 2:00 p.m.

Ben began to speak to his staff—us. He asked each block manager to raise his or her hand and come forward to get papers and clipboards as he called out each name. It was no surprise who Janet Hayashi was: I was the only woman in the room. I'd never thought of myself as a trailblazer or a woman who could function independently in a difficult situation, but here I was, thrust into this role.

"You have been selected for a function vital to the safe and efficient operation of this camp," Ben explained. "Each one of you is considered outstanding for your ability to speak and read both Japanese and English. You are also considered reliable and honest. These qualities will be crucial to your role as block manager. We at the WCCA are in charge of this camp, which is being guarded by the US Army. We don't want any trouble of any kind. You have been given a list of names of everyone in your block. Each manager has approximately two hundred residents he or she will be responsible for; you must learn the name and address of each person in your block. You also must tell your residents to stay far away from the fence; we don't want anyone to get hurt." I felt more and more nervous as he spoke.

"As you leave here, please take a kerosene lantern; you will need it each evening for your duties as block manager. Every night at ten o'clock, you will walk through the barracks in your block and do a bed check. For now, you will not need to report to us when your bed checks are complete if all residents are properly accounted for; however, if circumstances arise that necessitate daily reporting after bed checks, you will be notified. If someone is not in his or her room, come to the office, and report that person missing. We will investigate. If anyone in your block has a complaint, come to the office and report it to us." The responsibility of being a block manager now felt overwhelming.

"We will do the best we can to make living here as comfortable as possible, but keep in mind that we do not have any extra funds at this time. If there are disagreements in your block, please work to resolve them. If there is fighting or violence, the military will place offenders in a holding facility, if necessary. You will be the first person to intervene when there are quarrels. If a situation escalates beyond reasonable discourse, please report it immediately. Also, we will be setting up a canteen soon, where the residents will be able to purchase items at the discounted military prices." He paused.

"One last thing: we may have meetings here from time to time. You will be notified when to appear. Are there any questions?"

As Ben paused and looked around the room, all twenty block managers sat still, holding our papers and clipboards, and none of us asked questions. Maybe we were all too scared to ask anything or had heard most of these instructions the day before, or maybe we didn't have any idea what to ask. Clearly, none of us had experience as a block manager in an assembly center.

When no one raised a hand, Ben went on. "Spend time this afternoon going around and acquainting yourself with everyone in your block. You should be ready to begin your bed checks tonight starting at ten p.m. Thank you for your assistance. You are all dismissed at this time."

Chapter 7
Daily Life as a Block Manager

When I left the meeting, uneasiness encompassed me. How could I introduce myself to the residents of my assigned barracks in a way that wouldn't appear I was their boss of sorts? I could certainly tell everyone I hadn't volunteered for this assignment; they would surely understand my predicament. The most awkward part was going to be approaching men my parents' age, whom I looked up to as leaders of my community and temple. Yet I also knew what was required of me; all I could do was be as polite as possible and hope I wouldn't face any resistance.

It took all afternoon to meet and greet each resident of my block. Some I was meeting for the first time; others I'd known for years from school and Women's Club or as neighbors and family friends. Then there were those, such as business owners or leaders at the temple, whose identities I knew but who didn't know me. It was a challenge to tell these people I, on behalf of the WCCA and the US Army, was now in charge of the block where they lived. As I explained myself to them, it seemed they all understood this position was not my choice. What a relief! To many of the *Issei*, I spoke Japanese, but I spoke primarily English to the *Nisei*. I presumed this was why I'd been chosen to be a block manager—because I could easily communicate with both age groups. Still, I was one of them, and we were all anxious about what lay ahead.

While greeting people, I said I would pass any complaints they had to the authorities. The women replied quickly.

"We have no privacy in the bathrooms or showers," said one woman. "Please help now—this is awful."

Another added, "Get us fabric, and we will make curtains."

This was my complaint, too; now I could report it to the office as the complaint of every family.

Included in my block were horse stalls used during the county fairs; bachelors were assigned to these living quarters. Each stall had a swinging door with a latch. As I toured around the horse stalls, I detected a distinct remnant odor, not overpowering, but stronger than the general odor of the camp. These men were living atop years of accumulated horse manure.

One of the men I met in the horse stalls was Ray Konishi. Ray was cordial, so we chatted for a while. He was the nephew of Mrs. Arakawa, who owned the Star Theater, where I'd sold tickets until Pearl Harbor. I especially felt sorry for Ray and the other men who'd been given the most unpleasant accommodations in the camp. Surely, they told me, it would only be for a few months.

I couldn't speak with Ray for too long—I needed to meet all two hundred residents assigned to my block—so after a few minutes, I moved along.

After the general announcement had gone out asking for residents who were interested in employment at the camp, many accepted the opportunity. Mom and my sisters got jobs in our mess hall, assisting the cook, making sure the tubs were full of food, clearing off tables, fetching things needed by people in the mess hall, and cleaning up. Men were hired to wash and dry dishes. Pop got a job as a boiler man, heating up the tanks of water for showers, kitchen sinks, and the sinks in the laundry room every time people wanted to do laundry; women and bachelors primarily used the laundry room. Pop and some other men helped put up clotheslines after getting permission. There was never enough space on them, so we took turns hanging clothes to dry. All my family members were paid eight dollars per month for their work.

As block manager, I not only handled daily bed checks, made announcements, and reported grievances, but I was also responsible for keeping the order. If I couldn't do this, I would have to bring in the authorities for assistance. When I heard about peeping toms, I had to investigate. When I heard about small thievery, I had to investigate. When I heard about vandalism, I investigated that, too. Walking around, asking lots of questions, and lecturing the young delinquents was not a pleasant task, but it was part of what was expected of me as a block manager.

We were all living in tight quarters with no sound barriers between rooms—indefinitely. If you dropped any group of people in this environment, there would inevitably be conflict, whether within a family or between families. Whenever a situation developed, I went to the people involved and asked them politely to please cooperate and stop the disorder. By far, the most common problem I faced was getting people to just be considerate of others and keep quiet.

Amazingly, my block residents listened to me. I never raised my voice; I just explained that we all needed to follow the rules. Throughout my tenure, I never once turned in anyone for disobedience. Maybe my residents just felt sorry for this little twenty-two-year-old woman keeping order for two hundred people. I did hear stories occasionally of problems in other blocks—not extreme, but enough to require involvement of the office. I never heard whether anyone went to jail.

One incident happened shortly after we arrived. Someone stuffed the toilets to plug them up and wrote graffiti in places on the bathroom walls. These acts of vandalism remained unsolved petty crimes. Were they committed by annoying kids or by furious adults venting their disgust over their living conditions? Was it a single person or multiple people? These early incidents were dealt with and repaired by the camp officials. In short order, there was no more vandalism. Whoever was involved surely realized it wasn't going to change anything and that it was only disruptive to everyone in the block.

One complaint I received frequently was intense dislike of the food. And the reply from the authorities was simple: take it or leave it. We would be served the same food being served to military servicemen on their bases. The WCCA did hire cooks for each mess hall from the Japanese who applied, and we were thrilled to have the Stockton Hotel chef as cook in our mess hall. He could prepare food using only provided ingredients, but he would surely create the best possible meals from those ingredients; rice was provided at lunch and dinner every day. Chef Kamisono was pleasant, with a warm smile to all as we proceeded through the chow lines.

Despite this, the food complaints only got worse. Pork and beans were served regularly, and other offerings were also repeated over and over again; we all were sick of the food quickly. At first, some meat was offered, but as the war continued, meat became scarce. To extend what meat was available, the cooks often served stews with meat and vegetables in a broth, and sometimes hamburger was cooked up, crumbled, and served with vegetables, which the government purchased from local farmers. We often ate eggs for breakfast, thanks in part to an in-camp chicken coop that provided eggs. I also saw big boxes full of eggs arrive in the office. Milk or orange juice wasn't passed around, but you could request it, and one of the waitresses would bring it if it was available. Coffee and tea were provided at all meals. The young ones often refused what was available, but they learned eventually to just eat and be quiet. Surprisingly, our diet, while not appetizing, was reasonably healthy.

Before the camp, some Japanese had been mired in unrelenting poverty during the Depression; these people had stood in soup lines or found temporary hard labor working in the nearby fields, where meals were provided. These people thought the Stockton Assembly Center was grand. For the first time in years, they weren't hungry for days on end. I generally knew who these folks were in my block: I never received a complaint about food or anything else from them.

For Japanese of every socioeconomic stratum, camp was the great equalizer. Everyone received the same type of rooms, bathrooms, and showers, except for the bachelor men living in horse stalls. We also received the same freedoms—or lack thereof. The country people were used to living in cabins without interior walls and using outhouses, which was how I'd lived for the first eight years of my life. This made their adjustment to the barracks and our sparse provisions relatively tolerable from the start. For the wealthier Japanese, the adjustment was much more difficult. They'd left behind plush homes and furnishings and no longer had hired help to do their cleaning and laundry. Their money did them little good in this place, though they could afford to order merchandise from the Sears or Montgomery Ward catalogs to be delivered to camp. Maybe that was some consolation for them, but otherwise, we were all the same.

Our statuses in society at large seemed to carry over into the camp: the affluent Japanese tended to associate exclusively with each other, and so forth with the other various economic classes. I suppose it was just the natural way of people to have friends and acquaintances with a lifestyle common to their own. It wasn't snobbery to me, just familiarity.

The government set up a canteen in the camp—yet another similarity, in addition to the barracks, mess hall, and security, to a military base. The canteen was a welcome feature. It only carried a limited selection of products, but they included little hard candies, soaps, personal toiletry products, newspapers and magazines which were weeks behind, and kerosene lanterns. I was issued a kerosene lantern for making my rounds each night as block manager. I also used the lantern to find my way to the bathrooms after dark, so I could avoid the unpleasant situation of using the weeds as a toilet. Often, I used my lantern to venture out in the middle of the night to take a shower in privacy.

The *Stockton Record* was available at the canteen; those who didn't mind spending their money for the paper read it cover to cover. The news of the war was always a week or two old, but it was still news. The war was all anyone wanted to hear about. We also published a little paper called the *El Joaquin* at our camp, consisting of camp news the WCCA printed for us. It was more a bulletin than a paper. I passed it out to the residents of my block.

The residents could cash their government checks at the canteen, giving them a little bit of spending money. Also, the canteen cashed checks from our home bank accounts, but with no jobs putting funds in these accounts, most people were broke. My family never had a bank account; what money Pop had left from his last check came along with him to camp. Most, like me, only earned a meager eight to eleven dollars per month. The government would assist us with using our little bits of cash to order from the catalogs.

The US mail was delivered to our camp, providing us a connection to the outside world. Eventually, we received a typical government mail address to use, similar to military personnel. I wondered if incoming or outgoing mail was read by the authorities before reaching its destination. I had nothing to hide, so I really didn't care if they read my mail, but I hoped it traveled in a timely manner. As far as I know, the mail between Japan and America still went through to its destination, despite the ongoing war.

Amazingly, within two weeks, the greatly anticipated material for curtains arrived. It came in many nonmatching pieces, so it was no doubt remnants that the government got for free. The WCCA divided it up and gave it to each block manager to pass out as we saw fit for making bathroom and shower curtains. The government even agreed to hang the curtains once they were completed. The new curtains would only provide visual privacy, but that would be a huge improvement. Several women in my block gladly took on the job of cutting and sewing curtains by hand. I was too busy as a block manager to get involved with this big sewing project. Our completed bathroom curtains were colorful with all the material pieced together; my favorite was the shower curtain with cats and dogs, a rainbow, and primary-color balloons. With the combined efforts of the residents and overseers, the piecework curtains were hung in record time, to the relief of everyone. The curtains made our primitive facilities somewhat tolerable.

Next, the women set their sights on making curtains from the fabric remnants to cover the window that sat low on the wall in their own rooms. Some of the more affluent families were able to order lace for their curtains, or even some lovely sheer material. The bachelors in the horse stalls didn't have windows necessitating curtains: one very small advantage to their barracks.

Radios were considered contraband, but one of the soldiers, Charlie, did bring a radio in for us. What a treat! Everyone gathered to listen to it. Charlie was my favorite soldier; he understood the situation and reasoned it wouldn't cause harm to let us listen to the radio occasionally. If Ben, the superintendent, knew he was doing this, he didn't stop him. I appreciated Charlie's sense of humor; he enjoyed sharing stories about his children with me from time to time. He was married with a family and was just doing his job like the rest of us. We just happened to be together in the Stockton Assembly Center. Charlie's friendly Southern greeting was welcoming: "How are ya'll doin' today?" Getting to know Charlie helped relieve my overwhelming fear of every soldier. As for the other soldiers, they did their jobs and didn't communicate with us much.

One day, the staff told us about viruses sickening residents with a stomach ailment at one of the neighboring camps in California. The government quickly set up a "hospital," but luckily, the viruses didn't find us. Living together in such close quarters guaranteed the quick transmission of germs. Soon enough, the new medical center was fully staffed and operational, although it wasn't what one would think of as a hospital—there was minimal electricity and few medicines available—but at least the doctors were properly trained. I was asked to be a translator for female patients who needed treatment and spoke no English. This wasn't a paid position but rather volunteer on an as-needed basis; I said I'd be happy to assist when needed. It was one more role I received all because I'd studied so diligently for years at the Japanese language school.

Ben asked me to come to the office and assist some residents with translation needs. Many of the *Issei* wanted to write to their families in Japan or read Japanese letters they'd received but could hardly read or write Japanese. As word spread that I would help with translation needs, I was bombarded with requests. I both wrote and read letters, and this quickly became considered part of my role as block manager. I was busy every day. Every kind of translation need that came up, including assisting in the medical center, was added to the duties of my daily life. Sometimes I read love letters, and sometimes gossips asked me to share what I translated. I never violated anyone's privacy.

Overall, I was coping well with my new life. While I hadn't sought out or had any interest in being a block manager, as I hadn't when the FBI had asked me to translate for them, I thought I was doing my part to help. Being busy was good; I wasn't able to dwell on the what-ifs. Many others in the camp found the days long, and without the daily activities of their "former" lives, they grew bored.

Still, while I displayed an outward pleasantry conducting all my official duties throughout the day, I couldn't escape a deep-guarded uneasiness—fear wouldn't abandon my soul.

Chapter 8
Summer 1942

Many of us young ladies did our best to groom ourselves in the assembly center. We had to make do without fancy clothes, for starters, but since I sewed my own clothes, I could make myself more fitted dresses. My friend Bernice had given me a permanent before camp, which had been a treat. While living in the assembly center, I sometimes slept on brush rollers with pins in them—that was uncomfortable. The warm days made it difficult to keep my hair curled. I'd brought one tube of lipstick, which quickly ran out. None of my friends were fashion queens, but before entering the internment camp, we'd styled our hair, worn some makeup, and tried to look pretty. Now, life in the assembly center made us look and feel plain.

Camp was filled with men trained in every kind of trade. One in my block, Mr. Sugi, was a carpenter. One day, he took leftover wood from a heap in the corner of the grounds, borrowed a hammer and nails from the office, and started making dressing rooms for the girls in our block; the camp afforded so little privacy, so it was very thoughtful of him. He made frames, and we covered them with army blankets and put them in our rooms. Just big enough to slip into to change clothes, our dressing rooms were one more creative solution for making our living conditions as tolerable as possible by restoring some small measure of privacy.

When Mom found out there were chickens at camp, she asked about getting the down breast feathers to make pillows, as she had years before in the country. The US Army had furnished metal-frame beds and mattresses, but we were responsible for acquiring our own bedding, including pillows. Her request was granted in time. We'd brought pillowcases with us that we doubled up, as we did at home, to keep the pillow itself clean. Mom worked outside with the feathers, sneezing away, because she didn't want to get the feathers in the room. Eventually, these new feather pillows replaced our clothes-stuffed pillowcases.

One day, as I was in the office working on translations, I was stunned to see a familiar face walk in: Miss Humbarger, the high school sponsor for the Japanese Club, of which I'd been a member and one of the leaders throughout high school. She was not Japanese. It must have taken a lot of courage for her to walk through the entrance gate, past the towers and guards looking menacingly around; and if she wasn't afraid of the camp's security, would she fear she'd be ridiculed by others outside the camp who knew she'd visited us? Thankfully, she was admitted into the camp with no problem, and she walked into the office as I finished up helping Mr. Yamamoto write a letter to his family in Japan. When Mr. Yamamoto left, what a joy I felt as I sat down with Miss Humbarger. She was pleased to see how well I was handling the trauma of my life; I was struck by her kindness in looking in on us, many of whom she'd watched grow up.

Ben suggested I take her back to our mess hall so others could see her also. Miss Humbarger's eyes were wide as we walked back to the dining room, the gathering place for everything in the camp. She just said, "Oh my," to me as we walked past the barracks toward my mess hall. Word of her presence spread quickly, and within a half hour, dozens of former students had gathered to see Miss Humbarger.

Miss Humbarger began visiting weekly. Outside the camp, she ran many little errands for her Japanese friends, such as depositing or withdrawing money at the bank and picking up little things not available at the canteen, including balls, baseball cards, toys, or makeup. She was our link with the outside world—and more: she was an angel who came calling.

One day, Miss Humbarger brought in a kickball, which was like gold to the young boys. We had plenty of room in camp for outdoor sport. Tom joined in a pick-up kickball game, while Mom and Ed watched. The older boys divided the younger kids into two teams, and the game was on. It was so good for the boys to run around and burn off some energy; they played until they were all exhausted. Then the winners started bragging, and the losers promised to even the score the next day. Tom chattered happily about the game. I knew he couldn't wait to play the next day.

Some of the teenaged and young men acquired baseballs and bats. Some had even brought their baseball gloves. They started a game of their own, and after Will heard about it, he joined in too. I could tell they enjoyed it as much as a game at any park in Stockton. They planned to play again the next day. The various sports brought energy and vitality to the camp; eventually, people started wandering out to watch, even if they didn't know anyone playing. It was something to do and provided a bit of entertainment.

The younger ones, like Ed, just three, wanted to play, too. Mothers took turns watching the little boys in their rooms, where they could keep track of them. There weren't many toys, but the boys could entertain themselves with just a few blocks of wood. Sometimes they stacked them up or converted them into "cars." The boys flew around the room, and often one ran into a wall—making irreparable holes in the tar paper.

Finding entertainment in camp wasn't easy. Occasionally, the WCCA officials rotated old movies among the dining halls, mainly Old West cowboy shows or cartoons. I wasn't interested in them, but it was somewhere to go in the evening, so I often went with most of my family. The tables were already set up in the dining hall, ready for the show. Sometimes when I was doing bed checks, the men had gathered together for a raucous poker game, using pennies for chips. This was fine with me—what difference did it make if they were together in one room or separately in their own? Mrs. Arakawa encouraged the men to play poker in the room she and Mr. Arakawa shared, because she thought it would help keep the men occupied and give them something to look forward to in the evenings. I never played poker, but I knew Pop enjoyed it occasionally. Sometimes he joined in on the games.

Life took on somewhat of a rhythm for me. Being busy with many hours of translating and other block manager duties helped pass the time. My world was constricted and small but starting to feel relatively safe and secure. And my family was with me—that was key.

One day, I walked into the office as my coworker Shirley was sorting the mail. She greeted me and said there was a letter addressed to me.

"Thanks," I replied.

I took the letter with my name on it; there was no return address, but it had a Stockton postmark. I opened it up and looked at the signature first: "Your friend, Marie."

I read the letter from the beginning. Marie told me how quiet Stockton had become with seven percent of the population gone overnight. She was still giving piano lessons and now worked part time at the Stockton Hotel as a receptionist. There was, understandably, a shortage of workers. Then she said what must have been hard to write:

> *I am sorry I treated you like I did. My dad's rage at the Japanese made him irrational. I was scared to cross him when he told me to never speak to you again. I knew it was wrong. I hope you will forgive me. You will always be a special friend in my heart. I never could have made straight As at Stockton High without your help over and over again. Will you consider being my friend again? You can't write me back now, but sometime, I will find a way that we can write each other, if that is okay. I needed to send you this now. You have been treated terribly, Janet, and it makes me sad to think of what I did. Please know I think of you often and hope you are okay.*

> *Your friend, Marie*

I smiled as I read her words. Her abrupt departure from my life had been a blow, but I was never angry at her. I knew her dad, who had never had a kind word or look for me. He hadn't liked me before Pearl Harbor, so the attack gave him an excuse for his racial indignation. Marie was trapped in a home full of rage, and while she felt sorry for me, I also felt sorry for her. She was a kind and sweet friend, a complete contradiction to her insolent father. Just like I had no escape from internment camp, Marie, who couldn't afford to live on her own, could not get out of her father's tentacles. I knew she could only hope to find an acceptable man and get married.

Marie's letter brought me some cheer. I folded it up carefully, and when I returned to my room, I slid it into a corner of my duffel bag. I wondered when or if I would hear from her again. She was my special friend, even when she'd told me she wasn't.

As the days turned into weeks, the green wood that the camp constructors had used in their hurry-up, anything-goes construction began to warp. The wood planks of the walls were covered with one thickness of black tar paper, and as the wood lost its straightness, the tar paper began to rip. Holes appeared on both the interior and exterior walls, but there was no way to repair them. Our limited privacy began to shrink away before our eyes. The holes in the walls and the low-to-the-ground windows lured curious Peeping Toms, who had ample time on their hands and lots of pretty young Japanese women to check on. I caught some of these boys in the act of snooping, which slightly embarrassed them, but they were giggling. I talked to them for some time, explaining how important it was to respect everyone else's privacy, since there was little available at camp. I like to think they stopped, but more than likely, they just became more careful. So did the girls, who diligently checked for unwanted guests.

The tar paper wasn't our only problem. The thin layer of concrete poured hastily on sometimes uneven terrain started to crack all over in the barracks. The cracks were large enough that weeds popped through. As time passed and the barracks disintegrated, it was more like we were all camping in tents on the bank of the lovely San Joaquin River. But this was no vacation, and we couldn't pack up and go home. As fast as we pulled the weeds, more quickly replaced them. Heavy rains sent water seeping all over the barracks; thankfully, our bags were on our beds, so they stayed dry.

Richard, Henry, and George—a few of our Peeping Tom neighbors—found the wood pile, and, tired of climbing on beds and bags to peek into our room, one of them had an idea: they built a rough ladder that made peering over the wall easier than ever. Clearly, they had too much free time to spend tinkering around.

My sisters and I were not amused. By then, my permanent had faded from my hair, so one evening, I attempted to make pin curls with my fingers, using bobby pins to hold them overnight. When I looked up, I saw one of the boys smiling at me from over the wall.

"Could you quit peeking at us?" I asked politely.

Before camp, I never would have believed boys next door would climb their homemade ladder to look into our room. Besides being confined in the small room, I felt a deep loss of privacy; even what little space I had wasn't respected.

I saw Ben to report the tearing tar paper problem. He asked me to step into his office for a minute. I sat down, feeling relatively comfortable speaking with him. He explained that the WCCA had been established as the go-between agency to gather the Japanese and temporarily house them while another agency, the War Relocation Agency, was constructing better and more permanent housing.

"Everyone here will be taken to another camp somewhere inland; that camp will be constructed much better," he said. "The new camps are under construction now. If the war happens to end soon, this transfer wouldn't be needed; so either way, the Stockton Assembly Center will be emptied in a few months' time. Everyone will just have to tolerate the poorly constructed barracks for now. My hands are tied—I have no way of repairing any of the torn tar-paper walls."

He added that I should keep this news quiet for now, since it wouldn't be announced to the entire camp yet.

I thanked him for sharing the information, but my heart sank at the thought: we were going to be moved to a camp further inland, with more permanent housing; we'd still been hoping our forced relocation would be short term. We hadn't been promised this, but what else are 117,000 locked-up innocent people supposed to hope?

I couldn't keep the information to myself, so I told Mom and Pop what I'd learned and asked them not to repeat the information. They weren't rattled; they hadn't been from the start. They possessed the patience and courage for whatever lay ahead—*gaman*. I knew everyone would find out soon enough about what Ben had told me. Rumors were rampant at the camp. Any little thing was fodder for gossiping.

Pop said, "I am not sure the war is going well, but I have heard recently of a US victory in a huge battle at the Midway Islands."

It was the first time we'd heard of America winning a battle.

July 4 was an odd day for me. I recalled many joyful memories of going to the San Joaquin County Fairgrounds to watch fireworks with my family and friends, but now it was a prison. Everything had changed so much in such a short time. Years later, I would cry as I read the diary of Anne Frank, who, with her family, went into hiding on July 6, 1942, as the Nazis infiltrated Amsterdam. The world was consumed with hatred and war.

As our months of captivity multiplied, Ben asked me to help out in new ways in the camp, either because he'd grown more and more confident in me as a block manager or because he didn't have enough help with just his staff. I was surprised when he asked me to help with cash transactions. Almost everyone at the camp ordered something from the Sears or Montgomery Ward catalogs, and since they couldn't send cash through the mail and many didn't have a checking account or a way to get their meager government payroll checks to the bank, they needed help placing their orders. The canteen would cash their paychecks, which residents would save until they had enough money for the items they needed. Then, they received government checks to mail with their orders. I was allowed to write out these government checks and cash the paychecks for the residents. Of course, the cash drawer balanced out each day when I was processing transactions. I was a natural at math as well as languages. My years of experience working at the Star Theater ticket window had taught me well.

I continued my daily routine as block manager. After breakfast, I went to the office to see who needed translation assistance that day; sometimes I was needed at the medical center. After lunch, I finished more translation, dictation, and letter-writing or assisted with the cash and the canteen.

As I walked back to my barracks, I sometimes ran into Ray Konishi from my block. He always smiled broadly as he greeted me.

"Hi, Janet," he said one day. "It's great to see you more than— uh—just on your daily rounds." He spoke to me in his first language, Japanese.

"Nice to see you too, Ray."

"Janet, didn't you tell me you have four sisters and three brothers? The guys didn't believe me when I told them."

"You're right, and I'm the oldest—my baby brother is just three. We all have fun playing with him."

"Did you have a big apartment in town for your big family?"

"Sort of, I guess; we all fit into it. Mom made a curtain to hang in the bedroom to separate the kids from my parents. One of my sisters slept with me on the couch that we could make into a bed at night. Our apartment was big compared to the cabin where I was born."

"Where was that, Janet?"

"Bacon Island, in the river. The cabin had one bed for Mom and Pop and one bed for the kids. We all slept together—in those days, there were just five of us and a baby. We had no electricity and a pump outside to get our water."

"Wow—that is way different than how I lived when I was growing up in Japan."

"Ray, I'd like to hear all about that when we have more time. I have to run now."

He never stopped smiling. "Okay—see you soon."

Summer of 1942 passed, and I spent it serving as a block manager, supervising my fellow Japanese, in the Stockton Assembly Center, at the behest of the government: sometimes the reality of this would hit me. I would wake up startled at the thought.

On August 8, one of the soldiers gave me a copy of the *Stockton Record*. It reported that six Germans had been executed in Washington, DC, for participating in "Operation Pastorius," a sabotage that failed. No Japanese were mentioned, which was a relief. I'd heard that some Germans and Italians had been moved into camps, but I never knew how many or where. The paper also spoke of the US Marines winning another Pacific battle, at Guadalcanal, and about a new Walt Disney animated feature film: the story of a deer named Bambi. It was nice to see that some parts of America were carrying on in wartime.

Chapter 9

Second Internment Camp: Camp Rohwer, Arkansas

One day, the camp newsletter I delivered to everyone in my block along with the mail contained a brief article that stated that the Stockton Assembly Center would be closing in October and we would all be moved to Camp Rohwer in Arkansas.

Where is Arkansas, and how far away is it? we all wondered.

Ben told me the next camp was two thousand miles from Stockton and that we would travel by train for thirty to forty hours to reach it. I understood we needed to be moved far from the West Coast so we wouldn't pose a threat of espionage to the United States. But more than halfway across America? I'd traveled a bit with my neighbor to the coast and to conventions in cities around central and northern California, but I'd never left the state. I could only wonder how far this relocation would take me, how much farther it would remove me from my old life in Stockton. And would Stockton ever be the same again? If the United States won the war with Japan tomorrow, would we be welcome back home? We were at the mercy of the government, and the WCCA was passing us off to the WRA, our next rulers.

We would leave at eight the following Friday evening, October 16. Again, they didn't give us much time to prepare. But how difficult could it be to pack, since we'd never totally unpacked? Many wanted to reclaim their dishes they'd brought into Stockton Assembly Center. If we didn't pick up our dishes, the government simply packed them for us for the long ride to Arkansas. Most people took down their little handmade curtains from their rooms to take with them. Anything left behind would surely just go to the garbage dump.

I was apprehensive about the upcoming transfer. Would the new location be properly constructed with real walls and solid floors? Would it have electricity? Would the food be better? Or would it be just the same? And did this mean the war wasn't going well for the US?

The move suggested something else: our captivity would last until the war was over. After all, that was the term the government used for the new location: "permanent camp." After being at the Stockton Assembly Center for 160 days, at least we would get to see the outside world again, and for this reason, I concluded it was good to be leaving, even if it meant going two thousand miles.

On October 16, the four thousand or so fellow residents of the Stockton Assembly Center gathered near the entrance. Only Ben and one of the ladies from the office were there, along with, of course, the soldiers. Ben began logging everyone in but finally gave up, as it was taking too much time. He knew everyone was there. Who would want to remain in that awful place?

Meanwhile, I felt a moment of personal pride when I saw that many of my handmade duffel bags were scattered through the crowd. They'd held up well and, once again, were all packed full. It seemed a long time had passed since I'd made the bags. I'd been living as a free person then; so much had happened in the ensuing five months.

Immersed in the crowd, I enjoyed the anonymity, keeping close to the other nine members of my family. But I did make eye contact with Ben. We weren't friends, but we weren't enemies, either. He hadn't been unfair toward us. He'd simply been placed in a difficult situation with limited resources, and I understood that. He mouthed *thank you* and *good luck*. I smiled back and nodded. Our paths had crossed in the most unlikely of circumstances, and I knew he'd appreciated my daily assistance. As much as I'd originally wanted no part of being a block manager, I was content with my successful tenure at the Stockton Assembly Center.

We were loaded into the backs of trucks, carrying our precious bags, much in the same manner as our ride into camp. The trip to the train station was short, thankfully, and we were led off the trucks under the watchful eyes of armed soldiers. Then we were escorted through the vacant-looking station and onto the waiting railcars. It all went smoothly, and the trains were ready to go rather quickly. No doubt the timing of this was planned carefully. I saw a sign indicating that the last train of the day departed at 5:30 p.m. There was no mention on any marquee of four thousand Japanese taking a train anywhere. But we were all there, and so was the transportation. We Hayashis sat in adjacent seats, which helped Mom feel secure.

Then we were off.

As we rumbled along in the darkness, we could see nothing. The train continued overnight, so we tried to get a bit of sleep in our seats. I quickly learned that the toilets were almost overrun because of the full capacity of this train, so I waited to use one only when it was absolutely necessary.

Early the next morning, the train made its first stop. We were allowed to get out and walk around a bit, since this stop was seemingly not even in any town. It was a fuel stop. Barren land and tumbleweed lay everywhere as far as I could see. Pop remarked on how different this dry, crusty earth was from the fertile lands he'd farmed for so many years. Then we were back on the train, humming along. Meals were served in the last car, starting with a continental breakfast of a roll and juice.

During the day, we got up and walked around the train as best we could, after sitting for so many hours. We chatted with friends and acquaintances. Much of our conversations centered around curiosity and speculation about Camp Rohwer. Maybe it was contagious wishful thinking, but it seemed everyone was somehow convinced our new camp wouldn't have any soldiers. After all, the government had originally asked the Japanese on the West Coast to voluntarily move inland. Now they were forcing us to settle far, far away from the West Coast and its sensitive military locales, which we hoped would surely mean we would be free again in Arkansas—contained in a camp, yes, but provided meals and housing and allowed to carry on, without any need for barbed wire and machine gun–wielding soldiers. And once the war was over, the government would send the trains to return us to our former lives and jobs. It made perfect sense. These hopeful thoughts helped ease the tension of the uncomfortable train trip to what seemed like nowhere.

We would soon find out how wrong our assumptions were.

Sometimes, while my family walked around the train, my friend Ray came to sit with me when he saw the seat near me was empty.

He gave me a big smile with his big "Hi!" when he saw me. It wasn't difficult to figure out he had a crush on me. We would talk about many things, but beyond that I didn't give him much thought.

Once, Ray asked, "What year were you born?"

I replied, "Nineteen twenty."

"We are less than a year apart," he said. "I was born in nineteen nineteen. Did you know I am a *Kibei*, because I was born in California but raised in Japan? I only returned to America a year or so ago."

"Yes, I have known other *Kibei* who came to Stockton to find work."

When Loretta returned to reclaim her seat next to me, Ray politely stood and said he would see me later on the trip. I told him that was fine.

The next morning, one of the soldiers came through the sliding door, opening it with a thunderous noise.

"Listen up!" he shouted. "Everyone, pull your window shades down. We're passing a sensitive military area, so you are not allowed to see anything."

I learned years later that the soldier was hiding us from the locals in cities and towns we passed through, who might have been upset by seeing us Japanese passing by. At that moment, I didn't consider this, so I pulled the shade. I don't know whether I would have cared if they'd told us they didn't want anyone to see us; I'd become numb to insults in the months after Pearl Harbor. What more could the government do beyond locking me up? The train churned on through cities and towns that I never saw or knew the names of.

Overall, the train trip was hardly an exciting experience of taking in new sights and breathing free air. We rode in close quarters with minimally functioning toilets and stale-tasting food, and we couldn't even look out the windows except in desolate places. The journey was uncomfortable at best, but at last we arrived.

Our new camp was in full construction with lots of trucks and workers milling around. It was hot and humid outside; we'd been warned it would be, down in the South, only five miles from the Mississippi River. Then we saw the familiar barbed-wire fencing, towers, military personnel, and weaponry. Our wishful thinking of a camp without soldiers and machine guns evaporated.

Once everyone recovered from the realization that we'd still be living in a prison, we all knew exactly what came next; we'd gone through it before. With so much construction underway, we had the hopeful feeling that our new camp would be constructed with better attention than the Stockton Assembly Center. As we checked in, the officials asked what jobs we'd worked in Stockton. Mom and my sisters said they'd be willing to be waitresses in the new camp; Pop would carry on with boiler duties. As before, my name was marked for my experience as block manager. The new WRA representative wanted me to stay and speak with the new superintendent. As I looked down at the pages of Japanese names on the desk, she flipped the stack to the front page. It was titled simply "Inmates, Camp Rohwer."

Inmates. That word echoed in my mind.

The new superintendent, Rudy, asked me to sit down in a meeting room of some sort. He gave me some details of Camp Rohwer. It was built on ten thousand acres of land the government acquired during the Great Depression. There was a budget of around five million dollars to construct the camp, including clearing out the heavy marsh and woods that had covered most of the land. He explained this camp was spacious enough for the eight thousand or so Japanese being sent in along with me. Construction would continue for several months to get all the facilities completed.

He told me I was still desperately needed to assist with translation for the *Issei*; however, only men would be block managers in this camp. He thought this would be best in the event of trouble or violence of any kind. But since the camp was so large, I would serve as assistant block manager, for which I would be paid thirteen dollars per month. It was clear he wasn't asking me if I wanted this role; this was simply my new job. Once again, I wanted to say, "No, thank you," but I didn't.

"We will be in touch with you soon," he said.

At least I was getting a pay raise, however small! Maybe being the assistant block manager wouldn't require so much of me. Only time would tell.

I was resigned to accept whatever this new government agency, the War Relocation Authority, expected of me.

Chapter 10

Life in Camp Rohwer

I found my family in block thirty-two, where I discovered some news about Camp Rohwer: we were allocated more rooms in the barracks, so we wouldn't have to crowd five into a room. We could spread out over four rooms: Christine, Marian, and I set up together in one room; Mom and Pop had a room; Will, Tom, and Ed occupied another; and Fran and Loretta took the fourth room. It was a welcome change to have extra space. We began settling into our new home.

I'm not sure if I'd ever felt completely secure or at ease at the Stockton Assembly Center. I'd lived on edge, worrying something would go awry in the block for which I was responsible, that something terrible would happen in the war and we would be blamed, or that my family would be separated. The uneasy feeling of living in a situation where I was considered dangerous had crept into my mind.

Now, at Camp Rohwer, I still knew nothing about what my future held, and this was more unsettling. Would we be released after a few months? I held out hope. I'd heard enough about permanent camps to understand it was highly unlikely a few months of captivity would allay any fears about the potential threat the Japanese posed. I couldn't do anything to change my fate—only accept whatever the government chose to do with me and try to adjust to my life in the new internment camp. It was an odd feeling to have so little control over my own life.

Something seemed to change at Camp Rohwer. My first impression of the camp was of much more space, both in the barracks and in the surrounding open area; the buildings seemed competent, not thrown together. At Camp Rohwer, my raw fear was replaced, more or less, with acceptance and resignation that this was the way it was going to be—the new order for the West Coast Japanese—and I sensed a more relaxed mood from the barracks. Maybe everyone fully understood where we stood with the government. It had us where it wanted us now, confined and inland, safely secluded, and posing no danger. We'd been initially disappointed to see towers and soldiers at our new camp, but this feeling gave way to acceptance, since we'd already dealt with these things at our previous camp.

Although we'd received no communication about the government's long-term plan for us, I think we all felt we'd be there at Camp Rohwer until the war was over. There was no point in complaining; we might as well make the best of it. This had been Mom and Pop's attitude from the start.

Camp Rohwer's thirty-six residential blocks each housed 200 to 250 people. Each barracks building was 20 feet wide by 120 feet long, and each room measured approximately 20 by 20 feet and had one door. We were provided the same army metal-frame beds with accompanying thin mattresses, which we finished off with our own linens. Immediately, we wanted to hang our handmade curtains from Stockton in our new rooms. We were grateful the windows were higher, but they were also smaller, so the curtains needed to be trimmed. We were able to use most of the curtains in this second internment camp, and Mom set about making more with her scrap material.

My sisters and I considered several options about how to arrange our room. We laughed about the dirty socks and underwear we'd had to pack, since we'd had no time to wash clothes before leaving Stockton. I hoped we could find a washboard soon. Each room had only one outside door, akin to Stockton. However, these barracks were built several feet off the ground, because the land under them was marshy and because the Mississippi River flooded in the spring. The elevated buildings would hopefully help prevent mold and mildew—and weeds—from growing in the barracks. To enter our room, there was a set of three or four steps. Along with the rooms' elevation, the windows were also placed higher, the interior walls rose closer to the ceiling, and the floors and walls seemed sturdy and solid, with plenty of nails holding them in place, so hopefully we wouldn't have to deal with Peeping Toms in this camp. To reinforce this, the weekly camp bulletin made it perfectly clear that the camp rules absolutely prohibited anyone from attempting to peek into another room, so clearly, the WRA was stricter about privacy than the WCCA's temporary camp at Stockton. Even the bathrooms and showers were built with stalls, which was a relief. In the middle of each room's ceiling was a lightbulb with a cord hanging down—we had electricity. Not much, but a light. Our rooms wouldn't turn black as night here.

We resumed similar jobs to those we'd held in Stockton. Everyone had free time and no money, so most adults found jobs of some kind. I continued helping with translation, and this was no problem; in fact, it was a pleasure to help out so many *Issei* in this way. The hard part was being in charge of a couple hundred people in my block and ensuring there was no trouble. Women of the 1940s weren't in charge of anything outside their homes, so this was a role I hadn't experienced before I was thrust into it.

After setting up our rooms, we milled around the barracks, saying hello to our new and old neighbors. Naturally, I ran into Ray, wearing his huge grin, which I was already growing accustomed to seeing. He seemed to be on a mission.

"Would you like to go for a walk with me after dinner this evening?" he asked.

Although this was a bigger camp, the options for going for a walk were still limited. I replied, "Sure, we can tour around the barracks."

As Ray walked away, my sisters teased me. I told them a walk would be harmless.

In our dining hall, we learned that, just like in Stockton, we were assigned seats at picnic tables for meals, and our family was expected to be in place for each meal. This was fine with Mom; she would have insisted we eat together even if the authorities didn't demand it. Even though my younger sisters knew this was a camp rule, they still sometimes asked if they could sit with a friend. They pleaded and begged, but Mom and Pop made them follow the rule, and we Hayashis ate our meals together.

We were served familiar dinners in the dining hall, with plenty of food, including rice as well as pork and beans, which were high in protein and nutrition and readily available rations for the military. We'd been served these at least once a week in Stockton, and they awaited us in Rohwer. Rudy told us that food funding from the

WRA was thirty-eight cents per person per day. That was it. Further resources were needed for the war effort, they said, and the government didn't want to give the appearance of being overly gratuitous with the Japanese. This was no surprise to me; I didn't expect the food to be any better than what we'd eaten in Stockton. It was a pleasure to see Chef Kamisono back in my block. It seemed nothing had changed about our meals, despite the two thousand miles we'd traveled.

After dinner that first day in Camp Rohwer, Ray and I went on the walk I'd promised him around the barracks. Ray shared stories from his youth.

"Janet, I grew up in Hatsukaichi, just a short distance outside Hiroshima. My father was a very well-known businessman. When I walked around town, it seemed all the people bowed to me as the son of Mr. Konishi. These people were older than I was, which made me feel awkward. It has been nice in America, where no one bows."

"What brought you to America?" I asked.

Ray paused. "Well, it's my fault. I didn't do well at the university. My father was frustrated with me, so he gave me two thousand dollars and sent me to America to go to school here and grow up. I ended up living with my father's sister when I ran out of money. Last year, I was helping my aunt and uncle with little jobs and trying to figure out what I should do next when I found out my father was ill."

"I worked for Mrs. Arakawa at the theater for a while," I said. "Your aunt has been very nice to me. I bet she has enjoyed having you at her home."

Ray said, "She and my uncle are very prosperous and have welcomed me into their home, but I am a guest and surely not treated as one of their sons."

"I'm sorry to hear about your father," I said. "Do you know if he is better?"

Ray looked down and spoke quietly. "He passed away from alcoholism. It's very sad to think that my father is gone. I had no idea when he sent me to America that I would never see him again."

I wasn't sure what to say about this news, but I felt he needed a friend, and I wanted him to feel he could share his feelings with me. "Please know you have my very sincerest sympathy about this tragic loss, Ray. I can't imagine the grief you are feeling now."

Ray looked into my eyes. "Thank you very much. I appreciate your kindness. When I received the news, I couldn't get passage on a ship back to Japan for several months, and then it was Pearl Harbor."

"Do you have brothers and sisters? And how is your mom?"

"I never had a mom," Ray said. "She died in childbirth when I was little. But I had a couple of stepmothers who had no interest in being my mom. I have one younger sister, Kaito, who is in Japan now, but we don't get along at all."

I could see the loneliness on Ray's face, which normally had such a grand smile. "I'm sorry."

"Oh, please don't be sorry," he said. "I enjoy talking with you very much."

I tried to change the subject. "Have you enjoyed living in America?"

Ray smiled again. "Oh yes. My English isn't the best, but it's getting better all the time. I've made lots of friends at the university and around Stockton. But I am very upset about being thrown into this camp like I'm a criminal."

I understood this feeling, but I replied, "Yes, we are all disappointed with the government's decision to send us to this camp, but my family—we're all just following *gaman*."

"You are amazing, Janet," Ray said. "I am very happy you were assigned to be my block manager and that now we are friends. I will look forward to seeing you tonight."

We both smiled and went our separate ways. I walked away thinking how sad I felt for Ray, who was my age but had no living mother or father. I was happy to help ease his loneliness by being a friend he could talk to.

The following day, when I was back at the office, Rudy introduced me to George, the block manager I would be working with. We knew each other, but not well. He was also bilingual, which was a prerequisite for the job, but I'm not sure he had the same skills that I did. To translate properly, I needed to write Japanese, because many could understand and speak Japanese, but far fewer could write as I could. I don't think George could write Japanese as accurately as I could. Rudy gave us permission to sort out the duties between ourselves, which we did. We took turns with ten o'clock room checks, and if there was any fighting in our block, I got George to settle it.

That was a relief. The camp printed a bulletin each week on manila paper, and we were responsible for passing it out to everyone in our block. The bulletin contained news, announcements, and emphasis on the camp rules.

It was interesting to watch Mom take pride in her new "home," which was once again just an empty room with beds. She gave us strict instructions to clean off our shoes and remove them before entering; it was the way of the Japanese to remove shoes before entering your home or someone else's, which meant Mom was treating our government barracks rooms as home. This helped me to feel that this place in the middle of nowhere was my new home.

Soon, Loretta and Fran walked around with Ed and Tom to find out where boys the same ages lived. By that afternoon, each boy had invited a friend to visit, and as before, they found ways to play without toys. For Tom and Ed, life in the internment camps was fun and games.

One day, Ray came by again and asked me to go for a walk when we returned to our rooms after dinner. Off we went. On our walk, he told me about his job as a fireman at Camp Rohwer. The camp even had a firetruck. His job was like all other firemen's: sit, wait, and hope there would be no fires.

"Janet, can I purchase penny candy at the canteen?" Ray asked.

I said, "Yes, but I'm not sure when we'll get some in. I'll let you know."

"Thanks. Maybe I shouldn't say this, but I grew up on candy. My stepmothers didn't want to mess with cooking for me, so they just gave me money to go buy whatever I wanted to eat. So I ate all the candy I wanted. I never ate fruits and vegetables."

"Wow—that's funny. I guess you were very lucky. My dad had a garden and an orchard, so we ate lots of fruits and vegetables. How many stepmothers did you have?"

"Two, and the last one was sent away by my sister after my father died. Kaito never liked her anyway."

I was curious. "Is your sister alone now in your dad's big mansion? Mrs. Arakawa told us how grand it is."

"Yes, she is living there now, but it will belong to me when I return to Japan. I don't know about America, but women can't inherit property in Japan. I can't wait to get back to Japan and take care of my father's affairs. For now, everything is just on hold—at least, I hope so, since I couldn't leave before the war started."

"I am sorry, Ray—you have both the grief of the loss of your father and the worry about getting back to Japan and taking care of his estate."

"Yeah, but at least I've made special new friends in America— like you."

I smiled, and our conversation ended as we arrived back at my barracks. We told each other to have a nice evening, and we parted.

At Camp Rohwer, not only did the government organize our lives, but we Japanese made our own little cities inside the barbed-wire fences. All the residents did our best to take back some measure of control over our collective lives. This would be our community, and it was up to us to make it the best possible place to live.

Each block elected its own president and vice president, who served as resources for their block. The government promised schools for the children, and they opened within a month of our arrival. The president and vice president worked to make sure that children going to school were provided the pencils, paper, and books they needed. Government supplies were available but limited. The Japanese revered a proper education, so camp or not, the schools were a huge priority. Those who were teachers in Stockton resumed their roles, and additional local teachers as needed were hired from the surrounding area in Arkansas.

The president and vice president also coordinated gardens with other blocks. This was a major difference from Stockton: we could farm the land and grow our own food as an alternative to the food provided by the camp. Since many of the Japanese men had worked on farms, they saw the open space in the camp as a golden opportunity to plant their own gardens. Many men, including Pop, sent away for seeds. At that time, it was fall with winter coming, so planting would have to wait until spring, but we understood spring came early in the South.

Soon the hospital opened, using mainly Japanese doctors, as well as some military doctors, and Japanese women resumed being nurses. The hospital was reasonably outfitted with beds and equipment. I was often called to assist with translation. Outside, kids started organizing soccer, football, and baseball teams. It made me smile to find people playing games when I did room checks. The men preferred card games, especially poker; mahjong was also popular. As in Stockton, I didn't care if people played games in neighbors' rooms. As long as I knew where they were at ten o'clock, it was good enough.

Ray continued to stop by and ask to walk. Sometimes I said yes, but other times I was too busy with block manager duties. I told him gently to go find someone else to walk with him. It wasn't that I didn't like Ray—I was just busy, and I wasn't particularly interested in walking every day. He was a friend and nothing more. Sometimes Ray worked his fireman shift, which helped occupy him. He greeted Mom and Pop whenever they crossed paths, and they enjoyed speaking to him in Japanese.

Before long, June, the social coordinator of my block, arranged to have a party in the mess hall. We stacked the picnic tables in the corner, since they didn't fold up. Someone brought a phonograph and Japanese records. Had they carried them into camp, or ordered them from the catalog? I wasn't sure, but it was kind of them to share with everyone. There was no food served at the dance, but June promised to get Kool-Aid for the next one, although the sugar rationing would make this difficult. I didn't know how to dance, but I went just the same. I learned a bit of ballroom dancing, with some help from friends. It was a wonderful evening, full of happy faces of people having fun together. The room felt lively, with lots of conversation as well as dancing. Ray was working at the fire station that evening, so he missed the party. Of course, there was still a ten o'clock curfew, so the party wrapped up in time to allow tables and chairs to be moved back for breakfast in the morning and for everyone to arrive at their barracks before room checks.

When our block held the next party, Ray and I were both able to attend. I enjoyed talking with my *Nisei* friends whom I'd known since my grade school years, but I still wasn't much of a dancer, despite practicing at the previous party. June wasn't able to get Kool-Aid for the party, but she did get red food coloring, so we drank red water and pretended it was Kool-Aid. Ray wasn't acquainted with many people in camp. He was shy, maybe because he hadn't been raised in America and didn't have confidence in his ability to fit in. He was, however, at ease with me, and he talked nonstop when we were together.

During the party, Ray asked me to go for a walk again. He told me about how he'd received minimal guidance growing up. His dad was a businessman who traveled extensively, and when he was in town, he ate with his wife. As far as his father was concerned, the children were being taken care of. It was sad to think of growing up without the love of a mother, especially considering how very much I adored my mom.

Suddenly, Ray stopped walking. I did too. He looked at me and almost blurted out, "Janet, I know you would take great care of me. You are so nice to everyone and so friendly. You are the prettiest woman I have ever seen. You can do anything. You are so smart with your Japanese—you know it better than I do. I know you would be a wonderful wife. Will you marry me?"

I'm sure I blushed, but luckily it was getting dark. I smiled at Ray. His proposal was entirely unexpected; I'd had absolutely no idea he was contemplating asking me to marry him. I knew he was sweet on me, but as far as I knew, that was all.

"Thank you so much for your kind words. You are a dear friend to me. I didn't know you felt this way about me," I replied. "I must think about this, please—I promise to give you my answer soon."

We walked to my room together. He hugged me and kissed the top of my head as he said good night, then left for his room.

My heart was racing as I walked through my door at nine. Marian and Christine hadn't returned from the party yet. I was glad to be alone and collect my thoughts. To me, this marriage proposal was shocking. I visited the restroom quickly and then went next door to see if Mom and Pop were home. Mom had put the tired boys to sleep. She sat under the one lightbulb in the room making a pillow-case for a friend's upcoming birthday, and Pop lay on his bed, reading.

I asked Mom if she could come next door with me. She took one look at my face and put down her needlework. Quickly, we walked down her room's four stairs, then up the four stairs to my room. I told her the whole story of the proposal and how it had caught me completely off guard.

"How flattering that Ray thinks of you in this way," Mom said with a smile. But quickly she expressed her opinion. "Janet, you cannot marry Ray Konishi—he is from a world you have never known. Your father's family was considered more prominent than mine; as it turned out, it didn't matter so much here in America, but everyone thought I'd married well. We shared some similar relatives, we practiced the same Buddhism, and we knew each other's hometowns well. But if you married Ray and ended up in Japan, you would know nothing of the traditions and lifestyle of a family of this stature. You would know nothing of his village. You would be an outcast or, worse, left for a more appropriate woman who could properly fulfill her role. I regret to tell you this, but Ray is not a good match for you."

Mom's comments didn't surprise me. I understood. According to Japanese culture, I came from a poor family. I had nothing to offer to a prospective husband. I was, however, flattered by the proposal, even if I thought of Ray as my friend. He was interested in the details of my life and was a caring person with a compassionate heart for helping others. I wasn't in a hurry to get married—I really hadn't thought much about it—but I was disappointed that Mom quickly rejected the idea of marriage to Ray. Had Mom approved, I gladly would have accepted.

I didn't push Mom to tell me whom she anticipated I would marry or when. After all, I was twenty-two years old. Did she envision an arranged marriage for me and my sisters? I didn't necessarily think so, since she and Pop couldn't pay a marriage broker, but I believed she thought a *Nisei* would match up well with my background and standing.

I thanked and hugged her and told her I would tell Ray as soon as possible.

That night, I tossed and turned as I attempted to fall asleep. That was rare; I usually slept well. I knew Mom was right, but I dreaded telling Ray. How could I explain? Despite his status, he hadn't had a happy life growing up in Japan. While he had wealth and prestige, he grew up alone with an absent father and uninterested stepmothers. I'd grown up with a loving, secure family, making me the richer one between us, in my eyes. Family was everything, then and always.

I let my sisters think I was asleep when they returned from the party, and I listened to them talk quietly, as girls do, about the eligible men who had asked them to dance. It was a sleepless night for me.

In the morning, I didn't say anything to my sisters about the previous night. I would tell them later, after I saw Ray. It was a normal day at camp; I spent all afternoon assisting with translations and letter-writing in the office. It made me feel so appreciated to see the gratitude on the faces of the *Issei* I assisted. Communication with their loved ones in Japan was sacred to them, and we were very lucky that the letters were delivered both in Japan and America, despite war. Our military address gave no clue to anyone where we really were, but it worked. That was all that mattered.

I didn't see Ray for a couple of days. He was given evening shifts at the firehouse, and he knew I was busy in the office during the day. The following Wednesday, though, I spotted him while walking back to my room from the office. Maybe he was hanging around; he knew the path I took each day. My heart started pounding again. I could feel my hands get clammy, and I couldn't stop blushing. I asked if I could speak to him.

We walked down the pathway toward the construction area, where I could talk to Ray privately. I desperately didn't want to hurt him, but I knew what I needed to do.

"Ray, I want to thank you from the bottom of my heart for your proposal. I have discussed this with my parents, and they have advised me that we are a wrong fit for marriage. We come from different worlds, and they believe I would never be appropriate in your world. There is someone else who will be a very suitable wife for you—she will be someone who also grew up as you did."

Ray's head dropped down, and he no longer looked at me as I continued. "I like you very much, Ray, and so do my parents. My parents are honored you have proposed marriage to their daughter. But I am just a poor girl—not right for a man of your prominence."

Ray turned to leave. "Okay," he said as he ran off. I'm fairly certain he was crying. Tears filled my eyes, too, as I jogged back to my room and told my sisters the whole story. They sat still as I told them everything, and they hugged me when they saw how upset I was. I was relieved to put it behind me; I hadn't wanted my answer to drag on—there was no point. But I never wanted to hurt anyone, either. I felt awful for devastating such a sweet man.

Chapter 11
Winter 1942

Word spread quickly: Ray had proposed, and I had turned him down. My friends all had the same reaction and gave me the same surprised look. They couldn't believe I'd declined. For Japanese women, the route to marriage was about getting a good catch. It was an ancient custom for the families to match up couples for marriage, so the goal of each was to better themselves through marriage. Ray was a good man from a wealthy family. My girlfriends would not have turned down such a proposal merely because they didn't have the right upbringing for his upper-crust class. Ray was considered an eligible bachelor of enormous means at camp, which meant many admiring women were flirting with him. After rejecting him, I tried to avoid running into him, since I anticipated awkwardness.

Schools were opened in November. Japanese-trained teachers were hired, along with Japanese college graduates who had never taught before and Caucasian teachers from the surrounding area. One building hosted first through eighth grade, while a second building served as a high school. School began with the pool of teachers assembled and the limited resources supplied by the government, supplemented by camp residents. Seeing the children, including my brothers and sisters, walking to school generated a feeling of normalcy. School helped give a familiar routine to the weeks.

At home, we girls helped Mom work with Ed and Tom, since they weren't old enough for school yet. My sisters and I taught our little brothers nursery rhymes, which they could recite by memory. Will was a senior in high school then, Loretta a sophomore, and Fran in the eighth grade. Their afternoons and evenings soon became filled with homework and studying.

The weather was starting to cool down as winter approached. Mom stayed busy making needlepoint gifts for friends and family for Christmas. The WRA handed out heavy gray-green army blankets—the same blankets used by the soldiers—for us all to keep in our rooms. None of us Japanese had any experience with winter weather in southern Arkansas, and no one owned a heavy winter coat. We were told southern Arkansas got cold, freezing at times, but seldom stayed extremely cold for long. Mom had brought knitting needles from home, and she ordered reasonably priced yarn from the Sears catalog. I didn't have as much time to devote to knitting, so Mom took on the project of knitting sweaters for each member of her family. These thick, warm sweaters made all the difference once the air turned crispy cool. Some people also ordered plastic boots from the Sears catalog, not so much for warmth as for the mud; big rainstorms were common, and these turned the entire camp muddy. Some people even ordered scratching bristle brushes on little wooden frames to rub on the bottoms of their shoes to remove the clay-like mud.

Construction workers came around to each room in the barracks and installed a simple chimney, to which they attached a potbelly stove. This would be our heat in the winter. We were told to take big buckets to the coal pile and take as much coal as we wanted or needed; there was also a pile of scrap wood we could help ourselves to. Thankfully, Pop and Will did the hard labor of lugging the heavy coal buckets for our family. Generally, we lit the wood to get the fire started, which then ignited the coal, providing the longer-term heat. Every evening, we started our fire, and if we were lucky, the fire lasted all night. On the days it rained, it was a big challenge to get the wet wood to light. This happened frequently in the winter. If we couldn't get a fire started, we just wrapped up with our sweaters and army blankets. Amazingly, I never heard of a fire getting out of control in the barracks, but the potbelly stoves full of coal contaminated the air in our tiny rooms with coal dust. I often heard coughing at night all over the barracks.

When the winter nights dropped below freezing, I often shivered in our chilly room, even with the potbelly stove. Some of the women in the camp sewed pajama pants for themselves; usually, we women only wore dresses or skirts during the daytime and typically nightgowns for sleeping. Mom easily got Ed and Tom into bed, since they wanted to curl up and get warm. Other times, with the fires roaring in the potbelly stoves in adjacent rooms in the barracks, our rooms turned blazing hot, especially when the weather turned milder outside. The whole process was difficult to regulate. We all adjusted as best we could.

On some days, once we got fires started, the women kept big kettles of water on the stovetops, which Mom remembered doing in her early years in the country. We never cooked any food in the barracks; the women used the heated water and washboards to wash clothes. I generally wore my dresses for three days before changing, but with the mud and humidity in Arkansas, sometimes I washed my clothes more frequently. We all purchased our own soap and clothes-pins, and the women coordinated with each other, since there wasn't enough room on the clotheslines for everyone's laundry to be hung by each barracks. Even the wealthy ladies had to hand-wash their clothes, which they hadn't done in their former lifestyles; they also weren't used to hanging their clothes, and my sisters laughed about how crooked their clothes were on the lines. The women worked until the clothes were all washed and hung. It took the sun of the next day to fully dry the clothes.

We often used our mess hall for events in the evenings. I volunteered to teach Japanese to anyone interested. Many *Nisei* had been attending Japanese school at the temple before the war, and some were eager to carry on learning Japanese, even if they were overwhelmed by its complexities, to please their *Issei* parents. My class generally started at seven. in the mess hall, and I rang a bell to signal the beginning of class. I also used the mess hall, when it was available, to teach knitting and crochet; I'd learned these skills earlier in my life from Mom, but many others were motivated to learn to make their own sweaters as quickly as possible. Other times, the mess hall was used for a storytelling or book reading for the children. Occasionally on the weekends, the WRA showed a movie, but the films were usually the same as the WCCA had shown and were never current films. If you liked cowboys-and-Indians movies, they were available. Other evenings, *Nisei* friends gathered in the mess hall to write letters. After traveling two thousand miles from Stockton, we would receive no more visits from Miss Humbarger or anyone else friendly with the Japanese. Generally, the dining hall was emptied out by nine. The barracks were quiet in the evenings, since the children were engulfed with their studies. Then the school children took their showers and went off to bed. Breakfast was at eight the next morning, and the school bell rang at nine.

Some time had passed since Ray's marriage proposal, so I wasn't as anxious about seeing him. I tried to make George do the room checks in Ray's barracks, or I just scooted through as quickly as I could. I didn't enjoy being the subject of gossip in camp. Surely by now Ray had found someone else to take walks with him—hadn't he?

Despite my attempts to avoid running into him, he showed up at my room one evening. He smiled and acted like nothing had transpired between us. After a friendly greeting, he asked me to go for a walk. This seemed innocent enough, and I was glad he'd broken the ice between us. I thought he surely wanted to ask my opinion about a new girl he was interested in. My sisters smirked at me quietly, but I wasn't sure what that meant. Were they resisting laughing at me for heading out with my rejected suitor? Did they think I was stupid to be hanging around with him? It didn't really matter to me.

As we walked down the pathway, Ray looked over at me. "Janet, I miss you. Could we just be friends?"

I felt relieved. "Yes, Ray—of course we can be friends."

"Thanks, Janet." He grinned broadly. "You won't believe what happened the other day at the firehouse." Ray loved to tell me stories.

We were friends again, and that was all. I liked Ray as a friend. When I returned to the barracks and told my sisters about our conversation, they had none of my "just friends" talk. I tried to assure them he fully understood I was not marriage material for him, but they told me how obviously it was written all over his face: he hadn't given up.

Christmas approached, and we prepared for it. So many of us Japanese in camp had been raised as Buddhists, but we celebrated Christmas as an American holiday; my family had celebrated Christmas since we'd lived out of town, before we'd moved to Stockton. Many others in camp converted to Christianity through classes and services held by Christian missionaries. Our block threw a festive Christmas party in the mess hall, without refreshments but complete with Christmas music and plenty of handmade gifts.

Gift-giving was an essential part of our lives; it was how we were taught by our parents and our parents by their parents to acknowledge friends and family. My mom upheld this tradition; no matter how poor we were, she made sure we received small but meaningful birthday and Christmas presents, even if it was only a little bag of hard candy and a pencil. At camp, it was a challenge to find creative ways of gift giving. Mom made doilies for her friends and knitted us hats, gloves, and sweaters, and she and Pop usually saved enough money from their little paychecks to buy us some things at the canteen. I think our entire block turned out for the Christmas festivities, and it was a joyful evening for all.

For my twenty-third birthday on Tuesday, January 12, 1943, I received an amazing present: snow started falling at Camp Rohwer. Everyone ran around like crazy—none of us had ever seen snow! The little kids caught snowflakes as older ones shaped snowballs. It was exciting for all. But sadly, by the end of the afternoon, the snow vanished. Camp Rohwer didn't get snow often, so that show for my birthday was an exciting first.

We didn't get much news of the war, and what we did receive was usually dated a couple of weeks. It was hard to tell how the war was going, considering the many battles and reported casualties. It seemed America was fighting all over the world, in North Africa, Europe, the South Pacific, and the Philippines. We were glad to read that many of the navy ships sunk at Pearl Harbor had been raised, salvaged, repaired, and put back on the high seas. Meanwhile, the Soviets were retaking Stalingrad, and Jews were rebelling at ghettos in Poland. America had been fighting for well over a year by then, and we didn't know whether we were winning. We had no way of knowing.

In camp, arguments sometimes escalated into fistfights between men defending Japan or the United States. Frustration mounted with the unending imprisonment, and emotions ran high. The Japanese men quickly broke up fights without bringing in the authorities, but we learned of shootings at other camps when men tried to escape and other confrontations that spiraled out of control. We even heard of some being killed. This kind of news was shocking, but most of us fully understood we were in a prisoner-of-war camp. The guards were not there for show and would shoot to kill if provoked. Thankfully, I never knew of anyone shot at Camp Rohwer.

One sunny February day, my friend Grace Yamaguchi ran up to me, seemingly excited to say hello; we were all tired of two straight weeks of gray days. Somehow, Grace had ended up in a different block, so we didn't see each other unless we arranged a meeting. Just as during the years we'd been neighbors in Stockton, Grace's strong personality and inflexible opinions seemed to alienate her from other people in the camp. She was now easily in her thirties and still single. Perhaps she always would be single, but somehow I think she didn't care.

As soon as Grace caught up to me, though, I could tell something was wrong; she was crying. Had she had a heated argument? I would have believed it, but that wasn't the case.

"Janet, you won't believe the letter I got in the mail." The letter was crinkled up in her hand. She handed it to me, and as she wiped her eyes, I carefully opened the letter to read what she found so dreadful, while I also tried to calm her down.

"Grace, what can I do to help?" I asked. "Have you received bad news in this letter?"

The envelope was postmarked from Stockton and addressed to "Miss Grace Yamaguchi, Japanese Prison Camp." One thing the government executed well throughout the war was getting the mail delivered. Somehow, this little bit of information was enough for the post office to send it along to Arkansas and deliver it to Grace. Surely the Stockton Post Office knew everyone at Stockton Assembly Center had been sent to Camp Rohwer.

I read the letter:

Dear Miss Yamaguchi,

I am writing this letter to inform you I can no longer hold your apartment for you. I held your apartment through the end of the year, as you'd paid up the rent to that time. But now it is January, and since you have not returned, the apartment will be rented out to someone else. I cannot afford to wait for your return. If the new tenant does not want to use the furniture and other things you left behind, I will be taking them to charity. I am terribly sorry for this, but I have no choice.

Sincerely,
Mr. Schwartz

We hugged as the tears streamed down both our faces. I was crying more for her anguish than my own. She had nothing left at home. My family had stored some of our things in her apartment, and these would now be lost as well, but none of our items had been sentimental; they were just things, and it didn't matter. But Grace lost a lot. Her apartment had been so lovely, full of many knickknacks and all her little treasures. They were all gone now. She seemed terribly alone, separated at camp from her parents, with no family of her own.

"Grace, you will always be my friend. I am very sorry all your things are gone."

"Janet, I am lucky to have a special friend like you."

I wanted to reassure her. "Me too. We can count on each other—that's more important than stuff that's gone."

"I knew you would make me feel better. Let's find an evening we can visit each other soon."

"How about next Tuesday at seven?"

"That will be great—at my place. Bye, Janet."

"Bye, Grace. See you soon." And we each went our separate ways. At least our visit was something for Grace to look forward to, even if it was just sitting in our barracks and talking about the old days in Stockton.

Chapter 12
Spring and Summer 1943

Spring came early to southern Arkansas, and the men were ready with the seeds they'd purchased from catalogs throughout the winter. There was plenty of room in the camp for gardens. Many people planted as near as possible to the bathroom barracks, to keep the walk short for lugging pails of water. This was an unfamiliar climate and new soil the men had to till by hand, so they tried to plan ahead for any situation they encountered. The men were not only keen on planting gardens to produce fresh vegetables but were also working toward making our barracks look more like homes. They planted seeds along the perimeter of the barracks to grow small bushes and shrubs and even some grass.

Most of the men, especially the *Issei* men, had worked the soil by hand after coming to America. They were older now but knew how to be proper farmers, with or without modern tractors and tilling machines. Pop complained the soil was dense and heavy marshland, since we were just a few miles from the Mississippi River. The men, including Pop, tilled this new heavy claylike soil with only the spades and shovels they had ordered.

Beyond growing vegetables and improving the appearance of Camp Rohwer, the whole exercise was good for the men's morale, because it gave them some measure of control over their lives to be outside working the land. It gave them some purpose and a goal for improving the state of their lives while in captivity.

When green shoots came up through the earth, the collective jubilation of the farmers was apparent all over Camp Rohwer. They'd planted vegetables they thought would be easy to grow and that we liked; Pop planted radishes and carrots in his garden, along with Japanese daikon, negi, and napa cabbage. Daikon was similar in flavor to a radish—tart and spicy—and harvested as a root vegetable like a carrot, although it was white. When it was cooked, it had a similar look, texture, and taste to turnips. Negi was a type of leek that strongly resembled a green onion and was a common ingredient in Japanese cuisine, used in soups, salads, stir-fry, and other dishes. Another favorite was napa cabbage, which we called *hakusai*. It looked like an oblong head of romaine lettuce with a texture similar to cabbage; the outer leaves were tough and usable for soups or stir-fry. Sometimes, we cooked meats in the leaves. The vegetable gardens were an attempt to improve our boring, repetitious cuisine and supply the chefs with vegetables commonly eaten by Japanese, but they also improved the quality of our diets. The gardens were a welcome sign that the doldrums of winter were over.

Ray stopped by for walks with greater frequency. I knew in my heart that my sisters were right when they told me he wasn't giving up on marrying me. He would stop in and chat with Mom and Pop in Japanese. They didn't talk about anything in particular, but somehow it seemed Ray was striving to win them over. He knew my parents had forbidden my marriage to him, but this didn't seem to anger him. He understood their perspective.

I was often busy with teaching classes, helping people with translation, and block manager duties, so I wasn't always available. Ray also worked his shifts as a camp fireman. But when we were both free, he always seemed to appear to ask to go for a walk. So I went along with him. At least the awkwardness was gone. I wasn't going to worry myself about what was next.

Once, he said, "You are good at everything, but you're so nice that you never brag. All the other girls like to brag about something. You just carry on and help everyone." He paused. "And you are the prettiest, too."

I flushed and dreaded what might come next. I smiled at him, said, "Thank you," and quickly changed the subject.

We returned to my barracks and departed once again as friends—just friends.

A few days later, Rudy asked me to stop into his office to discuss something. He explained what was required of a block manager, which I already knew, then went on to explain in a diplomatic way how there had been an incident; it hadn't worked out too well with George as a block manager. Therefore, I was being "promoted" from assistant block manager to block manager, a promotion I hadn't sought or wanted. But as I knew from my WCCA block manager assignment at the Stockton Assembly Center, this role was assigned by the WRA, and one couldn't decline it—unless, I guess, you did a poor job, in which case you would be replaced. Rudy tried to compliment me by telling me how much everyone appreciated how well I communicated and treated everyone in the block with respect. I took my responsibilities seriously. I hadn't been aware of any incident with George, but I didn't ask Rudy to explain further. All I knew was I was the only block manager of my block again. I needed no further instructions—the only problem was they didn't give *me* an assistant.

The days grew warmer and stickier. I soon figured out humidity in southern Arkansas made the temperature feel much hotter than it was. This was a big change from Stockton, where the humidity was much lower. And summer was around the corner. May 10 arrived, and it was a solemn day for me—it marked one year of life as a prisoner of war, a year of no freedom, of daily following every rule established by the WRA, per the wishes of the president of the United States. It was time taken from my life and gone forever—a precious year spent accomplishing nothing.

Thinking of all this made me melancholy. I accepted my fate, but at times I was sad. I don't think anyone in my family realized when this date came and went. I didn't want to remind them and punctuate the moment for them as well. I carried on as though this day were the same as every other, hiding my sadness. Then Tom asked me to watch his soccer game; the boys were all running hard, and it made me smile to see the beehives' worth of children swarming the field. Still, I was relieved when the day was over.

Gaman had helped carry me, my family, and my fellow Japanese through our trials of the previous year. Surely, by May 10, 1944, a year from then, I would no longer be a prisoner of war.

The locals told me it was a typically hot summer in southern Arkansas. There was no air conditioning at the camp. There wasn't even any breeze. But there *were* ants, spiders, wasps, bees, and mosquitoes. The mosquitoes were the worst, thanks to the wetness and close proximity of the Mississippi River. At dusk, they were thick in the air, and within a few minutes outdoors, you could be covered with dozens of bites. Since there was no escape from being bitten or stung, we coped as best we could with the summer bug onslaught and with the heat. Sometimes I thought I couldn't breathe the heavy hot air. One brief walk to the restroom made me drip sweat.

Rudy's assistant, David, came by at dinnertime one night to make an announcement too important for the weekly bulletin: each male adult resident of our block was supposed to come by the office to complete a short questionnaire sometime in the next week.

Excellent, I thought. *I don't have to take care of this one.*

This Loyalty Questionnaire asked two questions, among others, of great interest to the authorities, confusing to many and quite objectionable to others. One asked if the man was willing to volunteer for military service in the US Armed Forces; the other asked the man to swear allegiance to the United States. After a year of holding us against our will, why did the United States see fit to demand an answer to these questions? As far as I knew, there was no trouble of any kind in the camps, except for a few isolated instances. Pop and Will answered yes to both questions.

I knew that forcing this kind of reply only served to further hurt and alienate the Japanese. Pop, who loved Japan, was disillusioned with his home country. My parents had taught us their fierce pride for their Japanese home, culture, and way of life, but they were not proud of Japan's leaders who massacred the innocents at Pearl Harbor. I myself was proud to be Japanese, as my parents had taught me, but I was also proud to be an American. I was being treated as a traitor and had been sent away to a prisoner-of-war camp far from home with no end to this imprisonment in sight, but despite this, I still loved America. How could I be more loyal to a country I had never seen—Japan—than to the country that was my home? But despite insistence from the FBI investigation of the 1930s that the West Coast Japanese posed no threat, the absence of any Japanese American acts of espionage or treason, and our largely peaceful acceptance of this year of imprisonment, the government was asking the men if they were loyal to America.

Meanwhile, the summer heat grew oppressive. There was no escape in camp. The air was so heavy and burning hot, all I could do was stay in the shade. Some people tried to cool down by putting their feet in buckets of water, but that was hot, too. Pop also used his bucket to water his garden before all his hard work burned up after weeks with no rain, and carrying the heavy load of water by hand even a short distance was arduous in the searing heat. Often I took a shower, only to be completely sweaty by the time I arrived back at the barracks. By the time I finished room checks, I needed another shower. I did my best to tie my hair up off my neck, but even this hardly helped.

Rudy wanted to do something to recognize the efforts of his block managers; he seemed to appreciate our daily work. We were invited to ride in an old school bus for a trip into the town of McGehee for the afternoon. I didn't have much money, since I was giving my meager earnings to my parents to order things needed for our family from the catalog. But this was a trip out of camp—certainly worth going to town, even if I couldn't purchase much. I was excited for this reward for us block managers.

The trip down bumpy country roads in the heat wasn't fun, but at last we arrived. I saw a theater, and we soon all agreed we must go see a movie. It didn't matter what was showing—we could sit in a cool theater and escape the camp and the heat all at once. Nothing could be more wonderful.

We were all smiles as we walked toward the ticket window at the theater—until we saw the two signs in front. One sign said "WHITES," and the other said "COLOREDS." It had been my idea to go to the theater, so, immediately, the other block managers looked at me and said, "What do we do now? Are we white or colored?"

"I have no idea," I said. "We better get in the colored line. I don't think the whites think we are the same as they are."

Everyone agreed. As we neared the front of the line, we realized this little town had probably never been visited by an Asian person. The ticket taker stared at us and then told us we weren't colored.

"Get in the white line," the ticket taker said.

We followed instructions, stood in the "white" line, and were sold tickets to the Charlie Chaplin movie we weren't especially interested in. We were allowed to proceed, despite not fitting into any racial classification, and with that, we encountered a new form of racism in America. It was almost refreshing to see the reaction of the people we encountered—they were curious. I preferred being a curiosity over being yelled at, insulted, spat at, or stared down with indignation. Maybe we'd left that sort of people in Stockton. The theater was cool inside, which made the embarrassment of purchasing the ticket all worthwhile. Soon enough, we returned to camp.

Pop was all smiles when he saw me walking down the hot, dusty pathway. He was proud to tell me how much he'd harvested from his garden. I told Pop that I enjoyed taking the trip into town, but I didn't give him a lot of details. He was thrilled with the fruits of his toil; he didn't need to hear about the white and colored lines in town. All the fresh produce was taken to Chef Kamisono, who was pleased with all of these vegetables and had managed to get the spices to prepare pickled radishes, or *tsukenono*—a favorite of mine and the other *Nisei*—and promised Pop he would serve sautéed daikon soon for dinner.

After dinner, Ray appeared at my door, wearing his normal big smile. He was quite eager to hear about my day in McGehee, and we walked for quite a while that evening as I told him every detail. He wished he could have sat in a cool theater; we were all tired of the heat that hardly lessened even at night in Arkansas. But Ray was glad he'd avoided the experience of not knowing which line to stand in. We wondered if there were two lines for everything all over Arkansas—was it this way throughout the entire South? What would happen if more Japanese moved to McGehee? Would they have a third line? We laughed together, pondering the perplexity of the two-line system.

As the summer progressed, it appeared some of the camp rules relaxed a bit. I don't know if Rudy was given the authority to set the rules, but he did let us know he would allow radios. Up to that point, we'd only used a phonograph for entertainment, since that was all that was available. A radio could give us news of the war. But who could afford one? Mrs. Arakawa, of course, so she ordered one right away. Since she was a relatively formal person who considered herself to be upper class, we only got to listen when we asked properly. She did share her radio for gatherings in the dining hall on occasion. Sometimes it was hard to understand the strong southern accent of the announcers, but I still understood most of what was said.

Rudy invited me several more times into town over the hot summer weeks. Generally, I didn't go, since I didn't have much money to spend, didn't feel like riding along the bumpy road and inhaling the dust kicked up by the bus, or wasn't interested in facing the two lines. But I did go again when Rudy offered to get us an ice cream cone. Just like before, the bus dropped us off at the edge of town, where we walked to the ice-cream stand. Rudy's assistant walked up to the counter with us and paid the lady for each of us. The Dairy King was a popular spot with kids in McGehee, and we were lucky to show up when there were only a couple of customers—and one line, which was a relief. It took a while for us all to be served our soft-serve ice creams in crunchy waffle cones.

That day, we were free to walk around McGehee, but Rudy's assistant, David, emphasized that we must be ready to go at the designated spot at 4:00 p.m. sharp. Only one of us wore a wristwatch, which was fine, because we all stayed together. It took us some time to eat our ice-cream cones. At first I dove right into mine and got a bit of brain freeze, so I slowed down. The creamy, cold, delicious chocolate ice cream was precious; I treasured each lick. But as much as I wanted to take my time and relish every last bit, it melted quickly in the summer heat. I didn't lose a single drip to the ground. Some of the other men attempted to eat their cones by licking from the top as it dripped off the bottom, which made me chuckle.

When we were all finished, we walked to the Kroger grocery store, which took around twenty minutes. Before we reached our destination, several of us needed to use the restroom, so we stopped into the Shady Oak Hotel. The clerk looked suspiciously at us but directed us to the white bathroom. This took a few minutes of our precious time, so we scurried to the store. Each of us had brought a few dollars, but none of us had a ration card, so many things were off limits to us. Even though I didn't have a sugar-ration card, I thought I could purchase several packs of chewing gum.

We all spread throughout the aisles, selecting our purchases. None of us had spare funds for picking up an extra something that looked appealing, so we only shopped for essentials. This process took longer than we'd expected, and we stood in the "white" checkout line, which moved painfully slowly. There was no one in the "colored" line, but we dared not attempt to use that one.

It was 3:30. One of the block managers, Ralph, warned us that we must leave in no later than ten minutes. Still, there were several people ahead of me in line. When 3:40 arrived and we were still in line, we panicked. I dropped my gum, toothpaste, detergent, and soap on the counter and ran out the door with the others. It was too big of a risk to be even one minute late. No one considered providing David a reasonable explanation or excuse of a long line, since none of us wanted any consequence from disobeying any rule, which could mean the end of all trips to town. I'd been looking forward to surprising Tom and Ed with a package of gum—but not today.

When I returned to camp, I explained I had run out of time and hadn't been able to purchase the soap and detergent. We would have to purchase what the canteen offered, which wasn't our preferred brand. I didn't mention the ice-cream cone—that would have annoyed my sisters and brothers.

Ray came by and wanted to hear all about my journey. I told him the whole story of my trip, complete with the ice cream cone. He laughed at me for dropping everything and running to be on time for the pickup. He would have finished the transaction, or so he said. Maybe there would have been no problem with being a few minutes late, but I didn't have the nerve to test the limits of my tiny bit of freedom. Leaving camp was at least something new and different to talk about. The rest of my life was routine. We were all waiting for some news of the war; our lives would remain on hold until further notice from the United States.

Chapter 13

A Wedding

Ray was persistent. He was persistent with Mom and Pop, stopping to visit and converse with them about anything and everything. He was persistent with my brothers and sisters, reaching out, being noticeably friendly, and almost acting like a member of the family.

Most of all, Ray was persistent with me. He accepted his role as "friend" and was determined to be my best friend. He didn't go for walks with the other girls, nor did he react to those who were obviously flirting with him or spend idle time visiting with other girls at our parties. He worked hard to be my friend, which meant sharing feelings, news, conversation of any sort, even advice, and somehow, by August, his persistence had made him important to me. I constantly told him about this or that; he was my "go-to" friend, because he worked hard to be that person for me. Thankfully, he accepted this role and didn't badger me about getting married.

At some point, though, Mom took note of Ray and how he hadn't gone away, despite being rejected by me. One evening, she asked me to go for a walk so we could speak in privacy. She said she couldn't believe that Ray had never left, that nearly ten months had passed since his spurned proposal and he obviously still wasn't giving up on me. Because of this, she and Pop changed their mind about Ray. While they still believed their original evaluation of our suitability was accurate, they were touched by his apparent unending affection for me. She said she completely understood why he was so committed to me despite receiving no commitment in return—she was biased about how wonderful her daughter was. But she was also a realist and wanted me to be happy; she'd devoted her whole life to the happiness of her children. She told me it was my decision, but now she and Pop supported a future with Ray Konishi as my husband. He'd proven over and over again that he wanted no one in the world but me, and they found this simply unbelievable. What more could any woman ask than that? All the rest would hopefully work out in time.

I was stunned about this development. "Are you kidding? You really think I should marry him?" I asked.

"Yes. You will never find anyone better, and you know he'll be able to give you more than you have known growing up in our Hayashi family."

This seemed to be true—Mrs. Arakawa had made everyone aware of the prominence of Ray's family. Mom added the exclamation point to her and Pop's revised opinion: how many men would fall so deeply in love with a woman who treated them only as a friend? She said it takes so much courage for a man to even ask a woman to marry, and when a man's ego is bruised as was Ray's, most would have moved on to find someone who wouldn't reject them.

"Do you realize how lucky you are to have a man who adores you like this?" Mom asked.

I knew Mom was right, but I hadn't thought any more about marriage since I'd told Ray no. I thanked her for her advice and told her I needed some time to think about it. She agreed.

"I just want the best for my precious Janet, the best daughter any mother could ever hope for," she added.

As we hugged and went to our own rooms, my eyes filled with tears. I loved Mom with all my heart.

I fell into my bed with my eyes closed but my head swirling. Was I ready for marriage? I didn't really want to leave my family. I felt like I was a second mom to Ed and Tom. But I was twenty-three years old, plenty old enough to get married; maybe it was time to start my own family. Ray and I were already close friends, and Mom was right about how much he apparently still loved me. Yet I worried about what my future would look like if I married Ray. Would I be ridiculed as a member of a lower class than Ray? Would Ray tire of my ineptitude and leave me? After all, Ray's father had left his second wife and married a third. Would I be taken to Japan and never see my family again? I felt highly conflicted. Usually it was the sultry night with hot, close air and no breeze in my room that kept me awake, but that night, I didn't even notice the sweat beads on my brow. All I wanted to do was lie there and be alone with my thoughts. Finally, I rolled over for the last time and fell asleep.

The next couple of days went by in typical fashion. I saw Ray, and we chatted—our routine. He knew nothing of what had transpired with Mom. I knew in my heart Mom was right, but I was scared to take such a leap. There were no guarantees of what the future would hold for me. I didn't want to leave my family. I was not a risk taker. My life usually unfolded in such a way that precluded independent decision-making. Maybe Ray really didn't still want to marry me; maybe I was kidding myself on this one.

I tried to process it all logically. He was a kind man. He loved me. He offered a life of greater prosperity than I knew. Was I some kind of idiot? I realized there was just one answer to this dilemma. There was no need to procrastinate with my decision.

It was time, and I knew it.

I stopped by Mom and Pop's home when I knew the boys were playing outside and told them I would marry Ray.

"I agree with Mom," Pop said. "Ray is desperately in love with you. How else could a man swallow his pride and risk more rejection to court you?" Pop added that I was not Ray's match in the ways that mattered to everyone else. "But Ray finds you his perfect match for everything that matters to him. That is the most important."

I smiled and thanked my parents for wanting the best for me. Pop said he would tell Ray they now approved if he would like to ask me to marry him again.

Pop wasted no time. Mom relayed Pop's comments to me after he spoke with Ray. She said Ray's face lit up and he could hardly contain his joy. Pop told him he hoped he held no grudges over their previous assessment of our compatibility. Ray assured him there were no hard feelings. He told Pop he wanted to get a ring and make it official.

Before this, one of the WRA workers had remarked often about Ray's fancy camera; no cameras like it were sold in Arkansas. The worker had added that he and his dad would be interested in purchasing Ray's camera if he ever wanted to sell it. Now was the time: selling the camera would help Ray raise cash to buy a ring. For Ray, it was a no-brainer. He never told me how much money he received for the camera, but the man brought in the cash, and Ray ordered a ring from the Sears catalog. He surely knew I knew he was going to propose, but I didn't let on. Neither did he.

Ray told me later that the little diamond ring arrived at Camp Rohwer quickly. Sizing the ring to my finger would have to wait. There was no romantic place in camp to propose, so it happened the second time much like the first. He told me how much he adored me and that he knew I would take such good care of him. He thought I was the kindest and prettiest girl in the whole world. I was the one and only one for him, and he promised to love me with all his heart for the rest of his life. This time, I wasn't caught off guard.

"Yes, I will marry you!" My face turned crimson when I gave him my answer.

We shared a romantic kiss that gave me goosebumps and made my heart thump. This was my first real kiss. Japanese courting usually didn't involve much kissing or physical contact, and Ray and I had never even held hands, though we'd walked many times.

Our kiss sealed the proposal. I was getting married! He pulled out the ring, which sparkled stunningly. I was overwhelmed with emotion in that moment—and a little scared, too.

Many men in Ray's position wouldn't have been as honest as he was in telling me he knew I would take good care of him. It's likely many men want a wife who will look after them as their mothers have, but few would admit it readily; it might scare away a woman who wasn't interested in becoming the maid. But I knew Ray had never known his own mother and that his stepmothers had showed no interest in mothering him, so it made sense to me that he was looking for a mother figure as his wife. I had grown up the oldest of eight children, and this had prepared me well for this domestic role. The idea of caring for children, cooking, sewing, cleaning, and any other matronly duties didn't intimidate me; my life was already full of domestic chores. But I could also tell Ray's feelings went far beyond just having a wife to take care of him. He made sure I knew how he felt.

My parents and most of the *Issei* in camp had been brought together through arranged marriages. Camp brokers even arranged appropriate marriages for fees. I'd wondered if I would also have an arranged marriage, and in a way, I did, since I never would have agreed to marry Ray unless my parents approved. His family and mine were from different worlds. His parents were both deceased, so he couldn't have had an arranged marriage; he could have hired a broker to find a suitable spouse, but he wasn't inclined to do that. He'd fallen uncontrollably hard for me on his own, and I don't think I encouraged him—I'd thought I was treating him like the other guys I knew. He was undoubtedly looking for a family where he could fit in and feel loved and accepted; my family seemed to already feel that way about him. He'd chosen me, and nothing deterred him—not even being told no.

My sisters and brothers were excited about the news. Christine was also spending time with a *Kibei* man—a Japanese man born in America, raised in Japan, and returned to America. Word about Ray and myself traveled through camp quickly. Phone lines weren't needed to spread news; there were over eight thousand of us living together at Camp Rohwer, and everyone knew everything about everybody that was newsworthy. In a way, no one in our block was surprised: Ray hadn't shown interest in any other girls at camp, though he certainly had every opportunity to take advantage of the interest shown by the eligible young ladies.

We decided to get married on Sunday, September 12, 1943. The dining hall would be available that evening for our reception of sorts, since usually nothing was planned for Sunday evenings. Beyond that, there wasn't much more planning to be done for our wedding in the internment camp.

Bernice came by after she heard the news. She lived in block thirty-one, close to mine. It had been a year and a half since Bernice gave me a permanent just weeks before Pearl Harbor. She insisted on giving me another permanent for my wedding, despite my protest that I didn't need one. I didn't want her to spend any of whatever cash she earned for supplies on me.

When I finally agreed, she ordered the chemicals from the catalog, brought in her little plastic curlers with the elastics, trimmed off quite a bit of my hair, and gave me a beautiful full permanent. It was almost like going to a fashionable beauty parlor. Bernice also gave me a wedding present—a brand-new tube of red lipstick. I suddenly felt pretty with my stylish, wavy hair and shiny red lips. We laughed when she told me not to get red lipstick on Ray's lips with all our kissing. She made me feel like a real bride-to-be.

My best dress was black, not white, but I'd made it myself, and it fit me quite nicely; there wasn't time to send away for fabric for a new dress. Everyone in camp understood. Who would have thought of making a wedding dress to take into camp? I had brought my heeled shoes with me, along with two pairs of nylon stockings and my garter belt. The stockings were heavy with a seam going up the back and were most definitely not comfortable to wear, but I'd thought I might need them for a special occasion, and they took very little space in my duffel bag; unfortunately, because of war rationing, women could no longer purchase nylon stockings from the catalog at that time. Now I had a special occasion to wear my stockings. So, I was ready to be married, with my best dress, my nylon stockings, and my pump heels to go along with my curls and shiny red lips.

On the day of our wedding, Ray came to my home all smiles, dressed in his suit. He carried a beautiful orchid corsage. His hand shook as he took the straight pin off the corsage and attempted to put it through my dress. I'd never been presented with a beautiful corsage by a man before; it made me feel complete and ready to get married. I wondered how he'd acquired the corsage; maybe one of the WRA workers had brought it for him. I was touched by his thoughtfulness. Ray's suit looked too big on his thin body. For a Japanese man, he was of average build, though much taller than my five-foot-one height. He didn't have heart-throb good looks, but the twinkle in his eye and his beaming smile made him appealing.

He looked at me after he'd successfully pinned the corsage on my dress, and he flushed a little. My brothers and sisters were looking at him, and Pop welcomed him into our family. There was small talk about the weather and what a lovely day it was. Pop said it looked like we were ready to get married. Pop, Mom, Ray, and I walked down the steps of my room. Ray quietly whispered to me how beautiful I looked, and I thanked him.

We first went to a Buddhist priest, who gave us his blessing for a long and happy life together. That was it—we really had no wedding ceremony or service. We signed the book at camp to make it official. Pop and Mom came along as witnesses; the whole thing took only a couple of minutes. Pop was sentimental about giving up his eldest daughter in marriage. He hugged me and told me how proud he was of the woman I'd grown up to be, then he looked at Ray and asked him to take good care of me. Ray assured him he would love me and care for me every day of his life, words I knew he truly felt with all his heart.

Our wedding reception in the dining hall that evening was full of well-wishes and greetings. It was amazing how many people we knew in camp, especially friends of our family. I almost cried when Chef Kamisono walked in with a beautiful white wedding cake adorned with white icing. He'd saved a spoonful of sugar each week from his ration just for this occasion. I was overwhelmed by his kindness. He apologized for not having Kool-Aid, but he colored the water red, and we pretended it was sweet, as we'd done at parties before. Japanese are known as gift givers, so everyone brought a little something if they possibly could. I received many handmade things from the ladies. Even Rudy and his wife showed up and gave us five dollars. With his slow-talking southern drawl, Rudy told us how happy he was for us and said maybe someday we might even be neighbors in Little Rock, Arkansas, where he was from. That was pretty incredible for him to say; I was amused and touched by Rudy's thoughtfulness.

When a couple married in camp, they received their own barracks room. Ray and I were assigned a new room to be our own, so we moved our two army metal-frame beds and mattresses to our new "home." We would have to make do with our twin beds and push them together. Soon after we signed the official book, Will and Pop helped Ray move our things into our new room. We were now husband and wife—almost.

Ray and I had both been raised in the Buddhist faith, which taught that our cravings caused unhappiness in our lives. Many considered sexual desire to be the same as any other craving; that's why the Buddhist monks lived celibate lives. But for the common lives of the faithful, did this mean sex was only for procreating? If so, sex to appease a sensual desire would be a craving to be avoided along the pathway to Buddhist enlightenment. Maybe this was why the Japanese had so little physical contact with the opposite sex; maybe Buddha wanted it this way, so we wouldn't have any cravings for intimacy. I wasn't sure myself. I'd attended services at my Stockton temple for years, but sex was never discussed there or at home. I'd always guessed I would find out what I needed to know when I got married.

That day was here.

We took off our shoes and left them by the door, then entered our new home together for the first time. Ray took off his suit jacket and put it on a hanger over the room's wall partition. He was quite keen to consummate his marriage with the love of his life—I understood that. He and I were both virgins, but he had undoubtedly gathered plenty of sex education along the way and surely had all the instincts of a man. My knowledge was limited to reading and discussions with a friend. Ray explained everything to me and couldn't wait to get on with it. He told me the firemen at his station gave him the best advice. They told him to make his wife happy—very happy. He said he couldn't wait to be my lover.

I felt anxious and embarrassed about what was expected of me. Ray loved the permanent Bernice gave me and told me how lovely the new waves in my hair were; now that we were married, he could run his hands through my hair. I knew my brand-new husband adored me, and I enjoyed that quiet moment in our new home, as we kissed and talked and kissed some more; all the while he stroked my hair.

Ray asked me to hold the hanger while he took off his suit pants, shirt, and tie. He stood in his underwear as he placed the hanger over the wall again. Then he slowly unzipped my black wedding dress and slid it off my shoulders and down to the floor. I stepped out of it, and he placed it carefully on the end of one of our beds. Next were my undergarments, which he was clueless how to navigate. He proceeded gently, slowly, as if I were a porcelain doll, savoring every second. Finally, he removed his own underwear as I stood waiting, unsure of what was next. Ray wrapped his arms around me and guided me down onto one of our twin beds. There was no more talk as our bare bodies lay together and the two of us found our way to becoming one. We were really married now.

I was greatly relieved to have complete darkness for our wedding night as my new husband gradually and totally revealed me. I trembled a bit, which I desperately tried to hide. I had never seen a naked man in my life—all I knew of a man's anatomy was what I'd seen in books or heard about from my friend. I'd been raised to dress privately at all times; I didn't even change clothes in front of my sisters. I was also raised to always be clean.

Making love seemed to violate all this. All I could think that first night, and the days following, was that I wished there were some way I could run away. I'm sure I wasn't the first woman to feel that way. More time brought relief, acceptance, and pleasure for me, as Ray worked hard to be my lover. He awakened the sexual part of me I hadn't known I had.

Chapter 14
The No-Nos

I faced many adjustments in my first months as a married woman. I'd gone from never being touched to having an adoring husband who couldn't keep his hands off me (strictly in private, of course). I was also adjusting to living with my new husband in our little room, which contained only two twin beds pushed together and a potbelly stove. We enjoyed plenty of togetherness. There was never a day I didn't know how much he loved me.

I liked my family surname, Hayashi, but now it was Konishi. Something didn't feel right about changing my name; I was still the same me. After many times of accidentally writing my maiden name, I finally made it a habit to sign as Mrs. Ray Konishi. That was who I was now.

It was ironic that Ray understood little about how things were done in America—my mom worried about me not fitting into his world, but it was I who was teaching him about how I lived. He was embarrassed at times about his lack of Americana knowledge, so I tried to minimize my explanations. After all, he'd only lived in America a year or so before the war. But he was eager to fit in as an American with his American newlywed. He liked Americans very much.

He also loved Japan; it was his homeland, and he was eager to return, especially since his inheritance was waiting for him there. He was also eager to show me his home and the Japanese culture. Japan was full of relics, gardens, statues, and pieces of ancient culture, he said, and he told me about many sights there which sounded grander than anything I could imagine. I looked forward to the day I could see them; more than anything else in Japan, I anxiously awaited seeing the cherry blossom trees in full bloom.

It was fun to sit and talk about our future; the day would come soon, hopefully, when peace reigned in the world and we would be off to Japan together. Then we could see and do everything Ray told me about. Money would never be a problem. Ray's family estate sounded like a dream to me. How had I been so lucky to marry this man who wanted to show me the world? But despite all the privilege Ray had grown up with, all the money showered on him by his family, and all the amazing travels he had enjoyed, I'd certainly had the better childhood. Ray talked about his many friends, but I wondered if his lack of a close family had left him lonely.

Living together was much different from being friends who chatted every day, only to return to their own barracks. I could tell Ray had been spoiled as a child and was used to getting his way; he would complain about this or that if it didn't go the way he wanted it to. I accepted this about him. Maybe being spoiled had given him the determination to do what he needed to do to finally get me, after waiting months and months. Maybe that was a good quality to have for success in life—never giving up. We were opposites in this way, and maybe this was part of what had attracted him to me.

We exchanged our wedding money and some of our own earnings for a check at the canteen, so we could order a double bed of our own. It seemed anything could be ordered from the catalog. Ray wanted to hold me close at night, so we squeezed together on one of our twin beds, which was not comfortable in the least. I was thrilled when our new bed arrived and I could finally have some room. I was used to all my years of sleeping on the pull-out bed back to back with Christine, but she and I had been careful not to touch. I didn't need a lot of room. With our new big bed, Ray and I occupied the same space as before, but it was much more comfortable. I wasn't used to being touched when I slept, but after being married for some time, I acclimated to my husband's warm, tight embrace.

When I ran into my girlfriends, they often asked me, "How did you find a rich one?"

I would just laugh and tell them I had no idea. "He found me."

Most of the single girls my age were trying to find a good husband. It was odd to think we were all starting new families while living in an internment camp, but this was just one more aspect of our attempt to make our own city in the camp and carry on with our lives as best we could.

The weather was cooling down, so Pop and the men laid straw over their vegetable gardens at night, in case there was a frost, then pulled the straw away during the day and let the warm sun reach the plants. They were determined to keep the produce coming for as long as possible. The men exchanged seeds and advice between the different blocks. They grew as many as one hundred different vegetables at camp, and all of that produce went to the chefs to feed everyone in each block.

One morning, I awoke feeling ill. I ran to the bathroom and threw up.

Later, I ran into Mom and said, "I didn't notice anything different last night at dinner, but something made me sick. I barely made it to the bathroom."

Mom smiled. "Sorry to hear you were sick, my dear. Could you be in a family way?"

I was stunned. "I'm not sure. Oh my."

Mom grinned coyly. "I remember getting pregnant right away with you after Pop and I were married, and how thrilled I was."

"Gee, Mom—I didn't think it would happen this fast. I need to get to the office."

She gave me a quick hug and told me to let her know of any updates. It would be our secret for now. I tried to act excited, but mainly I was anxious at the thought of being pregnant. However, I realized that if I was going to have eight kids of my own, like my mom, I'd better get started now. I decided to wait a few days and make sure I was really pregnant before saying anything to Ray.

I didn't throw up again, but my stomach was queasy. I was pretty sure Mom was right—I knew I felt different, so I must be pregnant.

I couldn't wait any longer, so I whispered in Ray's ear when we were going to bed, "Guess what? I'm pretty sure we are going to have a baby."

Ray sat right up. "Really? Wow, I can't believe it!"

I looked up at him and smiled. "Well, I haven't gone to the doctor, but I'm pretty sure I'm pregnant."

"What wonderful news, my love! Wow, so fast; I am a proud man!" He was wide awake and beaming, and he leaned down to kiss me. "Let's celebrate our news."

We were both happy, but I was still anxious about this development. The only birth control I knew of was abstinence, so most of the married women who were able, such as Mom, bore one baby after the next. I'd mostly thought that would be great, too, but only after we got out of camp. Camp or not, I was having my first baby. I was surprised, but I loved children, so I was excited to be expecting one of my own.

After another week, we shared the news with my family. It spread quickly all over our block and beyond. Mom was thrilled, though she'd already known and had kept it to herself. Pop said he was ready to be a grandfather. We all counted ahead to when this baby would be born; the summer of 1944 was our best guess. Tom would probably be seven, and Ed would be five; it was funny to think about my baby brothers becoming big uncles. Mom told me she couldn't wait to have another baby to hold and that I could count on her to help me out, just as I'd helped her so many times.

I went to the doctor at Camp Rohwer, and he confirmed I was pregnant. Since I didn't have any dates to offer him as to my cycle, he wasn't exactly sure of my due date, but he guessed near the end of July 1944. There was no charge to see the doctor in camp, and I received no pregnancy vitamins.

Unfortunately, pregnancy was hard for me. My equilibrium was thrown off, and I seemed to fall down all the time. I tried to eat extra, but not feeling well didn't help. I wanted to show a bump on my tummy, but it hardly looked pregnant. Ray was gentle, as he could tell I was struggling. He wanted to do whatever he could to help, but there really was nothing he could do; still, I appreciated how much he cared about how I was feeling. I managed to carry on with my daily block manager duties, but I returned to my room often to rest when I could.

Christmas arrived, and this year it was much different. I was married and pregnant, all in the past four months. Ray and I spent the day with my family. Mom and my sisters had managed to get many things ready for me and my baby. Mom made a maternity dress, with no waist, so it could hang down when my tummy got bigger—she laughed and told me it was easy to make. Maternity clothes were not flattering but would soon be welcome. Mom also crocheted a pretty baby blanket in yellow variegated yarn, and Loretta knit a little hat using tiny needles. It was stretchy and soft; I couldn't imagine it would fit my baby. They also made some sparkling-white cotton diapers. I remembered washing diapers; I was not looking forward to dealing with them again. Mom showed me a green outfit she was still working on that would zip up around the baby. I was delighted to receive the new baby things; while I knew there was plenty of time before I delivered, I was excited to start preparing for my baby. Ray thoroughly enjoyed the Christmas celebration with the Hayashi family. He was now a member of a big happy family, which he'd never enjoyed growing up.

In the New Year, my pregnancy moved along, but still it was not an easy time. I remembered Mom being well past forty when she became pregnant with Ed, and she'd carried on managing all aspects of our family. I definitely helped out in many ways, but still it seemed pregnancy wasn't agreeing with me as it had with Mom. Maybe the difference was that her body had been so experienced at carrying a baby. I hoped my next child would go much easier. I had passed the critical first three months, so although I didn't feel well, I was relieved I hadn't miscarried.

One day, Rudy asked me to come into his office because he needed to discuss something important. I could tell that he was about to share something serious with me. He said that another of the ten permanent Japanese internment camps was in Northern California. It was called Tule Lake. Japanese from other internment camps who were considered "disloyal" to America were being segregated from the other internees and transferred to this camp. These were the men who had answered "no" and "no" to the two main questions on the loyalty questionnaire, and who came to be known as the "no-nos." All such men, who were considered hostile toward the United States, would receive their notices of transferal soon, but Rudy wanted to tell me personally that Ray was a no-no. He would soon have to leave with the other men for Tule Lake Camp, and it was my decision whether I would accompany him to this camp, where the rules would be strict. A train would be coming soon for the transfers. After the war, the United States would supply transportation back to Japan for any of the no-nos who wanted to return.

When I found time later in the evening, I explained all this to Ray. He reacted immediately.

"If I must go, then you must go to Tule Lake with me," he said.

I didn't say much. I was a few months from having a baby. It would be a long train trip, and I didn't feel well. What if I went into labor on the train? When I arrived, I wouldn't have my family to help me when my baby was born. Ray was insistent he wouldn't leave without me, and he was being forced to go, so in his mind, there was no discussion of the matter. I must accompany him and leave my family.

I knew my family's reaction would be the opposite of Ray's. *Please stay.* Mom pleaded for me to stay safely in Arkansas with family close by. She understood Ray was being forced to go, but she also felt strongly that it wasn't safe for me to take a long train trip at my stage of pregnancy. She choked up when she asked what would happen if I went into labor on the long train trip; we all remembered the long, arduous journey from Stockton to Arkansas. Mom thought Ray and I could be reunited when the war was over and it was safe for all.

I knew Ray would not leave me behind. We were a family of our own now; he couldn't imagine one night away from me. He was upset at the idea Mom suggested—that he could somehow leave me in Arkansas. I belonged to him now, not them.

I explained to my family how important it was for Ray to get to Japan. I think my family respected him for his "no, no" answers on the loyalty questionnaire, though Pop and Will had answered with "yes, yes." They also understood the government putting all the no-no men together. But my parents thought Ray wasn't thinking about what was best for me—that I should stay safely in Arkansas.

However, I needed to support Ray; I was expected to be a good wife and accompany my husband, so I didn't really consider it an option to stay behind. I trusted him completely as my husband: he wanted to take care of me and our baby. We would go to Tule Lake together and start our family, and hopefully the war would end soon. We could then go to Japan, and Ray would take his place as the only son of his deceased father. I would have to just hope for the best with the long train trip. So it was settled: I told Rudy to count me in for the transfer to my third internment camp.

Almost simultaneously, my brother Will received a notice that he was being drafted by the US military. Mom, Pop, and the rest of us were concerned by this news. How could America put Will in a camp for a year as an enemy of the state only to turn around and draft him into the army? It seemed terribly wrong—but he'd answered yes on his questionnaire. Pop, who himself had left Japan so many years ago to circumvent being drafted, had to tell his son there was no choice. Will, who was just nineteen, was going to serve in the United States armed forces.

PART 4

LIVING WITH DISLOYALS

Chapter 15

Third Internment Camp: Tule Lake

It was highly emotional for me to leave my family. I'd never lived apart from them, except for briefly boarding in the Stockton temple as a young girl. My mom had left her family when she took a ship to America to marry Pop, and she never saw them again. I couldn't even consider that possibility—I loved my family too much. But we were also good Japanese who didn't display emotion; we desperately tried to conceal our heartbreak about being separated.

Tears filled my eyes as Ray and I boarded the train together. Maybe I was more emotional because I was pregnant. My future seemed so uncertain, but I would just have to accept whatever came next. I'd learned that lesson well. I trusted Ray; everything would work out. Every day, I was falling more in love with my baby.

I dreaded the long train trip to Northern California. We knew what to expect because of the similar train ride from Stockton to Camp Rohwer in the fall of 1942. On the long journey, Ray and I spent hours talking together about a myriad of topics. We discussed baby names, and by the end of the trip, we had agreed on girl and boy names. Actually, we found several names we both liked, so we decided we were ready for the next baby, too. It wasn't hard, and neither of us stubbornly insisted on a certain name.

Ray still couldn't believe it had all worked out between us. He said he loved me more each day, though he didn't think that was possible. He told me he'd fallen in love with me the first time I smiled at him, when I came around at Stockton Camp carrying my clipboard with the names on it. He said he'd felt my smile all over and knew immediately I was the woman he wanted to marry.

I was surprised. "Really? That's hard to believe. You're just kidding me now."

He said he hoped I hadn't married him only because my family had approved of him; I just smiled back at him. He told me he'd wanted to make sure another suitor didn't come along, so he would have just kept trying to win me over until I said yes, because all he'd known was he was in love with me. He also told me that our first few months of marriage were the happiest days of his life. He'd wanted to be with me all the time and loved to wake up first in the morning to just look at me. Whatever I was doing, he wanted to do also, if possible. He told me he would watch the clock, counting the hours until we would be in bed together. When I chuckled, he replied quickly: "And it isn't what you're thinking. I just can't wait until I can hold you all to myself every night."

I told Ray I loved him, too, but I hadn't married him because I was madly passionate about him. I'd married him because my parents approved, although of course, if I didn't like him, I wouldn't have married him. We'd grown close in that first year. I appreciated how he tried to make me happy. I didn't know if other men were like Ray in the way he'd fallen for me, but I was pretty sure they weren't. What was it about me that made him fall so hard? I decided to enjoy my doting husband, even if he was quite amusing at times. And he didn't mind me talking to other men; he knew I was friendly and enjoyed talking to people, but we were married, so he had nothing to worry or be jealous about. He felt secure in our relationship now.

He put his hand on my tummy and said, "Look what love has already started."

I smiled.

"You will be a great mom," he said.

I chuckled and replied, "And you will be a great father, too."

We both grinned, and then Ray suddenly looked serious. "I will be grateful every day of my life for your parents' permission to marry you. If I couldn't have married you, I just wouldn't have married at all."

"Ray, don't be silly. You would have found someone else in no time. You had to know all the girls were flirting with you."

"So what? None of them interested me."

I gave him a surprised look.

He said, "I was in love with you, and that was that."

Ray looked admiringly at me, and I'm sure he wanted to kiss me right then—but not on this train, never in public. I could tell from his face he meant what he said: I was the only one for him. I felt bad for all the hurt I'd caused him after the first proposal, but it needed to happen for him to gain the approval of Mom and Pop.

We made a fuel stop in Utah. We were allowed off the train and were amazed at the uniqueness of Salt Lake, which was almost thick with the salt. It was a natural wonder we all appreciated seeing. The rest of the trip was several days long, and all we could do was close our eyes and attempt to sleep in our seats. Ray tried to get me comfortable, but it wasn't easy.

I was quite relieved when we arrived; I'd been terrified that the rumble of the train would bring on early labor. When we received our room and set up our bed, I could relax. They'd stacked our bed frame, mattress, and box springs in the back car with many others, so we would have our own double bed in our new barracks at Tule Lake Camp.

I read a sign at the entrance of Tule Lake Camp: it had been established in 1935 during the Depression as part of the Civilian Conservation Corps to provide vocational training and work for unemployed young men at the Klamath Reclamation Project. Evidently, for this camp and the other nine WRA camps, the US government had sought locations that could be used or converted economically to house interred Japanese on a long-term basis. Tule Lake Camp was twice as big as Camp Rohwer, housing over eighteen thousand internees.

I noticed right away that military guards were all over Tule Lake Camp; it was heavily guarded. There was tension in the air—I could sense it the moment we walked through the gate. As Rudy warned me, this camp was run in a military manner. The authorities were on the lookout for any suspicious activity; after all, the camp housed men and their families whom the United States believed to be loyal to Japan, based on their answers to two questions. There was no escaping the reality of the situation at Tule Lake: everyone at this camp was a prisoner of war. I figured this didn't really matter, since Ray and I were harmless; we could just go about our lives as we had at the other camps. To my relief, no one asked me to be a block manager here. Rudy knew I was pregnant, wasn't having an easy time, and needed to prepare for my baby, so he probably didn't even pass along my qualifications; furthermore, the block managers at Tule Lake had been selected months ago.

Ray and I settled into our third prison camp, now as a married couple. We were glad we'd been able to bring along our double bed on the long cross-country journey, but our living arrangements were still as stark as could be—one plain room with zero privacy. We had to walk to another barracks to use the restroom, take a shower, or even wash our hands, and as newlyweds living together in our naked room that granted no modesty, we dressed and undressed together. This was fine with Ray; however, he understood I wasn't used to living in this way, so he tried to make me feel quite comfortable and complimented me on everything. I wondered how the other Japanese men treated their wives in private, because they never showed any public affection. Was Ray like this because we were newlyweds? Maybe it would be different in a few years, but we were married and happy now, and I knew my husband just couldn't get enough of me. Eventually, it seemed like we weren't newlyweds at all; it was like we'd been married for years.

I wasn't nervous about the strict rules at this camp, but I was nervous about delivering a baby soon. I was relieved to learn from some others that Tule Lake's hospital was adequate. The one-floor, fifty-bed hospital had been built in the camp. When I inquired about a doctor for my pregnancy, I was directed to Dr. Hasegawa, an obstetrician and pediatrician who had previously practiced in Hawaii. When I met him, I thought he was an attractive man, but I figured modesty would be the least of my concerns when my time came. It was comforting to know I would have a real doctor with experience in delivering babies; this knowledge relieved the many worries I'd considered on the train from Arkansas to California.

When I met Dr. Hasegawa, he was concerned that my tummy wasn't as large as expected for my length of pregnancy. He encouraged me to eat and drink as much as possible.

"I will do my best," I promised. I still wasn't feeling great and still struggled with getting dizzy and falling down. But Dr. Hasegawa thought I was entering my last trimester. He estimated my due date as the last week of July.

I wrote a letter to Mom and Pop, telling them the details of our travels and a bit about Tule Lake Camp. Even though Tule Lake was in California, it was in a different region than Stockton. It seemed more arid; I don't think Pop could have grown all the vegetables here that he grew in Arkansas unless he watered them often. I didn't mention anything about the heightened security to Mom and Pop— there was even barbed wire around the office, as if the officials were afraid of being attacked—because I didn't want to worry them. I told them I did feel great relief about one thing: to be a resident without block manager responsibilities. I was busy making things for my baby, and I teased Mom that her dress was plenty big on me, since my tummy wasn't that large. I was glad I didn't have an enormous baby belly, but it did bother me at times when others said I barely looked pregnant. I promised Mom and Pop I would write often and give them progress reports on my pregnancy.

Mom wrote back, and I was excited to learn that Christine and Mitsuru were getting married. Maybe Ray and Mitsuru would be fast friends, since they were both *Kibei*. Mitsuru's father in Japan was ailing, so he was also intent on returning to Japan after the war ended. Mom said Christine and Mitsuru would possibly also be taking the train to Tule Lake soon. Mom didn't mention whether Mitsuru was also a no-no or if he just thought transferring to Tule Lake was his best chance of getting on a ship for Japan. Still, it was a thrill to think of having my sister in camp with me.

In my spare time, I worked on making things for my baby. I needed plenty of bibs, swaddling blankets, and sleepers, and I wanted to be sure to have everything once the baby arrived. There were no cribs at Tule Lake; you could have an army bed for a baby, so that is what we got. We knew our baby wouldn't need a crib for many months, so the army bed would be fine for now. I wished Mom were around to tell me what to expect when I went into labor. I had no instruction whatsoever, other than to go to the hospital when the pains started. Mom had delivered me with just a midwife and encountered no major problems, so hopefully I would be just like her. It was reassuring to know my doctor was a real obstetrician and I was going to have my baby in a real hospital, even if it was just one thrown together by the WRA.

In our barracks, I could hang up our clothes by poking a little hole in the plaster walls to push in wire hangers, so the clothes didn't get wrinkled after I ironed them; Mom had taught me years ago to iron my clothes before wearing them, so I diligently kept everything neatly pressed, even though I didn't feel much like ironing while pregnant. It was fun to look at the little clothes now ready for my baby. Ray and I didn't have lots of clothes, but I hung up Ray's suit and my dresses. I still wore each dress for several days before changing. No matter what I put on for the day, Ray often commented about how great I looked. He kept my spirits high, even though I really wasn't feeling well.

My neighbor stopped by one morning with big news: the Allies had invaded France. They'd enacted a huge operation by sea from England to the beaches of Normandy; there had been many casualties, but the push was on to liberate France. I was excited about the news, although Ray didn't say much when I told him. Maybe the war was finally turning in the Allies' favor. There was no news of Japan. It seemed the military might was being used in France. Maybe this was the beginning of the end of Nazi Germany; then the Allies could finish off Japan, and the war would be over.

Meanwhile, our incarceration as Japanese in America passed the two-year milestone. I'd spent 8 percent of my young life coping with the emotional and physical difficulties of being confined in a prisoner-of-war camp. At least my life in the last year hadn't been totally wasted; a year ago, I hadn't thought I'd spend another year confined, but I also hadn't expected I would be married and expecting a baby by this time. At Tule Lake, Ray made some new friends who had also lived most of their lives in Japan and wanted to return. I didn't ask many questions about his new friends; I was happy he'd found acquaintances. He enjoyed getting together with them, and I knew he looked forward to their meetings in each other's barracks and rooms.

Chapter 16
A Baby Is Born

The cramps started. *Labor.*

Ray picked up my little ready-to-go bag, and we walked to the hospital, where I was whisked away while Ray was shown the waiting room. My labor progressed, and Dr. Hasegawa arrived to check on me. He informed me my baby was breech, or coming feet first, and that this was dangerous as the baby could suffer oxygen deprivation and brain damage. So he worked hard to push the baby back up as high as possible in an effort to turn it around. Thankfully, the labor stopped, but the procedure was torturous as the doctor and nurses tried to shift the baby both internally and externally.

The hours went on, and nothing changed. I felt contractions, but I couldn't push. Daytime turned into evening, nighttime, and morning again. I was getting weaker, exhausted with the process, never mind the pain of it all. After two days of this arduous labor, the doctor was determined to get my baby righted. He didn't mention possibly delivering the baby by surgery; maybe he didn't have the equipment for that. Somehow, he rearranged the baby, and it was coming head down.

Doc securely grabbed the head with his forceps and pulled out my baby. All I heard were the sounds of tools, a splat, and people scurrying around. I did not hear the cry of a newborn baby. I didn't see a baby, either. The nurse quickly wrapped up my baby and exited the room. I was bleeding heavily, and the doctor worked on me, obviously panicked. The long hours of labor and manipulation had torn me up. I heard the doctor barking orders and asking for ice; nurses were running around. I was trying to ask about my baby, but I was just too weak. I passed out.

Ray told me later that after working on me, the doctor walked out to where he was still in the waiting room, exhausted. He told Ray he had a son, but his son had been damaged in birth and I had lost a massive quantity of blood. The doctor didn't know whether either of us would survive the night. He told Ray he could not see our son, as he was highly discolored.

When my baby was born, Doc thought it was a stillbirth. He barely weighed four pounds. But after breathing his first breath, he was quickly placed in the oven; there was no incubator at Tule Lake Hospital. The nurses were doing everything they could, and Doctor Hasegawa never left my side. It took all his experience, training, and determination to deliver my baby—and save my life. Ray thanked him for everything; he would wait to hear any news. Ray wasn't a deeply religious man, but he told me later how he'd closed his eyes as he sat the long hours waiting for a progress report and pleaded with God to watch over his wife and son.

I was packed with ice, and the bleeding stopped. I received an IV with fluids, but there weren't blood transfusions available. When I came out of my stupor, the nurse told me I had delivered a baby boy. She also told me he was in critical condition—and I was, too. I drifted in and out, but I quickly stabilized, to the great relief of my doctor. The doctor told Ray I was doing much better but they were still concerned about his son. Neither of us would be allowed to see him. But Ray, after putting on full hospital attire and facemask, was allowed to see me. We were overjoyed that our baby boy, Norman, was alive, although of course we were still worried about him.

I was awakened for lunch. The nurse's assistant said I needed to eat my whole tray to regain my strength, so I forced it down. How was my baby? The nurse assistant told me to expect Nurse Gladys soon. She didn't share much information with me, other than telling me Nurse Gladys would be in charge of us.

Soon, Nurse Gladys arrived. I hadn't seen her before. She was a large woman, probably Mom's age, with dark-blonde hair tied back securely in a bun. I don't think Gladys wore any makeup, and I could see the years carved into the prominent wrinkles crossing her forehead. Her skin was milky white and sprinkled with freckles or age spots on her face and arms. When she smiled, I noticed her teeth were missing. Despite her appearance, her manner and approach gave her an air of assurance that increased my confidence in her.

Gladys cranked up my bed until I was almost sitting up. She leaned over, untied my hospital gown, and pulled it down to my waist, exposing my chest. She grabbed my left breast with her big hands and started massaging, rather gently, then harder and harder, like she was kneading a loaf of bread.

"Yo and me gonna be a team," she said. "Yo baby needs its milk, and he needs it now. Doc told me I needs to git him some of mamma's milk every two hours, even if it be just a few drops now. He real weak, and I knows Doc is real worried about him. He look bad, too—real bad. I just picked him up. He needs yo milk. I gots to get yo mammary glands producing. The first milk that comes out—that is the best of all. Yo baby needs it. Needs it bad."

At first, I asked Gladys to repeat herself, as her heavy southern country drawl was hard for me to understand. But in time, I grew to understand her by listening intently to everything she said. Gladys's hands looked big and strong as a farmer's, probably part of the reason she'd been given this job. She also was a pro.

The ward only had women in it, so by this point, there was nothing left to be embarrassed about. Gladys moved over to my right breast, massaging with every ounce of strength in her mighty hands. I was scared—really scared. But all I could do was let her do what she had to do. I knew how important mother's milk was, so I was only too happy to cooperate.

Maybe I flinched during her increasingly aggressive work, because she said, "Honey, I knows yo man loves doing this with you, so just pretend it's him now. Just enjoy. I do all the hard work, and you jest get to set there. We gots some work to do with these breasts. You see how big they is today? Just get me a few days. I am the best at getting the most milk from my ladies. Those breasts will be twice as big in no time. Yo be happy having some big ones soon—I mean real big."

Funny, I already thought they had grown large through my pregnancy. But Gladys did make me smile. "Oh, yes, that would be great," I said.

"Jest you wait. We be a good team." I wasn't sure if she was talking to my breasts or me, but it didn't matter.

After massaging for a long time on one breast and then the other, she washed her hands thoroughly. She brought a warm washrag over and scrubbed my breasts clean. Then she started working on my nipples. "I can tell this is yo first baby. We gots to build up those nipples. We got to get them nice and big for yo baby to latch on." Now she was squeezing and pulling and squeezing harder and pulling harder. "Look, this one is coming up nice." Then she pushed down hard on my breast and pulled up just as hard on my nipple, pinching hard on it. And there they came: the first droplets of milk.

We were both excited. "Look at this, honey child." Gladys hollered for the assistant nurse, who held the flask up to my breast as Gladys continued to push and squeeze with all her strength. "I am the best at getting every drop of milk. I jest keep working and working until it's all done for now."

She repeated the same process with my other breast. She made the same comments again, and I understood what she meant then. As odd as this was for me, I appreciated her dedication; I knew my sweet baby boy was in poor condition. When she expelled every drop, it was over, and she spread a salve on my nipples.

Gladys thought I might be sore soon. I was sore already. But I was ecstatic when she returned to tell me she'd used a syringe to feed Norman every drop. "He needed that bad." Then she made me drink a big glass of water. "You gots to drink all day, then I be pumping it out later. You can rest a little bit now."

When Gladys said I could rest a little bit, she meant it. She was back two hours later for the same routine. "Yo little boy needs to eat every two hours now. Doc orders. He needs mo milk. I gots to get him fed right away."

The nurse assistant captured the milk in the vial, making sure to get every drop. She didn't want to aggravate Gladys. Gladys was considered the best at getting milk; all the nurses told me that. This routine went on every two hours for the next twenty-four hours. I was definitely sore but not complaining; I was getting reports that my sweet Norman was slowly gaining strength.

A day later, Gladys lowered the breast-pumping frequency to every three hours. It was such a relief to hear that baby Norman was improving. The doctor was pleased with how much milk he consumed. Gladys said he told her, "Good job." But still I wasn't allowed to see him. Somehow, Gladys knew it would be a long time before he would be brought to me. But she let me know how much I was directly contributing to his growing health.

"Honey, we done good together," she said after feeding Norman again. "They is working real fine. Yo baby was fill up, and the bottle was just gone. Some of the moms, they ain't got the gift of makin' milk like you, and their babies be crying," Gladys went on. "Is it okay if I give yo leftover milk to one of them? They be nursing on their own, so they don't have any idea how much milk their baby is drinking. They don't want me working on them like you, but I know I get them producing just like these beauties if they would let me. It's yo decision if yo want to share."

I smiled, glad to help. "Oh, of course, as long as you are sure my baby is full."

"Oh, he be full, and he be sleeping now."

It felt so good to know I helped out another mom and baby. It didn't matter if it was my milk; all mothers' milk was good.

Gladys didn't let up with me, but at least the pumping sessions backed up to every four hours. "Pretty soon yo boy be ready to nurse on hees own. You wants to be sure he latches on. That's what we want—to make it easy on yo boy."

I had to hand it to Gladys—was she ever successful! My breasts and nipples didn't resemble their former selves. They would quickly fill up with milk, get hard, and ache, often after just a couple of hours. There were times I called for Gladys; I needed relief.

"Way to go," she said as she massaged my breast. She hardly did any massaging now, as all she needed to do was get the breast to let down, and the milk flowed.

Six days had passed since Norman's birth. Ray came every day and was only allowed to see me briefly, but he was relieved to hear both Norman and I were improving. I told him I wasn't good at being pregnant and I wasn't good at delivery, but I was good at producing milk. Ray was surprised when I told him I produced enough milk to share with other babies in the nursery. Every day, I asked if I could see and hold my baby. I was told he was improving, but no, I couldn't hold him yet.

Gladys had already told me several times that the more bottles a baby was given, the harder it was to get the baby to take the milk from its mom's breasts. "But yo nipples lookin' so good," she said. "But be careful—baby boys like to hang on to their mama's teat. They git the milk, and then they don't let go. It's always the baby boys. The girls git their milk, and they be done. But the boys, they like to jest hang on. They be like that their whole lives."

What could I say to that? I just looked at Gladys and smiled.

As the days continued, I noticed the milk pumping was good for my health. I was feeling stronger; my body was in full gear, and the routine of the pumping sessions stimulated it. It just seemed right and wholesome. Even the pain passed. I was relaxed, and the milk pumping was working as it should.

I was into my second week in the ward and still wasn't allowed to see my son, though I was told he was gaining weight and looking much better daily. It was agony to wait without holding my precious baby, even though it was customary for a new mom and baby to stay two weeks in the hospital after a normal delivery. I was getting friendly with the other moms in the ward. We were all excited to be first-time moms. They thanked me many times for sharing my milk with their babies. I wasn't worried anymore about Norman; the nurses kept assuring me I would be allowed to hold him soon.

After two full weeks, Gladys came in for what I thought was a normal milking session. She squeezed on my left nipple to start the milk—and quickly stopped. Then she squeezed on my right nipple—and stopped again. She took the milk she'd just extracted and smeared it all around. "They ready to go."

In came another nurse with my precious baby boy. Then I was holding him. He sucked a little, then a little more. Then he latched on. Success!

Gladys and I wanted to scream for joy. I looked down at my baby. I couldn't believe how perfect he was. I already loved him more than I could imagine, and I was on top of the world. *I'm really holding my baby!*

Later, Gladys told me Norman had been born completely black and blue and stayed that way for days, which was why I wasn't allowed to see him. My body had produced precious little amniotic fluid, and my frequent falls while pregnant, the hours of manipulation to turn Norman during labor, and the tortuous delivery, Norman had been bruised many times.

After a few more days, Ray was allowed to enter the hospital without wearing scrubs. We were going home. I promised another new mother I had become friends with, Virginia, I would continue to help nurse her daughter, since she was going home also. And I received good news as we left the hospital: the cost of care for Norman and myself was free, courtesy of the US government.

Before we left, the doctor wanted to speak with us. He smiled and remarked how good Norman and I looked. Then his face grew sober. "I do have some unpleasant news for you," he said. "I am sorry to tell you Norman will be your only child. It was a miracle you became pregnant, with your anatomy, but the delivery has destroyed your ability to conceive again."

Ray was stunned and speechless.

I quickly replied, "I am sorry to hear this, too, but I want to tell you that Ray and I are very grateful for everything you and all the nurses, especially Gladys, did for my family. We will be indebted to everyone at the hospital for the rest of our lives. Thank you from the bottom of my heart."

We said goodbye. Our family of three walked out of the hospital to our "home" in the Tule Lake barracks.

Chapter 17

Internment Camp Life as New Parents

Ray carried Norman as we walked carefully to our barracks. Norman started to fuss, so I told Ray he must want to nurse. I was new at nursing on my own and didn't have Mom there to ask her questions, but I decided it was best to assume he was hungry. To me, Norman was still a small baby and needed to eat often. I was going to make sure he got all the milk I could get in him, even though I was pretty sure I was supposed to get him on a schedule. I was expected to bring him back to the hospital the next morning so they could weigh him to make sure he gained more weight, even though it would probably just be an ounce.

I unbuttoned my dress, removed one breast for feeding, and asked Ray to hand Norman to me. But before he did that, he said, "Wow—look at you . . ."

"Oh yeah, the nurse worked hard to make me a big milk producer," I joked.

Ray couldn't believe his eyes. I laughed and told him they belonged to Norman now. He laughed too, and said, "Well, they belonged to me first."

We laughed as Norman fussed. He latched right on to me and began to suckle. After a while, I made him take a break and get out a good burp. Then on to the other side; he suckled for a while, then fell fast asleep. I carefully pulled him off and patted his back to get a good burp again.

I wrapped him up tightly and handed him to Ray. "You hold him now and walk with him," I said.

I redressed and told Ray I needed to help Virginia with her baby; I'd told her I would come to feed her baby after Norman was done, because her daughter was a big girl and Virginia didn't have enough milk for her. "I'll be back as soon as she is done," I said.

"What should I do if Norman cries?" Ray asked.

"Just hold him and pat his back; he will be fine."

He decided to join me on the four-minute walk to Virginia's home. He would wait outside and walk with Norman. Once we arrived, Virginia was delighted to see me and woke up her little baby for my breast milk. I remembered what Gladys had said—that it was important to take my breasts down completely each feeding. Nursing Virginia's baby and Norman definitely drained me well. I told Virginia I would be back in the morning, but not at night. She was grateful and hugged me.

We returned to our room. Norman was sound asleep, so Ray put the baby on his giant twin bed. He looked funny on it, but as a new resident of Tule Lake Camp, he'd received the same bed and mattress as everyone else at camp. I'd wrapped him up nice, tight, and secure as they'd showed me at the hospital. We both sat down on our bed, looking over at our baby.

Suddenly, I felt myself tearing up. I tried to stop, but the more I tried, the worse it got. I started sobbing uncontrollably.

Ray hugged me. "What's wrong?"

"Look how perfect he is; I just can't believe it." I could barely speak. "We are okay now, and we are a family."

I sniffed, and then it got even worse. I never cried like this—I was the easygoing one in my family—but suddenly, all I could do was take deep breaths. Nothing seemed to help. Finally, I blurted out through sobs, "I'm not a good wife now. I can't give you any more children. We talked about a big family, and I can't provide you with any more. I saw your face when the doctor told you. You were devastated, and so was I. It is all hitting me now. I will never even have a daughter."

Ray tried to speak. "Janet, I didn't marry you just to have babies. I married you because I want to spend the rest of my life with you."

I looked into his face and wanted to believe him, but I was inconsolable. "You say that now, but you will change your mind someday; I am sure. Mom was worried you would leave me someday—she thought you'd think I was inadequate because of my poor upbring-ing. She would be shocked to hear I couldn't bear any more children. I am already inadequate as your wife."

Ray realized I wasn't listening, so he just held me tightly. There was nothing more he could do.

My outburst lasted for a while, until I finally calmed down and could talk without crying again.

"Did you forget already about all our conversations on the train trip to Tule Lake?" Ray asked, once he felt it was safe to talk with me again. "You thought it was amusing that I fell in love with you the moment I met you. Nothing has changed. You are still the same Janet, and I am still the same Ray. I told you I love you more every day, though I didn't think I could. But it's true, and it always will be. I married you to be your husband forever. How can you even think I would ever leave you? We have a beautiful baby boy, and together we will raise him to become a fine man someday. What more could we ask?"

I looked into his eyes, and I knew he meant every word. But I thought I no longer deserved him. The problem was me. "I never would have married you if I knew I could only give you one son," I said. "I am so sorry. You know the royalty would cast aside the women who couldn't reproduce."

Ray stopped me. "Janet, you aren't making any sense. I would have married you even if I knew we couldn't have any children. No one is ever guaranteed they will have children. And we have a son—look at him!—I think he looks like you. And to think you were a little overwhelmed about being a mother so soon. I am the happiest man in the whole wide world."

I slumped in his arms and didn't say any more. Then I shut my eyes. I'm sure Ray was wondering how he could perk me up.

"You know what, my love? This doesn't mean we can't keep prac-ticing and hoping for another baby. I wouldn't be surprised if the doctor is wrong; you could heal in time and turn up pregnant again," he said, his voice gaining optimism. "It just doesn't matter. Some women won't let their men come around for a couple of weeks every month because they don't want to be pregnant, and they argue about it. We have no restrictions. We can make love anytime we want. As soon as you feel up to it, you let me know. There is no hurry. You are my life and my love always, and don't ever doubt me."

It was hard to explain to Ray how hard this was. I always did what was expected of me and never let anyone down. When I got married, I was expected to be a good wife. It was my duty to oblige my husband; it was also my duty to have his children, however many came, and to be a wonderful mother. Men wanted their wives to bear their children, the fruits of their loin, and I wanted to have his children, who would bring us much joy and fulfillment, like my siblings and I did for Pop and Mom. How was it possible I could have only one? I hadn't expected to have eight, but I saw myself with at least four or five. Eight would have been fine, too.

Ray leaned in to kiss me, and we fell back on our bed. He leaned against the back wall and pulled me between his legs, my back lying on his chest. He put both his hands around me. "All I ever want or need in this life is you. I don't know how I ever got so lucky to find you. We can never be separated. We are one together and will be forever."

We were both comfortable and tired, so we nodded off together for a short nap. Ray helped me to relax and never let go of me.

I knew I must put this sorrow out of my mind. I couldn't undo the damage I'd suffered while delivering Norman, so I must accept I would not have more children and just live my life.

Then I remembered one more thing Gladys told me: to watch out for crazy hormones for a while. She said hormones could make me emotional and subject to big mood swings. I'd dismissed her comment, as I had never been overly emotional about anything, but my new irrationality now made sense. Yes, I was sad about the news of my health. But the hormones were surely why I'd lost control over myself. How lucky I was to have a husband who didn't care that I was now a barren woman.

We walked to the mess hall for dinner. Ray and I took turns holding Norman while we ate. I needed to keep eating and drinking. As badly as I felt about myself, I was proud of my mighty milk production. It was a relief to at least be good at that. I would work hard to maintain my ability to produce milk for two babies; I would keep nursing Virginia's little girl, and maybe another friend's baby, too, but Norman would soon need all of my milk for himself. I made sure my breasts were drained out at each feeding no matter how much Norman drank, which gave me something to think about and plan. But as I held Virginia's sweet daughter to nurse her, it hurt to think I would never have my own daughter.

It was weird to think that, a year ago, I was doing my daily work as block manager. What a difference a year made. I was married to a man who adored me, which had made me think we would conceive many babies together, after conceiving one in such a short time.

Enjoy every moment with this baby, I thought. I now knew I would never have any more babies, but I needed to think about all I was thankful for.

After dinner, I tried to sneak in a nap while Norman slept. Soon, he stirred, so my nap was brief. I changed his diaper and immediately put him up to my breast. I smiled and thought of Gladys. The doctor said he could go three to four hours between feedings, but since I had plenty of milk, if Norman fussed a little after only an hour had elapsed from the last feeding, I fed him. And if he just wanted to hold on after he ate, that was okay, too—sorry, Gladys. That left me without much sleep, but there was nothing else for me to do but take care of Norman. The doctor wanted him to gain weight, so that was my job—to supply all his nutrition. It made sense now, how nursing bonded a mother and baby. It was wonderful, indescribable, and worth the ordeal in the hospital.

I began to keep my emotions in check. Ray and I hoped to get four or five hours of sleep before Norman awakened.

"You know, I have been thinking about everything the doctor said," he said one night. "I think it turned out for the best. You've told me how hard your mom worked over the years taking care of all her children. She cooked and cleaned all day, then gave baths and put the kids to bed, and then sat up making something they needed. And then she would be up early the next day, making lunches, getting breakfast, getting some off to school, and caring for the others at home. Taking care of her kids was hard work—exhausting work. I know you wanted to be just like her. But I think we have it perfect now. We have Norman, and you will do all those things, but it will be easy with just one. Your evenings will be free to spend with me. And we will spend a lot of time with your family and enjoy their children, who will play with Norman. And we will be able to travel and see many places and will have so much time to be together—that's the best part. We will have the happiest life together. I think I am the luckiest man in the world."

I was afraid I would cry again. I managed to thank him and tell him no, I was the lucky one. He was sincere; how could I ever think his love for me would ever change?

The three of us became our own little cocoon. Ray and I didn't have jobs in Tule Lake Camp, so we spent much of our days with baby Norman. I encouraged Ray to get together with his friends. Sometimes we walked around the barracks, just like the old days, only now we carried our baby along with us.

The nurse had told me to wait at least six weeks before resuming marital relations, but to be safe, I waited eight weeks. When I told Ray we could make love again, he was thrilled.

"Can we start right now?" he asked.

I laughed. "After Norman is asleep tonight," I said. That night, we went back to being a normal married couple again.

Slowly, I let go of my sorrow over my loss of fertility. I was going to savor every precious minute with my baby, all I would ever have of motherhood. I didn't bring it up with Ray anymore. He thought the issue was behind us; he loved his wife and son more than anything and couldn't have been happier with his family.

Luckily, I didn't have to endure another Arkansas summer. The Northern California summer was warm but nothing compared to the searing heat of the summer of 1943 in Arkansas. We still had no air conditioning, but at least it cooled off at night. With my new routine of nursing and hand-washing diapers in addition to our dirty clothes, I was grateful for the milder climate.

Norman was a dream baby. He only fussed when he was hungry or needed to be changed and started sleeping through the night quickly. All I did was look at him, and he smiled and cooed. I held him all I could, maybe because I knew he would be my one and only. Ray often held Norman in his arms as we walked. I teased Ray that he might break Norman by holding him so tightly; he said he just didn't want to drop him. To help Norman get to sleep, I walked with him around our little room, humming a song. His darling eyes gazed into mine until his eyelids grew heavy with sleep.

I hadn't told Mom and Pop that I would just have one child. They probably still worried about the news of the traumatic delivery. But now Norman and I were feeling and looking healthy; Norman was thriving. I didn't even have to take him back for weight checks. It was time to let my parents know about my situation. They needed to be told—Mom would otherwise wonder why I didn't get pregnant again and whether something was wrong.

I wrote a long letter detailing the whole story. I also told them about how Ray had helped me cope with this loss and how he loved me no matter what. Still, I'm sure Mom was sad for me; raising children was her whole life, and she knew I'd wanted to follow in her footsteps. I finished by telling them how much I missed and loved them all.

The summer of 1944 had started with the Allies invading Normandy, and all the news seemed to indicate they were crushing the soldiers of the Third Reich on their march toward Germany.

Meanwhile, in Washington, DC, a noteworthy thing happened in July of 1944: Public Law 405 was passed, allowing an American citizen to renounce his or her citizenship during wartimes. The law specifically targeted the no-nos at Tule Lake.

Chapter 18

Fourth Internment Camp: Santa Fe

On September 12, I woke up around seven to find Ray already dressed. He told me to go to the restroom but to be sure to come right back to our room. He scurried out the door, and I did as he asked and then lay back down. When he returned with his hands full of food, he told me, "We are having breakfast in bed together to celebrate our first anniversary."

He'd secured permission to pick up breakfast from the mess hall. In his arms were two cups of tea, two hard-boiled eggs, and two biscuits. It was just like Ray; I thanked him for his thoughtfulness and told him what a wonderful year it had been, even if he was a little annoying at times. He agreed, and we both laughed. I pulled out a handmade card I'd prepared. I had tried to be clever and write a poem, but it just didn't seem to work. I wrote to him of falling in love over that year. I knew how lucky I was to have a husband who loved me and was willing to wait for me so long; we were blessed to have our son, who filled our hearts with more love than we could have imagined. I thanked Ray for his tender and sweet love. His eyes were watering as he put the card down and told me he would keep it to reread often, and he promised great things for future anniversaries. I told him I didn't need things. I was content with just us.

We shared some intimate moments together before Norman woke up. We both remembered our anniversary in a special way, and we were ready and excited for year two to begin. For the time being, we had no choice but to remain a married couple with a baby living in an internment camp.

Mom sent news of Christine's wedding and said they would soon be joining Ray and me in Tule Lake. I was sorry to have missed the wedding, but I knew getting married in camp meant a limited celebration anyway. I was excited for their arrival.

Meanwhile, in Tule Lake Camp, word traveled that I was good at translating. Once again, as in Stockton and Rohwer, I received many requests for translations. Some saw it necessary to test me first: they asked me to translate a short passage, and if I got it correct, then they carried on with me. I thought this quite odd, but I smiled and helped them out. Tule Lake Camp was just different; many people were mistrustful. As before, I wasn't being paid for my translation help.

We'd been in captivity for about two and a half years. It seemed like a lifetime. It was hard to remember life before camp and having the freedom to do as I pleased. I understood how hard it was on everyone, so I happily helped others, including by translating letters for free. But my baby added a complication; I couldn't plan on meeting someone in camp, so often people dropped off letters at my home, and I would translate them, either from Japanese to English or vice versa. The people would return, retrieve their translations, and maybe dictate letters for me to write back. Some letters were newsy, others romantic, but all full of love for someone far away.

I gave many, many hours to translations after Norman was asleep. Some recipients were grateful; others seemed to expect my service, hardly acknowledging my work. Many were simply mad at the world, and rightly so. The principle of *gaman* wore thin after so many months of confinement, with no end to the war in sight. We were all in the same predicament. I never turned anyone away. If I could help, it was my duty to give of myself any way I could.

I also mended clothing using the portable sewing machine I owned. One person would tell another about my skill, and before long, I was fixing a tear here or a seam there for several people. I told them I would get to their mending as soon as I could, and once again, I was never paid.

On December 17, 1944, as war raged on in Europe and Asia, huge news arrived for us: the US Western Defense Command had rescinded the order excluding Japanese Americans from the West Coast military zone. All relocation camps would be closed in six months to a year.

It was a time to celebrate, right? That's what the US government thought. They expected jubilation from us interned Japanese, but they didn't get that reaction. Most of us were terrified at the prospect of leaving the camps without money, places to live, or even job prospects. Further, we were understandably concerned about how the world at large would accept our return to society. After all, America was still at war with Japan. Would we be outcasts and still considered the enemy in America, just because of our ancestry? We read plenty of articles quoting state and local officials who wanted no part of "the Japs' resettlement in California." Many other officials continued to say that all the *Issei* should be deported immediately.

However, the relocation-project director ended the conjecture:

> The closure of the relocation camps . . . imperiled the security of thousands of residents who, at the price of being branded disloyal, believed they had attained war-duration refuge. For all of them, forced resettlement . . . loomed if not as certainties at least as disturbingly high probabilities.

Consequently, everyone in the camps would be classified as either free to settle anywhere in the United States or needing to continue to be restricted due to renunciation of citizenship.

Thousands of Tule Lake Camp residents signed a renunciation of their citizenship so they would be restricted and could stay in the camp till the end of the war. They assumed wrongly they would subsequently be allowed to resettle in America. However, once they renounced their citizenship, they really became American aliens.

This led to mass confusion, paranoia, and misinformation. It seemed the new order was directed at Tule Lake, since my family in Arkansas didn't even hear about this announcement. My family assumed they would be staying at Camp Rohwer until the war was over. Why, suddenly, was the government contemplating releasing the captive Japanese back into society? Was it to save funds? Was the government finally convinced the Japanese posed no security threat? Were they concerned at all about our future, with no jobs or homes to return to once released?

It was ironic that we'd waited patiently for freedom for many weeks, months, years, sometimes saying we didn't think we could take the camps much longer, and then panicked at the prospect of gaining that freedom.

When Ray mentioned he'd joined a men's club at camp, I didn't think much about it. But looking back, I understand now what I didn't then. Ray had lived his first twenty years in Japan; if Japanese were anything, they were loyal to their homeland. Ray never discussed the war with me—he knew I was American and my family wanted the United States to win the war—but I knew Ray was hoping for a Japanese victory. Whichever way the war went wasn't an issue between us. Japan had never lost a war; neither had the United States. One was now going to lose—or was it possible there would be a negotiated peace with no victor?

When I think of the hurt and anger developed over the thirty long months of our unjust imprisonment in America, I easily understand how many who had grown up in Japan's intensely patriotic culture were becoming increasingly agitated. In the fall of 1944, the members of Ray's men's club convinced him to openly pledge his allegiance to his homeland, Japan, thereby showing his contempt for his oppressor, America. Returning to Japan for his estate was no longer his priority; returning as a patriot who loved his homeland was what mattered to him now. Ray, in his state of anger, defiance, and allegiance to his club, now considered a despicable gang, signed a renunciation of his US citizenship.

Ray was such a gentle soul. We never fought; he treated me with such love and kindness and the utmost respect. I sometimes heard other people arguing bitterly in our barracks, and I was grateful we did not have those problems. Ray never displayed a temper with me, and he never said anything to me against the United States.

However, he had another side I didn't see at first, filled with rage for America and an all-encompassing pride for his heritage and country. I don't think his radicalization ever became violent; it was pushback against the centurions keeping him confined, a way to scream back at his captors. *How dare you, America? Long live the emperor!* It was the opposite of *gaman*. His patience was gone.

Maybe Ray's enmity had started when the US government made all the men fill out the "loyalty questionnaire," which had been highly offensive. Maybe Ray's upbringing had made him vulnerable, without the firm foundation of a strong family bond. Maybe he also lacked a strong faith, an anchor, since he hadn't attended Sunday school and services to learn about following the Buddhist way. Maybe Ray's personality was impressionable, able to be easily persuaded. Perhaps his stubbornness—which I knew firsthand—made him a good candidate for the cause; he'd never give up on his country. Or maybe, and quite possibly, he was inspired by a bunch of kindred-spirited men who lived immersed in the prideful Japanese culture and were fed up with America and our ridiculous jailing.

As for these men, perhaps their frustrations fed off each other's. Maybe they sensed the war was turning in America's favor, at least in Europe, where the Allies were now closing in on Germany. The men in the gangs at Tule Lake began to openly express disdain for America and love for the Land of the Rising Sun. The government took note, and I didn't, even though I was married to one. These men truly became enemies of the state. They just couldn't take it anymore. But what real harm or imminent danger could they cause to national security? They were angry. They ranted and raved. But their actions were not violent.

Regardless, the WRA decided these men needed to be removed from Tule Lake and from its jurisprudence. These 350 to 400 men were transferred to the authority of the Immigration and Naturalization Service, to be deported to Japan, at the earliest possible time. They had renounced their US citizenship. They were not welcome.

Just before Christmas, Ray came home one evening and told me in a calm voice that he was going to another internment camp.

"What are you talking about?" I asked, shocked.

He said Norman and I would be staying at Tule Lake, but the members of his club were all being sent to Santa Fe, New Mexico. He needed to pack, which only took a few minutes; almost everything was already in his bag. This man who adored his wife and son was going to leave us all alone. He simply said it wasn't his decision; everyone in his club was being transferred to another camp because of their un-American activities at Tule Lake.

I didn't know what to think. I don't think I understood the gravity of the moment. So much had happened in the last few years, I thought I could handle anything, so I took this news as just the next step in our continued imprisonment. As much as Ray loved his family, his new association and their "Organization to Serve Our

Mother Country" meant more to him at that moment. He didn't know how long he would be gone. I wasn't angry; I didn't know what to feel. I really wasn't sure why he was leaving, other than, as he said, it was not his choice.

I just knew I was now going to live at the heavily guarded Tule Lake Camp, clearly the most severe of all the internment camps, alone with my baby and no family.

About a year and half prior, Ray had been committed to convincing me and my family I should marry him. I knew he still loved me and his infant son. However, he had become radicalized for this cause, and nothing else seemed to matter. I accepted my fate and whatever the United States did to me as a result of the war with Japan; he did not. It was all he could think or talk about. Still, as surprised as I was that Ray was leaving Tule Lake, I was even more surprised he didn't appear tormented about leaving me. When we left Arkansas for Tule Lake, Ray couldn't imagine a day without me; he never would have departed for California and left me behind. I knew how much he loved me, but now, he wasn't thinking straight. I wasn't number one anymore. Suddenly, nothing was more important to him than defending his homeland. I didn't fully grasp this because he didn't give me any details; I had to just accept he was leaving and do my best to carry on. We could write letters. Because the government was taking him from his family, there would be no postage charges for our letters. Eventually I learned that, as soon as the war was over, these men would be placed on the first ship to Japan, no matter who had won. Their offensive attitudes sealed their fate.

A policeman came to our door to escort Ray to the gate and the transportation waiting for him and his comrades. We embraced for a long time before he left. He told me he loved me—and then he left for his new number-one loyalty, standing up for his country. There was no crying or carrying on. He picked up his bag and walked with the policeman toward the next chapter in his life, while I watched him walk away from me and his baby boy. I desperately tried to conceal my fright. My heart pounded in my chest as I held Norman in my arms, walked back into our room, and pondered our future, filled with questions but no answers.

In a few days, my fortune improved. Christine and her new husband, Mitsuru, arrived. How thrilling to see them at the door! It was great to see my sister and have family with me. The authorities also managed to assign their home close to mine. Christine couldn't wait to pick up her new nephew.

"How beautiful! He looks like an angel!" she exclaimed.

We chatted nonstop. Christine was surprised Ray was gone. She didn't ask a lot of questions because she could tell I didn't know many of the details. I told her I'd already written a long letter to Mom and Pop and told them Ray was now in his fourth internment camp.

Meanwhile, Mitsuru noticed I was just using an army bed for baby Norman. He told me he wasn't the most talented carpenter, but he thought he could put together a simple crib. We all knew Norman would be crawling soon, and he needed to sleep in a crib to be safe. I was quite excited and touched by Mitsuru's kindness. My sister had married a fine man. The crib was completed in less than two weeks and was perfect in its simplicity. I was so grateful; I knew Norman would be rolling over soon, and now I wouldn't have to worry about him falling off the bed.

I managed the daily activities of my life as best I could without my partner to help out. For each meal, I tried to make sure Norman was napping. I left him wrapped up cozily in his bed, dashed out to the mess hall to eat, and dashed back as quickly as I could. I feared he would awaken and cry and I wouldn't be there to pick him up. I became skilled at managing his feedings and mine; I continued nursing him to provide all his nutrition. I went through diapers quickly, so I was doing more hand laundry than ever. Scrubbing dirty diapers on a washboard was hard work.

After several months of nursing both Norman and Virginia's daughter, Virginia said her own nursing was now sufficient for her daughter along with supplemental rice cereal. This was good news, although I'd been happy to help. I had already cut back to two feedings for Virginia's daughter a day. My body quickly adjusted, but since Norman was growing quickly, I continued producing as he consumed more than ever.

As the weeks went on, I heard more about these men who were thought to pose the gravest threat to the United States. The Santa Fe camp was men's only, and they were being called the Tuleans. They were angry at the United States and, at times, at each other as their long confinement dragged on. Many shaved their heads and wore headbands. They chanted, bugled, and goose-stepped. They rejected anything American; they only wanted to live as Japanese. The authorities in Santa Fe seemed to understand and tried to accommodate them as much as possible, setting up Japanese-style baths with the hand-washing station followed by the rinse in clean water, serving Japanese cuisine as much as possible, and tolerating their anti-American behavior, to a point. They even allowed the men to celebrate the birthday of Emperor Hirohito.

I received letters at least every other day from Ray. He didn't dare write anything about the war. He mainly talked about what he did during the day, what he ate, and how much he missed me. I started keeping a daily diary of Norman's progress, and I copied my diary into letters for Ray. I also wrote him often. I missed him, too, but I was managing quite fine. Once again, I was staying busy with translations, washing, sewing, and most of all, caring for my beloved son.

As was the case in all three camps, there was no shortage of gossips. Many people asked me about Ray. Where was my husband? What had he done to get himself sent away? Why had he left me with a new baby? I was quite embarrassed, but being embarrassed was nothing new; I'd endured that feeling on many occasions. I was strong. I could carry on, and other people were not going to rattle me.

Deep in my soul, though, I was worried about what would happen next. My life was in limbo; my husband was in trouble with the US authorities. When would I see him again? My family, except for Christine, was thousands of miles away in their own confinement. When would I see them again? How much longer would the war carry on? How much longer could everyone in these camps handle putting their lives on hold for months and years? How much longer could we cope with no freedoms? Would it ever be possible for us all to find jobs and reestablish our lives once we were all released?

All I could do was take care of myself and my baby. No one knew of my personal anguish, not even my sister; though she surely knew I was anxious about Ray's forced removal, I was grateful she didn't dwell on it.

In November of 1944, it was time for another presidential election. FDR was running for a fourth term against Dewey. No president before FDR had been elected to three terms, let alone four. I knew FDR approved the Japanese imprisonment, so I rooted for

Dewey. Two thirds of us in camp were Americans by birth, but that just didn't matter; we certainly would not be allowed to vote. FDR won again. I guess people thought it made sense for him to carry on leadership until victory was achieved.

One evening at dinner, a lady was passing around a paper. It contained a long article about the Japanese flying airplanes like bombs directly into ships as suicide missions. They were called kamikaze pilots; I was amazed that Japan would resort to killing its own pilots and destroying its airplanes. The landing gear was built to detach as a pilot took off, so it could be reused for the next mission. The article said this made it impossible for the pilot to change his mind, with no ability to land his aircraft; other planes were sent along to confirm the kamikaze pilot executed his mission. The article said the US military called the kamikaze planes "stupid bombs," which made sense to me too. The United States was developing defensive strategies to keep the kamikaze pilots from reaching the aircraft carriers and battle groups. Years later, I read a letter written by a kamikaze pilot to his family as he departed.

> *It is easy to talk about death in the abstract, as the ancient philosophers discussed. But it is real death I fear, and I don't know if I can overcome the fear. Even for a short life, there are many memories. For someone who had a good life, it is very difficult to part with it. But I reached a point of no return. I must plunge into an enemy vessel. . . . I am pleased to have the honour of having been chosen as a member of a Special Attack Force that is on its way into battle, but I cannot help crying when I think of you, Mum. When I reflect on the hopes you had for my future . . . I feel so bad that I am going to die without doing anything to bring you joy.*

This letter touched my heart; I couldn't believe what Japan was willing to do in desperation.

Christine, Mitsuru, Norman, and I celebrated Christmas of 1944 together. We didn't have much to exchange for gifts, but we did talk about the good old days growing up in Stockton. Christine and I both missed Mom's Christmas feast; we'd had it every year before camp life.

It was my twenty-fifth birthday on January 12, 1945, and no one knew. Christine no doubt forgot. My big family, who had always sung to me while Mom brought out a cake she'd baked at home and a couple of gifts, was in Arkansas. My husband, on top of the world a year prior on my twenty-fourth birthday, was absent. He'd bought me my own portable sewing machine from the Montgomery Ward Catalog so I could make lots of clothes for our baby. He'd wanted to please me. On this birthday, I did have my son, so my present was seeing him crawl for the first time. It was all I needed. It was a wonderful twenty-fifth birthday.

The next day, I received letters from Ray and my family saying they all wished we could be together to celebrate my birthday. All my family members signed the letter from Mom. I missed them all. Ray's letters grew more sentimental as the days turned to weeks; however, I was starting to understand how consumed he was with this passion that had overtaken him.

Norman wasn't feeling well; he was teething. He woke up at night, and I held him and tried to quiet him. There was no medicine of any kind to help him. But I did get a chunk of ice occasionally from the mess hall, wrapped it in a cloth, and rubbed it on his gums. He was also fighting a cold, likely a result of the teething, and had a messy nose, which didn't help. After a week or so, he was better. Luckily, those were the sickest days of his early life.

Ray and the others seemed to be coping well in New Mexico—as much as I could tell from his letters. I heard from the clerk in the office about a riot at his camp, but I was relieved to learn there were only minor injuries and that Ray was not involved.

I managed to stay quite busy caring for Norman and helping others with a constant flow of requests for translations or mending. It was good to stay busy; it helped pass the time. Each day, it seemed Norman was doing something new; he was such a joy in my life.

We heard news at the end of January that the concentration camp Auschwitz had been liberated. In time, the world would learn that this camp had gas chambers to exterminate the Jewish people. While we American Japanese were hated after Pearl Harbor and were taken from our homes and livelihoods, I never heard of abuse or torture by the government. However, we did hear of a couple of people shot to death in other internment camps for trying to escape, so we were afraid of the soldiers in the towers.

In late March, the camp released a newsletter with news that seemed quite significant: Hitler had ordered all industries, military installations, machine shops, transportation facilities, and communications facilities in Germany to be destroyed. He would not allow the Allies to take over any of these. Many in camp were suspicious about the reports, but I could feel the tide turning. Hitler was about to be defeated.

Chapter 19
Spring 1945: Victory in Europe

The news shocked us all: On April 12, 1945, President Franklin D. Roosevelt died of natural causes. Vice President Harry S. Truman was immediately sworn in as the thirty-third president of the United States.

Who was Harry Truman? I didn't know anything about him, but we all talked about our new president at dinner. He was now in charge of everything pertaining to the war, including all Japanese in the camps. We all wondered if he would disdain Japanese Americans. Would he realize what a mistake his predecessor had made in considering us a threat to the country?

Most at camp celebrated the news of the downfall of Hitler and Mussolini. Those two tyrants would never bring harm to this world again. The UK lost 25 percent of its national wealth defeating the Nazis. Soon the world learned of Hitler's concentration camps and gas chambers which took the lives of millions of innocents. Because we Japanese that were put in the US camps weren't tortured or abused in any way that I ever saw, I thought over the years that my story wasn't all that historically important.

Sadly though, the Allies were also aligned with a tyrant not all that different from Hitler: Stalin. I imagine FDR and Churchill understood the evil that was Stalin, but needed the Soviet Union to provide the eastern front of the war. The Soviet Union lost over thirty million people during the war unrelated to combat deaths, from starvation, disease, mass shootings, and labor camps. Stalin wanted to cleanse his country of any remnants of the previous Russian dynasties. I was sick to my stomach when I learned that Stalin told his soldiers to consider the German women to be a prize of victory. As the German battalions approached, thousands of women committed suicide to avoid being raped. Nearly two million women were raped by the Soviet soldiers with the blessings of their commanders. We Japanese faced emotional trauma, but we were kept safe from physical harm.

None of us could have imagined our captivity would carry on for three years—and counting. We'd expected it to be more like three months. Two of the three members of the Axis were now defeated; Japan stood alone against the Allies. Was it just a matter of time before Japan was finished off?

I still wrote my family and Ray often. Some letters were short; it was hard to find new things to write as life varied little from day to day, except for the new things Norman was doing. Communication was how I felt close to my family. I told Ray how much I looked forward to and enjoyed reading his letters, even if he didn't have much to write about either. It was like getting a hug when I opened them.

A letter from Mom arrived with news from Arkansas. Will, now a private in the US Army, had come back and visited the family. He was looking well and said the training wasn't nearly as intense as he'd feared. The army promised he was not drafted for combat duty: they were preparing for the end of the war with Japan, and they needed as many soldiers who spoke Japanese as possible to help with rebuilding the country. Maybe all along, the intention of the loyalty questionnaire had been to find men for the Japanese rebuilding. If so, what a shame the questionnaire created so much heartache and apprehension for the interned Japanese men. Will, Mom, and Pop were not at all happy about the government's plans to force Will to go to Japan as part of the occupation whenever the war ended. Mom knew Will would be hated as an American but at least protected as a soldier. She also sent news of Loretta: she was becoming friendly with a *Nisei* man from Hawaii. Mom said she would tell me more as the courtship continued. The letter made me homesick for my family. How I wished I could have seen Will myself.

In the summer of 1945, I was sitting in the mess hall holding Norman when another presidential proclamation affecting the Japanese Americans was announced; this time it came from President Truman. If you were an enemy alien (and anyone who had renounced citizenship would be considered an enemy alien) and you were considered dangerous to public safety, you could be subject to deportation.

After we heard about this order, I talked with acquaintances at breakfast. Tule Lake was the epicenter for placement of the disloyals, so it was surely also the place where people would be selected for deportation. I also knew this meant my husband would be the first to go, because he had already been sent off to Santa Fe; however, I wasn't alarmed, since this had been Ray's plan all along. Everyone wondered whether the no-nos would be deported now. We all knew that almost everyone who had renounced US citizenship didn't really want to leave America; they'd just been afraid of leaving camp before the war ended. I was a little embarrassed that my husband was still considered a troublemaker. I wasn't aware of any trouble he'd caused, but he'd clearly joined the wrong crowd.

Still, the question really frustrated me: How was it possible that, after we'd spent three years following US government orders and causing no problems, they were now prepared to start deporting us? The new uncertainty bred fear and hysteria in many of us. Many who had renounced citizenship began going to the authorities and begging to retract their renunciation. Now, we who had been sent to the camps and followed the rules were terrified of being released from the camps with no way of earning income and no homes to return to.

Coping with these fears after thirty-six months of confinement was especially cruel. Everyone seemed to be anxious, and each of our stories was unique. There wasn't much small talk at meals and gatherings any longer—only serious discussions about our common fate. The faces and eyes said it all; smiles were rare and greetings short, and many people made no eye contact at all. Some looked worried, others frightened, others angry, and still others sad. We felt almost the same way we had on the day we'd stepped into camp life, only now it was worse. We'd endured excruciating stress and anxiety throughout our long incarceration—and uncertainty over our future still remained in all our lives.

Chapter 20
Summer 1945: Victory over Japan

One of Mom's letters arrived with news of graduation day at Camp Rohwer. The teachers decided it was time to recognize the students who had completed a curriculum sufficient for graduation since starting high school classes in camp in November of 1942. Mom thought it symbolic and gratifying to have a Camp Commencement Day, complete with diplomas. Will was gone with the army, but Mom happily accepted his diploma, as he'd easily finished high school in camp; he'd been only a month shy of graduating from Stockton High School when we were interred. Now he could say he'd graduated from Camp Rohwer, for what it was worth. So could Loretta and Fran, who graduated that day too. Tom and Ed were in grade school. I wished I could help my little brothers with their homework.

I'd missed seeing changes in my young brothers as they grew up in the year since Ray and I had left for Tule Lake. I loved hearing about everything in Mom's letters, but at times, it made me homesick. However, this made it even more enjoyable to have Christine at Tule Lake. We talked about the different pieces of news we each heard from Mom. Pop's garden was looking better than ever; he'd learned just what to grow in Arkansas's humid climate and soil and was excited to take his freshly grown produce to the kitchen. Mom said she and Pop couldn't wait for news of every new thing Norman was doing. Likewise, she was missing seeing her first grandchild, now almost a year old, grow up. But she also said how happy she was that he was healthy and growing after his hard start.

We were starting to get daily updates at camp. In July of 1945, the WRA official told us the Imperial Japanese Navy was decimated; the papers talked about the United States preparing for a ground invasion of Japan. Once Japan's navy and air force had been soundly defeated, Japan still had an army of over two million men and an untrained civilian militia of twenty-eight million men. I would learn later that the Allies planned Operation Downfall to invade Japan on the ground. The United States estimated four to eight hundred thousand Americans would have perished in a ground invasion, along with untold millions of Japanese. Plans were in place if needed. At the same time, in July of 1945, President Truman was notified there had been a successful test of an atomic bomb in New Mexico.

In the middle of this, Norman's first birthday arrived on July 24. We celebrated with Christine and Mitsuru; his father, grandparents, and other aunts and uncles were missing from the celebration. He was walking now, almost running, and curious about everything. I watched him every minute as he investigated anything and everything. One day, while I was standing and chatting with some ladies, he picked Christine's beautiful flowers and handed them to me. *Oops—thank you, my darling.* I started bringing him to the mess hall for some meals and feeding him rice. It seemed time to wean Norman from nursing. I started him on milk in a bottle from the mess hall during the day and nursed him only at bedtime, which relaxed him and usually sent him right off to sleep. I loved this special time together; it was such a bond between us as mother and son, and it was hard for me to let it go. I knew that when I stopped nursing completely, I would never have that joy in my life again.

We sang "Happy Birthday" to Norman, and he listened intently to us. I bought him some animal crackers from the canteen, and I could tell he enjoyed eating them; it was his first real treat. That was it for his first birthday.

I looked down at him, at how big he was now, and thought about how grateful I was. We'd both nearly died in childbirth. Norman was such a dream child in that first year; he rarely cried, always smiled at me and melted my heart, even understood the word *no*, and was already almost fully toilet trained. What more could I have asked for? I wrote this to Ray; I'm sure it was difficult for him to be away from us.

Since I'd told myself to stop nursing, I skipped a night, then another night, and soon I began drying up. Before many more days had passed, I was done nursing. Remembering my time in the hospital with Gladys made me smile—I would never forget those days.

Nursing had been the one part of having a baby that worked well for me. It was such a beautiful part of being a woman, doing what was natural and good for my son and feeling the bond of motherhood. I was grateful for those memories and a little sad it was now over.

On August 7, a shocking statement was read to us in the mess hall. President Truman had announced the successful drop of the world's first atomic bomb on Hiroshima, Japan. My heart sank—I knew Ray's hometown was near there. I thought of so many innocents who surely perished from this new catastrophic bomb. Ray was safe in Santa Fe, but was his family mansion destroyed? I'd heard a lot about Ray's home; could it all be gone now?

We all wondered whether Japan would surrender after the massive destruction and aftermath of the atomic bomb blast, but we heard Japan wasn't giving up. Once a Japanese physicist confirmed it was a nuclear attack, the Japanese war council published four conditions for surrender:

1. The Imperial Institution and the authority of the emperor would be preserved
2. Imperial General Headquarters would disarm and demobilize
3. No occupation of Japanese homelands, Korea, or China by the United States
4. War criminals would be delegated to Japanese government

I knew enough from what Pop had told me through the years that Japan never lost a war; they would fight to the death. These terms were not acceptance of defeat in any way. President Truman was furious. "If they do not now accept our terms, they may expect a rain of ruin from the air, the like of which has never been seen on this earth. Behind this air attack will follow sea and land forces in such numbers and power as they have not seen and with the fighting skill of which they are already well aware."

Then several days later, we received the news of a second atomic bomb hit, now on Nagasaki. Emperor Hirohito feared Japan's very existence could be threatened; he finally announced a full surrender in a public address to his people. This was the first time the Japanese people had ever heard their emperor speak. September 2 was the date set for the Japanese Instrument of Surrender to be signed on board the USS *Missouri* in Tokyo Bay. China, Korea, Hong Kong, Vietnam, and the Philippines were all liberated. To this day, the only public holiday celebrated in both North Korea and South Korea is August 15, Victory over Japan Day. World War II was over.

At Tule Lake, the reaction to victory over Japan seemed quite guarded; I saw smiles around camp, but not exhilaration. Everyone was relieved the war was over, the camps would be closing, and we would be freed, but I still saw the conflicted emotions in the eyes of so many. After these long years, the Japanese had become dependent on the government for their room and board and management of their lives. For us, freedom meant challenges for basic survival in a world where we feared we would still be outcasts. Could we even find jobs or places to live in a community with non-Japanese people? Would the government care at all about our future? We internees were consumed with a myriad of emotions. We desperately wanted free and normal order back in our lives, but we were afraid to be sent out into the world to fend for ourselves.

I was proud of my people through our long captivity. For some, the psychological burden was too much to be sure. I read years later about superstitions and hallucinations being prevalent at Tule Lake. I also read about the Japanese becoming highly ritualistic, loosing grasp of reality. No doubt these detailed accounts of events at Tule Lake occurred as the articles describe. But for me, I never witnessed any of these things. I would certainly consider these situations to be the exception and not the norm, based on my many months at Tule Lake.

A few days later, our Tule Lake paper carried an article with the details of the Japanese surrender as it applied to all men at the Santa Fe camp. They were already on their journey to Japan; when they'd been transferred into the control of the Immigration and Naturalization Service, their deportation began. They were no longer US citizens. They belonged to the defeated Land of the Rising Sun.

My heart sank when I read this. I had hoped Ray would be returned to Tule Lake before leaving for Japan. Surely, many of the men had families, as Ray did, waiting for them in Tule Lake. However I didn't have any friends related to men at Santa Fe. I couldn't talk to my husband, see him, or touch him. The men were gone. The thought of Ray not even being in America anymore made me miss him more than ever.

I knew Ray would write as soon as possible, so as our second wedding anniversary approached, I waited for a letter with news of his arrival in Japan. This anniversary was dramatically different from our first: he'd lived in Santa Fe the last nine months and would be on a ship to Japan on our anniversary; there would be no breakfast in bed or romantic cards. I knew he loved me as always; I wasn't concerned our marriage was over. But I had an uneasy feeling about where we would be for our third anniversary and whether everything would be okay. So much of our future was up in the air.

I was eager for news about my family in Arkansas. What were they planning for their future? Would they be coming back to Stockton? Would Pop be able to go back to work as a foreman for Mr. Zuckerman? If not, was Pop alarmed about finding a job at his age?

I was staying put for now, waiting for news from Ray. My daily life continued the same way after V-J Day as I waited patiently for what was next for Norman and me. Luckily, I didn't feel the overwhelming stress that so many felt contemplating their future: I knew there was nothing I could do about the situation, so I might as well relax and wait for whatever happened next. I trusted Ray; he would take care of everything.

PART 5:
A BIG MOVE—JAPAN

Chapter 21
Victory over Japan: The Aftermath

A letter arrived from Mom. Surely she was excited the war was over, as was I—or was she worried about her family's future? Mom could be a worrier at times. We'd waited for the end of the war for so long. It was like someone had taken the handcuffs off, opened the doors to the world, and set us free, but our freedom meant reestablishing lives in a community again and hoping we weren't hated. Mom's letter told of her apprehension to walk out of Camp Rohwer with no job, no home, and the twenty-five dollars cash per person that was being provided by the US government. She and Pop faced the daunting task of starting their lives over at forty-nine and sixty-one years of age. Nothing in their lives had any permanence or stability. Pop was only promised a laborer job if he returned to Mr. Zuckerman's farm.

Mom told me she and the rest of my family would not return to Stockton. The cost of the journey from southern Arkansas to Stockton and the thought of navigating the trains with their broken English seemed overwhelming to them. And besides, why bother enduring the arduous journey to California with no job prospects? Stockton offered nothing anymore. Everyone they knew in Stockton was gone, and it seemed no one they knew was returning.

Some California officials had even publicly decried allowing the Japanese return to their state. "According to the law of every Western state, no Japanese can marry a white person. And that means no matter how long these people are here, if they are here a hundred years or two hundred years or five hundred years, if that policy is continued they will always be a group set apart with other racial characteristics, and that situation will be a focal point of friction. We cannot melt every single colored person into our population." Anti-Japanese groups formed in California, including the Remember Pearl Harbor

League and Monterey Bay Council on Japanese Relations. Their goal was to "discourage the return of persons of Japanese ancestry to the area."

WRA officials came to camp to offer some assistance with the internees' resettlement, but their financial assistance consisted of twenty-five dollars for a train ticket and a few dollars for food along the way. Mom and Pop also had some money saved from their camp jobs. But they were leaving camp homeless, jobless, almost broke, and extremely anxious about how they would be treated by society as they tiptoed back toward living as free Americans. The WRA officials recommended taking the train to Chicago; jobs were available in the Windy City. Since the prospect of work was priority number one, Mom, Dad, and the rest of the Hayashi family at Camp Rohwer would be boarding the train for Chicago the next day. Pop would find a job somewhere. She promised to write as soon as they arrived.

Mom thought many others would be joining them on the train ride in hopes of finding employment. She was hopeful everything would work out, but she thought it was most important to keep the remaining family together. Only four of Mom's children were with her as the family departed camp—Marian and Fran, now adults, along with Ed and Tom, who were still in school. Her letter was the most somber I'd received from her since I'd left Arkansas. From the start of camp, she'd been grateful to have her family together. Now Christine and I were both married and at Tule Lake, Will was in the US Army headed to Japan, and Loretta was about to marry a Hawaiian man. She obviously was overwrought with apprehension for Norman and me when she composed her letter.

> It is only because I love you so much that I plead with you to stay in America. You are an American. If you go to Japan now, you will be hated. You will still be the enemy. I grew up in Japan. I know the people. Even though you had nothing to do with the war, they will despise you. And you will face the added problem of not knowing the ways of Ray's class. He is wrong to ask you to enter this impossible situation. He should know what to expect. He is only being selfish to ask you to bear this burden. Come and stay with us wherever we settle. There will always be room for you and Norman. Ray can then choose what he wants

to do with his life. He can close his father's inheritance, come back to America, and be your husband if he chooses. Or he can choose to stay in Japan, if that means more to him. You can divorce him and start your life over. You are just twenty-six years old. You have your sisters and brothers, and Pop and I will be there to help you raise Norman. You will never be alone. It is a hard task for me to write this to you. My dearest Janet, you have already endured much in these last years. Through it all, you have given endlessly of yourself to help others and your family. I can't bear to think of your suffering anymore. If you go to Japan now, I fear your life could turn unbearable. Please, I beg you, don't leave. All my love—Mom

My eyes filled with tears, as I fell down on my bed and reread Mom's letter. Norman napped quietly in his homemade crib while I cried. This was supposed to be a time for celebration of victory. Finally, the Japanese Americans were no longer to be feared. What if Mom was right? Was Ray wrong to expect me to join him in Japan? Then again, how bad could it be? After all, he'd inherited land and a mansion. And besides, how could I just walk away from my marriage? I'd known Ray wanted to return to Japan after the war when I married him. But if I did stay and live with my family, would Ray ever return to be my husband? Would Norman and I become a burden on my family? Would I have regrets that I didn't even try to live in Japan?

I wiped my eyes, but I continued to shed fresh tears. I wished Mom were with me so we could talk about this agonizing decision. The limitation of pencil and paper was part of my struggle—I wanted and needed my mom; I missed her every day. Now especially, I felt alone in my thoughts. The time was now to decide what I was going to do with my life, and the life of my one-year-old son. I'd thought getting married was the hardest decision of my life—this one was even bigger. Stay or go? My decision would devastate either my mom and family or my husband.

When Norman woke, I took him quickly to the bathroom, where he used the potty. He was quickly catching on to toilet training. The sign was when he started rubbing on his leg: *Get me to the potty.* It worked. He almost trained himself. One advantage of having time on my hands was I was able to work closely with Norman on everything.

We walked over to find Christine pulling weeds in her garden. I asked her if she'd received a letter from Mom. She had. Before I said any more, she told me she and Mitsuru had decided to stay in America. It was a hard decision for Mitsuru, as he knew his father wasn't well. Maybe in a few years they would travel to Japan. But not now. Mitsuru would take the English name John when they left camp. He'd heard of jobs available farming grape vineyards south of Tule Lake.

Christine asked what I was going to do.

"I don't know," I said. "Mom asked Norman and me to join them wherever they settled. Ray's still en route to Japan; I'm waiting to hear from him."

Within another week, we received more government news: all renouncers would be transported to Japan in two months' time. People looked more panicked now than when we'd first arrived in camp. Many begged to reverse their renunciation. A civil rights attorney, Wayne Collins, took up their cause and appealed to the authorities that these people had renounced because of "true duress," thinking they must renounce to stay in the camp until the war was over. He contended the renouncers were petrified to be turned out into society after the government announced the camps were going to be closed. It was a confusing mess. Amazingly, many newly freed people were not flocking out of the camp exits.

I felt badly for these people who wanted to stay in America, but I was wrapped up in my own thoughts as well. Then I learned something that directly affected me and the decision I was facing: I could only board the ship to Japan if I renounced my US citizenship. The clerk told me Japan wanted it that way. But how could I do that? How could I just sign away my citizenship? If I did this, could I ever return—or see my family again? America was my country and my home; even though America had treated me badly these last three years, I couldn't imagine leaving forever. After thinking for so long the end of the war would bring relief and jubilation, I was deflated and dejected.

The decision was torturous. It was all I thought about. All along, I'd expected deep down I would be going to Japan, but I hadn't known

I'd be forced to renounce my citizenship to get there. I thought through various possibilities: What if I left and renounced? What if everything Mom said was true and I couldn't even come back to America? Was I crazy to risk this? What if I stayed? Would I ever see Ray again? Would it be wrong of me if I didn't follow Ray to Japan? Oh, how I knew he would be crushed if I told him I wasn't coming. Could Ray take care of things in Japan and join me in America? Even if he wanted to return to the States, would he be allowed?

Then I considered something even more important: What was the right thing to do for my son? He would have a big family around if we stayed with my parents. But he wouldn't have his father. How could I not take my son to be with his father?

I think I knew all along what I was going to do: honor my marriage and join my husband. Even though I managed quite fine by myself, I missed Ray terribly. I also knew it was important to bring him his son. I believed I could handle any difficult situation I encountered in Japan; I thought of myself as strong. Ray thought that, too. Many women would have been terrified at the thought of boarding a ship for a fifteen-to-twenty-day journey overseas with a small child and no man to accompany them; I'm sure most of my girlfriends would have found this impossible. *What if you encounter a problem on the ship? What if your husband isn't there when you arrive? What will you do? Where will you go?* I thought of many of these possibilities also, but for me, these concerns didn't pose an impediment. The logistics would be manageable, and I knew I need not worry about Ray not being there when I arrived.

Although I don't believe this had much of an impact on my decision, a part of me also looked forward to being the wife of this man of prominence. I didn't know what to expect, but it did offer promise of a comfortable lifestyle. Growing up poor had made me content with that lifestyle; I didn't need riches to find happiness. But I was curious—just what did his mansion look like? Had the bomb dropped on Hiroshima left Ray's estate in some state of destruction?

I was delighted I received a letter from Ray. He had arrived in Japan and was staying in Tokyo for a few days before returning to his home. I was equally surprised to read he planned to help the US Army as a translator. Ray trusted the government, and they trusted him? Evidently, they needed anyone they could find to help out, and although Ray's English wasn't perfect, he understood both languages well, so he'd agreed to help. That made me smile; this seemed like a sign the war was truly over. Would his willingness to help mean he could return to America, though he'd renounced his citizenship during the war? He sent me his home address to write him back.

As I read the letter, I realized it hadn't occurred to Ray I might consider staying in America after I left Tule Lake.

> *All I think about is you, my love. It has been unbearable to be apart for all these long months. I can't believe what I did to be taken away from you. I am very sorry for that. You are my everything, now and forever. How my heart aches for you every day. And I feel like I haven't even been a father yet. My son is walking, and I missed his first steps. I want to be close to him, not running around with my business or whatever else, as my father was. I love you both with all I am. I was devastated when I learned we wouldn't be allowed to return to Tule Lake, but they promised a ship would be available to transport our families to Japan as soon as possible. Do you have any word yet as to when your ship will be departing from San Francisco? I know you will send me word on your departure, and I will count the days until you arrive.*
>
> *The atomic bomb went off just miles from my home. My home is still standing, but many others aren't. The devastation is everywhere here. I must sign off now and get this letter posted. From your husband who loves you more than anything—Ray*

I appreciated his remorse for his gang involvement, and I decided I wouldn't bring up anything more about Santa Fe—there was no reason to. I sat down to write him back and knew I would mention only that Norman and I would come as soon as we could. He didn't need to know I'd ever thought of staying; it would crush him. He also didn't need to know Mom had begged me to stay in America; he wouldn't understand her interference in our lives, although I knew it wasn't anything personal for Mom: she liked Ray, and her concerns were real and understandable about my future in Japan. I told him my family was leaving Camp Rohwer and weren't returning to

Stockton. And I told him about the cute things Norman was doing and some words he was saying. I knew Ray would enjoy that.

Christine and John came by to tell Norman and me goodbye. John had received confirmation of his job working in a grape vineyard, so they were leaving. They would find an apartment when they reached their destination, which was only several hours from Tule Lake. And they also shared other big news: Christine was expecting a baby. She'd told me before anyone else, since she was still waiting for confirmation from a doctor. As I had, she also experienced nausea, but otherwise she seemed quite fine. The big Hayashi family was growing again.

I felt a knot in my stomach. When would I get to see Christine or her baby? I didn't show my inner turmoil; we hugged and promised to write. Off my sister and her husband walked, carrying everything they owned in their bags, to begin their new lives away from government supervision, while looking forward to the birth of their first child. I was happy for them.

By then, Norman was running everywhere and keeping me busy, so I didn't have much time to sit and chat with the many acquaintances I'd made at camp. I was waiting to hear from Mom and Pop and knew I needed to write and explain my decision to go to Japan. Norman ran around so much, he wore out his first pair of leather shoes. There was no time to order more, so he just kept wearing them, holes or not. He was eating well, and it seemed he was growing fast. I was just taking one day at a time. I knew I would receive news about the ship for Japan eventually, but in the meantime, I just tried to relax and wait.

And then a letter from Mom arrived; I couldn't wait to hear about Chicago. Mom was full of news. Loretta had married just before leaving Camp Rohwer, so she and her new husband were on their way to Hawaii. Loretta's husband was going to join the family insurance business, and Mom was optimistic for her daughter's future. While Hawaii seemed a long way off, it was still America. I was thrilled for Loretta; she and I were very close, even though she was six or so years younger than I was. We both liked school, and our similar personalities made us close. Mom said she would send Loretta's address along as soon as she got it. Mom hoped we could save our money to go visit her and that she would come and visit us too. Her letter went on:

> We all loaded onto the train with your wonderful duffel bags in hand, packed full. We were happy to have many people from camp riding together for this journey. We all hoped we would find a new home and life. It was a long train, and it seemed to be full. Our train started out and made a brief stop in Little Rock, Arkansas. We then headed north, and the conductor announced the next stop would be St. Louis, Missouri, in five more hours. We all settled into our seats and rested for this next leg of the journey. When we were getting close to St. Louis, the conductor came through the train again and told us we would have a one-hour layover in St. Louis, so we could leave the train if we so desired.
>
> As the train rolled to a stop, we looked out the window and couldn't believe what we saw. There were many people standing on the platform, smiling and waving at us, and there was even a homemade welcome sign. As we all walked down the aisles, down the long steps of the carriage, and outside, we were flabbergasted. The people gathered there handed out sandwiches, cookies, and even chocolates to everyone. We all took one of each, started eating, and said thank you many, many times. We just couldn't imagine this kindness directed toward us. It wasn't so much the food as the feeling—they didn't hate us. They were smiling at us. It was shocking and unexpected, and it lightened our hearts. We didn't know how to react—we all stood together frozen in our tracks. For these people, the war was over. Maybe they never did resent the American Japanese. It didn't matter. As long as I live, I will remember that moment in my heart. I am sure everyone there felt the same as I did. Some of the men gathered together to talk, then more, and then they spoke with the rest of us, and then we all decided the same thing—the entire train of us Japanese leaving camp would stay right here in St. Louis. No one climbed back on board to journey farther north to Chicago, despite the fact we'd already paid our passage.
>
> The local people were happy to assist us in any way they could. They knew of employment agencies the men could visit. They also knew of inexpensive apartments available in a town

about twenty-five miles west of St. Louis called St. Charles. We took a bus along with many others out to St. Charles and have rented a small but cozy apartment. The rent is reasonable, and we even put down enough money to cover a month of rental fees. Pop and several other Issei men found jobs with a landscaping company. They can take a bus to a location, and someone from the company picks them up. Marian and Fran are each going to move in with a local family; they will cook and clean for their room and board. So it is just Pop, Tom, Ed, and me together in our apartment. There is plenty of room for you and Norman.

Janet, I can't tell you how happy we are here in St. Louis, even though it has just been a few days. None of us has been insulted, stared at, or looked down upon. We are just regular citizens here, living as everyone else. How is it possible to be accepted? More than worrying about finding work or a home, we have all worried about finding peace in the world where we live. It is here. We understand we will be poor—we expected that. But now we are truly free from the government and from prejudice—free to just live our lives. It has been exhilarating. I can't wait for you and Norman to join us.

What a joyful letter. This was the happiest Mom had seemed since the day of Pearl Harbor. It was a huge relief for me, too, as I'd worried about what would happen to my family when they ventured out into the world. But I needed to tell her about my decision to leave America. She would be sad and worry about Norman and me, but she would accept it. It was the first time in my life I didn't listen to my mom or follow her advice—this made the decision even harder. I loved my parents very, very much, and I was tortured by the thought I might never see them again. Both of my parents just wanted me to be safe and happy. All I was I owed to my parents, and I was grateful. They deserved all the credit for raising me into a woman who could feel confident about facing whatever lay ahead in Japan.

I wasted no time to write back. I was excited to hear about their arrival in St. Louis—such wonderful, surprising news! And I was thrilled to hear about Loretta's marriage. One more thought on my mind, which I didn't include in the letter, was the possibility of seeing Loretta on my journey to Japan. Often the ships stopped in Hawaii en route—but would I be allowed off the ship into America, as I would no longer be a citizen? I stored the idea away to pursue if it proved possible. Then I got to the hard part of my letter: explaining my decision and thanking them for their concern. They knew I appreciated their sage advice, but I didn't doubt it would be hard for them to read the letter, so I tried to explain everything as best I could. Almost everything: I left out the part about renouncing my citizenship. There was no need to worry them about this—that was my private agony.

Tule Lake officials gave us a date for departure: December 26, 1945. It was almost funny to think I would spend one more Christmas in camp. Now I could plan in my own little way, and I could make sure Norman and I were both well rested; we were lucky the government had continued to cover our room and board since the war ended. I was going to wait as long as I could to sign my renunciation letter.

Soon enough, I received a return letter from Mom. She seemed quite content since leaving Camp Rohwer and relieved about how well she and all the others in camp were received back into society. She understood my decision to join Ray and told me that if anyone could make it work, it was her precious Janet, whom she and Pop had taught to do the right thing and never cower under pressure. She asked me to write often, since she would be anxious for news. At the end of her letter, she wrote, "Be careful, my darling daughter. You are leaving on a dangerous journey. We pray for safe travels for you and Norman. All my love—Mom."

I signed and mailed my last letters in the United States, one to my family and one to Ray, on Christmas Eve, 1945. Hopefully, Norman and I would be reunited with Ray within a month.

Chapter 22
Traveling to Japan

It sure didn't feel much like Christmas—no tree, no gifts, no family around, no happy conversation. Would I ever have another Christmas with my family in America?

The day came to take the next step: leave US soil for what could be forever. I was leaving my third internment camp after approximately 1,320 days of imprisonment. I'd spent so much precious time of my young life held captive by my government. My life in Stockton seemed long ago, like a memory of my youth. I was twenty-two and single then; now, I was a twenty-five-year-old married mother of a son.

I needed to stay calm, and I desperately wanted to be joyful, but I couldn't escape a feeling of loneliness and simple resignation about my decision to renounce my citizenship and leave for Japan. I knew enough from Mom and others to have real feelings of terror about my future, but more than anything, I wanted to protect my son. Soon he would be reunited with his father. I knelt down and prayed for safety.

I bought a little cardboard suitcase at the canteen for Norman's things. I decided to leave behind my portable sewing machine, because I didn't have room to take it along. Of course, I would also leave the double bed Ray and I had bought, which had brought us such relief and was the best purchase of our marriage to date. I still wore several dresses I'd brought along when I came to camp, along with new ones I made for myself. My homemade duffel bag was packed full for a journey across the world.

Norman was seventeen months old and didn't know about Christmas. We went to the mess hall for our final internment camp dinner; I thought to myself it wouldn't bother me if I never ate on a picnic table again. Then I took Norman for his final shower in our bathhouse—another aspect of camp I wouldn't miss. We both went to bed early, since I hoped we could both get a little extra sleep. Norman fell asleep quickly, as he typically did, but I lay awake. So many thoughts swam in my brain, and one thought especially: I had finally signed the paper to renounce my citizenship. I was now a citizen of no country on earth.

I also wondered about accommodations on the ship. Around eight thousand people were headed to Japan after the war, mainly from Tule Lake Camp, and I didn't know if we would all be on the same ship or not. I'm sure I finally fell asleep, after hours of lying awake, full of thoughts about the last few years and what was next. Christmas Day 1945 was an emotional one for me.

The next day, we were up, to the bathroom, dressed, packed, and ready to go by eight. We ate our last meal and walked back to our room, our home at Tule Lake, and I shut the door on three and a half years of my life. I carried my duffel bag in one hand and Norman's bag in the other and asked him to hang on to me. We waited at the front gate, as instructed, to take a bus to the train station for the southbound train to San Francisco. Many people were leaving with us, but unfortunately no real friends of mine, although I recognized plenty of people I could speak to. At Tule Lake, I was known as the mom of the cute little boy running around. Many also knew me as a translator, and I still continued to assist anyone who asked, but unlike in Stockton Assembly Center and Camp Rohwer, where I'd been a block manager, I was more anonymous in Tule Lake. The difference in camp size was also a factor; after living together for over a year in Camp Rohwer, everyone seemed to know each other's name, but in Tule Lake, which was significantly larger, I wasn't acquainted with many residents beyond my barracks. So, there were just a few people to say goodbye to when I walked out of Tule Lake with Norman holding tightly to my dress.

On the journey to San Francisco, all transfers went smoothly, and there seemed to be a kind man to help me with my bags each time I struggled. The officials found our names on their clipboards, and we were checked in. While we were directed onto the gangway of the ship, I turned to look at America one last time. I would always belong to her, no matter where I lived. In a way, I felt silly fighting tears and saying goodbye to no one. But I couldn't deny the ache in my soul. My nerves and raw emotion almost took over, and I feared I could collapse momentarily. I loved America, my homeland.

I managed to stay strong and continue putting one foot in front of the other, and soon Norman and I were safely on board. This was actually a navy ship, so sailors and soldiers were on the ship around us. That was fine with me. More and more people boarded, until the outdoor deck was nearly packed full. Getting my bearings helped me dispel my agony over leaving; Norman and I became immersed in the sea of people traversing the ocean to Tokyo with us.

We were assigned a hammock for sleeping in a large room full of hammocks that were hung up, one atop the other, in stacks of five bunks that reached the ceiling. At the end of each row, there was a ladder to climb to access your hammock. Our hammock was on the first level, which was a relief; Norman and I would have to sleep together for the next sixteen days or so, and if we'd been assigned a spot up higher, I don't know what I would have done, since I would have been terrified of Norman falling over the hammock's edge. I was even concerned he'd fall out and hit the floor on the lowest level; I wondered if I should tie him down, but I didn't know how I could do it. I decided to hold on to him so hopefully, if he stirred, he would awaken me, too. There were convenient shelving units down the length of the outside wall, and I found an empty cubby and slid both our bags right in. I had no way to lock up anything, but I doubted anyone was concerned about that.

We walked around to find the dining area, where we learned dinner would be served at five, six, or seven. We were assigned the first hour, which would work best for Norman. Then a loud blast from the ship's horn startled us, and the ship slowly crept away from the dock. We were on our way.

The loudspeaker announced a fire and emergency drill, and we were all called on deck and shown where the life jackets were. I couldn't swim, and I sure couldn't imagine the little orange puffy vest jacket would keep both of us alive in the big ocean, so I trusted the mighty ship and crew would get us to our destination safely.

Within an hour's time, the ship had increased speed until it cruised along at a fast clip. Norman was having fun checking everything out and running around. It was hard to explain to a seventeen-month-old he had to walk slowly, but I held on to him tightly until he understood he wasn't in the camp anymore.

Outside, the deck was crowded and chilly—we were out on the Pacific Ocean in January. I put several layers on us, including heavy sweaters I'd knitted in the last couple of months, in the evenings after Norman was asleep or while he napped during the day, in anticipation of this trip. I was wearing heavy knee socks under my dress to stay warm, and Norman wore heavyweight pants I'd sewed. I bought him a cap with flaps that tied under his chin, which fit just right, and I wore a big scarf tied on my head to protect me from the constant stiff breeze on the deck. We were ready for the brisk weather of our journey.

That first night, an hour before dinner was to be served, I started feeling nauseated. I found a chair and bent over with misery, held on to Norman, and told him Mommy didn't feel well. I must have looked bad, because a friendly voice asked, "Ma'am, can I help you? You look like you're seasick." It was a soldier; he offered me some Dramamine to help ease the seasickness. I thanked him and swallowed the pill with no water. Maybe it helped a little, because I didn't actually throw up, but I still felt awful. When it was time for dinner, I took Norman and sat down, but I did not want one bite. The ship tossed back and forth like a roller coaster. I knew from my days at the Stockton County Fair that my tummy couldn't handle carnival rides. We weren't through day one yet, and I was already dreading two more weeks of the trip.

Dinner was served on a conveyer belt because the motion of the ship would make carrying our own plates to our table impossible. We were instructed to simply choose a seat and eat from the plate that stopped on the conveyor in front of us. After Norman and I sat down, he took a bite. As the ship swayed, plates started scooting down the conveyer, and Norman took another bite off the plate in front of him, which was no longer his. And on it went. At first, I didn't notice this was happening. When I realized Norman was taking food off other people's plates, I asked him to stop, but he didn't understand. He was just eating his dinner; no one around seemed upset, if they realized what was happening. The scene looked like something out of the *Three Stooges*, but I wasn't feeling jovial, because just looking at the food made me nauseated.

I took Norman to the bathroom before bed. There was a sink and toilet, but no showers or baths. I'd thought ahead and brought several washcloths and small tea towels to clean up both Norman and myself as best I could, and after doing so, we dressed for bed. I put a sweater on for some modesty before we walked to our hammock and climbed in. The hammocks swayed with the ship, which Norman thought quite entertaining. I didn't find it much of a thrill, but I think it did help with my queasy tummy; I'd taken some crackers from dinner and managed to keep them down. We got situated in our hammock, and I kept one arm around Norman so he wouldn't fall and hit the floor. He fell asleep quickly; it had been a long day without rest for him, except for a brief nap on the train to San Francisco.

Around our hammock, a crazy scene unfolded. Lights turned off and on. People searched for their assigned hammocks, then some climbed up the ladder at the foot of my hammock and kicked my feet. Others talked, and many were just inconsiderately making noise, clearly oblivious that they were in a room with a couple hundred people trying to sleep. At some point, all the lights went out, and the talking stopped. Everyone was falling asleep—and then, almost like a switch was flipped, snoring erupted all over the room, like a chorus. *Oh my*, I thought. That night, cat-napping was the best I could manage.

Norman woke early, and we climbed off our hammock quietly and headed to the bathroom. I was relieved to find a stall open—I'd seen the evening before how a long line developed—and amazingly, Norman was still dry. I tiptoed to our bags and got the same clothes we'd worn the previous day. There was no laundry available on board, so I would need to plan out our clothes carefully for the duration of travel.

We walked outside to the fresh air on deck. Gale-force winds greeted us, and our layers of clothes felt good. Breakfast for us was at seven.; we were ready when the mess hall doors opened. Once more, we sat down at the conveyer belt, where scrambled eggs with toast and a spoonful of canned peaches came by on plates. The peaches were supposed to help with seasickness. I asked one of the helpers if I could get some milk for my son, but he said they didn't have enough milk for the guests because there was limited refrigeration available. He apologized. What would I do for the next sixteen days with Norman? For now, he would have to just drink water.

After breakfast, we got up and walked around a little bit; the deck wasn't as crowded this early in the day. I saw the soldier who had given me the Dramamine. We said good morning, and he asked how I was feeling.

"Better, but not normal—thank you," I said.

"This is the roughest time of year to be out at sea," he said, "and most likely we will encounter some pretty good storms along the way, too." He introduced himself as Donald, a soldier from Illinois. He already knew I was from the internment camp, and I told him my name and thanked him once more for the medicine the day before. Norman was curious about everything hanging from Donald's belt. Donald was good humored and not annoyed by Norman's pushiness. He handed Norman his flashlight. Oh, was that ever fun to turn off and on! He told me to let him know if I ever needed any more Dramamine.

"No doubt," I said, and he reached into his pocket and handed me a small package. He encouraged me to take one before I felt ill, as it worked better. Some other soldiers came over, chatting, so I returned the flashlight, and Norman and I moved on.

As I walked away, I noticed several nearby Japanese travelers giving me a look. They were faces I didn't recognize, but I understood the look: they despised American servicemen. I was fraternizing with the enemy. I had never harbored hatred for any of the soldiers or administrators at camp; they were just people doing their jobs. From the first to last day of internment, I'd understood my fate was a result of wartime paranoia of the leaders. Why would I dislike the soldiers or the administrators? I carried on with Norman and pretended not to see the disdain the travelers wanted me to see.

My concern for the lack of milk for Norman grew—and then I had a brainstorm. After all the breakfasts were completed, we slipped down to the dining hall, and I found someone who worked in the galley.

"Can I have some of the leftover rice from the evening meal?" I asked. "And can I use a burner on the stove?"

The man checked with the head cook, who said that would be fine.

I held Norman's hand, and we walked back to the big stove. I added water to the rice, simmered the rice until it turned to paste, and then added more water until it reached a smooth, flowing consistency. Then I sprinkled in a wee bit of sugar, removed the mixture from the heat, and let it cool a bit. I grabbed a bottle from Norman's bag, took a paring knife from the big drawer of knives and other large metal cooking utensils, and made a big slit in the bottle's plastic nipple. By then, my brew was tepid, so I poured some into the bottle, put on the top, and handed it to Norman. He took it and immediately started drinking. He liked it—success!

The kitchen worker told me I could store my handmade rice milk in the refrigerator and showed me where to find it. I could use a little saucepan to reheat it when I needed to fill the next bottle. I was relieved and pleased that I'd found a way to make milk for Norman. Maybe rice milk didn't have the same nutrition as cow's milk, but the rice was good for him, and I knew he needed more fluids, because he barely drank any water. I thanked the kitchen help for their assistance.

By then, the outside deck was quite full, but there weren't a lot of other choices of places to take Norman. I did my best to entertain him by looking out at the sea and talking about every new thing on this big ship. I could feel the surface swell increasing and sky filling up with clouds. Maybe a storm was developing. The increasing turbulence turned me green once more. I found a chair and curled up, holding on to Norman's pant leg. Just like the day before, Donald appeared again, this time with another soldier standing nearby.

"Janet, would you like me to take your son for a walk with my buddy here?" Donald asked. "We have nothing to do. Maybe we can help you out a bit."

"Oh, thank you very much," I said. With that, Norman walked off with Donald, holding his hand. Then the second soldier took his other hand, and the two men pulled him up and down for a thrill.

Meanwhile, I couldn't escape my queasiness. I swallowed a pill but still felt miserable. Thankfully, the men wore Norman out during their long playtime. After I told them how grateful I was, Donald said it was fun for them, too, since they'd been just standing around. I took Norman inside to our hammock, and we took a much-needed rest.

Donald and the other soldiers all helped out with Norman at different times. I varied between feeling okay, being nauseated, and throwing up. I wrote letters to Mom, Pop, and Christine to mail when we reached port, and I tried to keep Norman entertained. Though he was a curious toddler, he really didn't give me any trouble; he was such a good boy. There was one other boy about his age on board, and they played a little bit. But most of the children weren't walking yet, so their parents carried them. Norman drank his bottles of homemade rice milk every day. At meals, plates on the conveyer belt often slid back and forth with the ship's rocking, and Norman continued to pick up a piece of food he wanted to eat off any plate going by. I tried to eat to keep my strength, but often I just sat with him.

Nighttime was the hardest, with all passengers hanging together in the rafters. On top of all the snoring, I heard a loud thump nearly every night, which always startled me. *Boom!* Someone had fallen out of bed. The next day, I would see another person walking around with an arm in a sling. But swinging a bit on the hammock did help ease my nausea. During the whole voyage, I never had a decent night's sleep, but at least Norman did.

One morning, I heard an announcement over the loudspeaker: "We will be docking in Tokyo harbor at noon tomorrow. Be sure to have your belongings together; we will disembark immediately. As soon as we deliver the ship's roster to the Japanese officials, the gangway will be available for you."

Finally! I'd been keeping track of the dates; I already knew tomorrow was our scheduled arrival. My tummy was looking forward to being on dry land once more.

I found Donald and the others. They knew how much I appreciated their help with Norman; they'd been lifesavers for me when I fell ill. They were all smiles and wished me well. Although they certainly didn't expect any gift from me, I wished I could give them something, as that would have been the polite thing—the Japanese thing—to do. But there was nothing to give.

When I closed my eyes for the last night of noise and commotion, I thought about Ray. I knew he would be waiting for us and would no doubt arrive early, just in case we did. I wondered if there would be some awkwardness between us; since we'd been married, we'd been apart for nearly as many months as we'd lived together, and Ray had left me at Tule Lake thinking only about the war, not his family. But he'd apologized, and I could tell from his letters he realized the error of his ways. Beyond the Santa Fe part of our lives, I was anxious we might feel like strangers simply because so much time had passed. Would he still feel so strongly about me now? I knew he would be thrilled to see his son, and I told myself I couldn't possibly question him and his feelings for me. If we felt at all odd or unfamiliar at first, hopefully this feeling would just slide away in time. My other concern was that I was traversing the ocean to a country where I wasn't a citizen. Would I feel trapped in this country where I might not be welcomed? Would we be a happy little family of three?

There was no turning back now, nor were there alternatives if I encountered trouble—and maybe this was why I was anxious.

Relax, I told myself.

Eventually, I put the snoring and my worries aside and drifted off for a bit of sleep. In the morning, I couldn't wait to see my long-lost husband.

Chapter 23
Reunited

The ship docked, and I walked into a new country with no papers. Though my son was still an American citizen, I was no longer an American, and I wasn't a citizen of Japan, either. I tried valiantly to put these thoughts out of my mind and not worry about it, but it was impossible to vanquish my fears completely. Japan had forced me into this situation, but I had accepted their terms, hard as it was. I signed away my rights in the United States, but I hadn't signed away my love for the land of my birth.

My duffel bag was bulging as I zipped it up, along with Norman's smaller cardboard suitcase. Once more I was leaving for a new destination carrying everything I owned in my homemade duffel bag, which also served as a dresser drawer for my clothes. As we waited to disembark, Norman was too young to understand he would soon see his dad, but I know he could tell I was thrilled. I knew Ray would be equally excited.

As Norman and I walked down the gangway, I struggled to carry both our bags and negotiate the uneven boards intended to prevent anyone from slipping. Instantly, I spotted Ray in the throng, waiting in the dock area. When I made it to him through the crowd, I dropped the bags, and he hugged me as hard as he could; he didn't want to let go. Then he picked up his son and looked admiringly at him.

"What a beautiful boy we have!" he exclaimed. When Ray had departed from Tule Lake, Norman was just an infant. Now, he was almost eighteen months old.

We started walking, Ray carrying our bags. I could feel his euphoria; I was all smiles, too. It only took a couple of minutes off the ship for me to realize there would be little or no awkwardness between us.

Ray was jubilant. He was talking nonstop, and he couldn't stop smiling. I had felt seasick for most of our long voyage and hadn't eaten much, so I asked Ray if we could find some food. Luckily, it was only a short bus ride to the US Army base.

"They will have food for you—I am sure," Ray said. He went on to explain we would be staying at the barracks together for four days, where he was helping with translations for the military.

Ray explained that General MacArthur had been appointed by President Truman to be the supreme commander for the Allied Powers while the United States took control of Japan. He brought in five thousand military personnel to assist him, including my brother Will. MacArthur's first priority was to demilitarize the country and destroy its ability to wage war again. Over two hundred thousand hard-line military, political, and business leaders were prohibited from serving in any elected capacity. Political prisoners were released. The "thought police" were abolished. The International Military Tribunal for the Far East was formed to hold trials for the war criminals of Japan. Ray said that after the Japanese people learned of horrific crimes committed by the military, many were disillusioned with their proud military in the samurai tradition. The Rape of Nanking, the Bataan Death March, the Burma Railway—these were permanent stains on Japan. Japan was just as guilty as Germany of torture and execution. A new constitution was being prepared that would give women the right to vote; in the new order, women would also have the right to own property and the freedom to divorce. Labor unions were now allowed. These were huge, unfathomable changes to the ancient traditions and order of Japanese society.

Many years later I learned of one more atrocity at the hands of Emperor Hirohito.

> He ordered the military to expand its so-called comfort stations or military brothels during the war. . . . Women were rounded up on the streets of Japanese-occupied territories, convinced to travel to what they thought were nursing units or jobs, or purchased from their parents as indentured servants. . . . Once they were at the brothels, the women were forced to have sex with their captors under brutal, inhumane conditions. "It was not a place for humans," Lee [Ok-seon]

told Deutsche Welle in 2013. . . . "There was no rest," recalled Maria Rosa Henson. . . . "They had sex with me every minute."

It's estimated hundreds of thousands of women were enslaved in at least 125 brothels during the war and that 90 percent of the "comfort women" died by the end of the war. Shamefully, the military tribunals never charged or convicted anyone for these despicable crimes against women. Enough women survived and were willing to document for all time what transpired at Japan's "comfort stations."

With the soldiers now working on the rebuilding of Japan, they were in constant need of translation assistance. Ray had worked out a little deal with a colonel. The base was crowded, since there hadn't been much time to set up barracks, but because he needed Ray to stay on for two more weeks, the colonel had given up his quarters for us to use for the next four days. Then, Ray would stay for ten more days in the barracks with the men, and Ray's old friend Chuji would take Norman and me on the train out of Tokyo and to our new home. Ray would join us after he finished helping the colonel.

Ray had even tried to get me a job before I arrived. He told the colonel his wife was the best translator in the world, but the colonel was appreciative of Ray's help and was only interested in having him translate. Maybe Ray didn't have perfect English, especially written, but he was quite competent.

We laughed at the happenstance of residing in military barracks after the war was over. Ray told me the colonel's quarters had a private bathroom, so it would be much better than our camp-life barracks. That was all fine with me. We were reunited, we were together, and we were safe and sound.

At the next bus stop, our little family of three stepped off together. After being on my own for so long, it hit me: we were really a family again. At the military base's mess hall, the cook was happy to serve lunch leftovers—rice and braised beef. While I ate, Ray dropped off our bags in our room. I felt much better; I was relieved my tummy had finally settled.

Ray returned and said he'd made arrangements for Norman to sleep in a crib just a few doors down. When he'd asked about a crib for the few days we'd be staying at the base, a friendly lady had said she would be happy to keep Norman overnight and would bring him to us when he awakened. We were delighted with this setup. When we finished eating, we walked to Mrs. Johnson's room so we could all get acquainted. She spoke to Norman sweetly and showed us the spare crib. When we departed, I told her I would see her just ahead of eight, Norman's bedtime, to get him situated.

We walked to a small grassy hillside near the base and sat down. Norman ran around in circles and laughed as Ray pretended to catch him. Then he really caught him, threw him up in the air and caught him several times, grabbed him under his arms, and twirled him around and around. We were all giggling. Norman didn't want his dad to stop. He put his arms up for more. They played and played until both were tired. Father and son, playing—this was the way it was supposed to be. Ray didn't stop grinning. I hadn't seen him smile like that since we three had left the hospital together after Norman was born.

After playing in the park area, we walked several blocks around the base. I looked around and said, "So this is Japan. This is it." For my entire life, I'd heard how beautiful Japan was from my parents, friends, and of course, Ray. But the war had just ended five months prior, and everything around us was messy. It would take much work to clean up Tokyo. Devastation from Allied bombings still showed. There was damage and destruction all around. But at least the people looked like they were getting on with their lives.

As we walked, Ray told me what people were talking about in Japan while I'd been traveling. The emperor had admitted he was human, not divine. I told Ray that my parents and friends in America thought Emperor Hirohito was their leader, but not a god. But to the Japanese in the homeland, Hirohito was their god on earth. Ray explained that the United States had insisted Hirohito confess the truth to his people as a condition of surrender. We both agreed it was a good step to take, even though Ray said his statement was written in the ancient dialect that few people could read or understand. But in time, Ray said the masses understood their precious emperor was mortal. Ray said it had been discussed often on the base; the emperor could have been considered a war criminal like so many under him, including Prime Minister Tojo, because of the barbaric crimes against humanity committed by the Imperial Army.

We returned in time for dinner in the mess hall. There were plenty of offerings, so we all ate heartily. Milk was available too, and I gladly served it to Norman after over two weeks without it. Many military men walked around in simple-looking uniforms; some sat together telling stories and sharing big, raucous laughter. The pressure and stress of war, which had weighed all of us down for so long, was over. These men had a big job ahead in rebuilding Japan, but with the war behind them, they were relaxed.

After dinner, we went back to Ray's room, and I got out Norman's pajamas. It was a thrill to have a private bathroom, so I let Norman sit and enjoy his warm bath before getting him ready for bed. I told Ray I would carry him over to Mrs. Johnson's room and stay with him until he was asleep. I wrapped up Norman in a heavy army blanket and headed outside into the cold night air. It was just seven thirty, but Norman almost fell asleep in my arms. I got him comfortable, kissed him good night, and sat down with Mrs. Johnson for a few minutes. He was quickly asleep.

"It is a big relief to know Norman will be safe in your crib, Mrs. Johnson."

"Oh, it is my pleasure, and please call me Sue. Where I'm from in Texas, our door is always open to helping others."

"I only wish I could return the kindness to you." I'd been raised to always return kindness, but at that moment, I had no idea what gift I could present to Sue Johnson. "Norman is surely very tired and will likely sleep for twelve hours."

"That's no problem—I am up early if he gets up early."

"I'll be sure to be here by seven thirty in the morning, if that's okay."

"You go relax after your long journey," Sue said, "and don't worry a second about your sweet boy."

"See you in the morning, and thank you again."

As I walked back briskly to the colonel's room, the winter air hit me in the face. When I opened the door, I wasn't prepared for what I saw, and my mouth dropped open: Ray had transformed the colonel's room into something amazing. The lights were off, and he'd lit at least twenty-five candles. There were candles on the nightstand, on the table in the corner, on the big foot lockers, and on the lampstand. It looked magical.

Ray rushed over to greet me. "Happy birthday!"

Indeed, tomorrow was my birthday. He took my hand and closed the door behind me. Then he said he wanted me to know how much he loved me and had missed me, and he walked us into the colonel's bathroom. After no privacy for many years, it was quite special to have a private bathroom. There were more candles burning on the sink top. Ray lit a cylindrical piece of sandalwood incense, and the narrow, wiggly smoke filled the room; it smelled divine. Then he set up a Japanese bath for me.

"You are no doubt weary from all your days on the ship," he said. "If your ship was like mine, I'm sure you were barely able to wash at all. I want you to enjoy a traditional Japanese bath with me, and I will take care of everything."

Ray took off his clothes. Then he unzipped my dress, carefully removed it, and did the same with everything else, slowly and deliberately, with much more confidence than he'd showed on our wedding night. It was chilly standing on the cold bare floor, but Ray quickly took his warm cloth and soap and began to wash me, sometimes kissing me as he worked. The candles flickered with enough light for him to see what he was doing, and the incense was aromatic. He was just as thorough as Mom would have been out in the country when I was five years old. That was the last time I'd had a Japanese bath, although Mom and Pop's backyard country bath was not a favorite memory for me.

However, this Japanese bath was a night I would never forget.

My personal hand cleansing took a long time; Ray made sure he missed nothing. Then he helped me into the bathtub. The water was still quite warm, almost hot, and it felt wonderful. I looked up and saw my admiring husband. Next he went through the same handwash procedure with himself, taking only a fraction of the time, and stepped into the tub behind me.

Ray leaned against the back of the tub, and I scooted back to lie against his chest. He put his arms around me, and I put my arms on top of his. We both closed our eyes and soaked up the moment. Neither of us said anything as the water caressed us. I couldn't have been more relaxed and felt a million miles away from the outside world as Ray's arms squeezed around me; I was totally engrossed in this moment of pure pleasure. After some time, I looked down and noticed my fingers had turned to raisins and the water was cooling down. We laughed and decided it was time to end our bath. Ray jumped out, wrapped up in a giant towel, and handed me the biggest towel I'd ever seen. It was full and fluffy and could have wrapped around me twice; I felt like royalty with such pampering.

Ray picked up a beautiful silk garment. "Touch it," he said. I did; the negligee was the softest thing I'd ever felt. "This is for your birthday. I will put it on for you."

He put my towel on the rack. The lovely ivory-hued negligee had buttons all the way down and elastics opposite the buttons that made loops on the edging. The collar stood up, and the sleeves were short. Ray put one of my arms in the sleeve and then the other, then fastened the elastic around the button up by my neck. It was snug. "It seems this isn't my size," I said.

He smiled broadly. "It's just the perfect size."

Ray had found a lingerie shop open in Tokyo and taken the bus there. When he'd told the clerk he needed the most wonderful piece in the store, she'd brought him this one. Without asking the price, he'd told her he would take it. The silk was smooth and soft, almost sheer, intended to be tight so as to highlight every bump and curve. Ray pulled the elastics around the buttons, and the silk adhered to my skin. There must have been thirty buttons, all of which required pulling the silk tightly across my skin to secure. The last button was midthigh. As luxurious as the garment was, I thought I couldn't move. Ray laughed and said, "the material will move with you." I took a small step or two. "You should be in the royal palace," he added.

"Right now, I feel like a princess," I said.

The silk was like a soft, completely transparent piece of skin on me. It did move with me as I moved. I'd never felt anything like it before. Ray thoroughly enjoyed gliding his hands all over the silk that now enveloped me as we reclined on the colonel's bed. I suddenly felt incredibly spoiled. Ray had spent a long time preparing for that moment; he'd thought of everything—the candles, incense, towels, and silken masterpiece.

He wasn't done. He hopped up and brought me a wrapped package. What more could he possibly have to give? Not knowing what to expect, I untied the bow and opened the box. Inside was a stunning kimono, obviously expensive, the colors smashing, the finest detailing sewn into the garment. *Wow*—I hadn't expected I would ever own anything that grand. Ray told me I would need it to wear in time. Once we were living in the family mansion in Hatsukaichi and all the war cleanup was completed, Ray thought we would be a grand couple in the local social circles. There would be many society events for us to attend, and on occasion, I would be expected to wear a gorgeous kimono, such as this one. I kissed him and thanked him for everything, overcome with emotion. I was so touched by his thoughtfulness for the entire evening, I almost couldn't speak.

Ray blew out the candles and the incense. He joined me under the covers and began to unbutton my silk, releasing me from the fabric that touched everything. It was now time for the climax of the evening. After thirteen months apart, we returned to being husband and wife again.

After our dreamy night, I woke early, thinking about getting over to Sue's. But I didn't want to arrive too early and be rude. My internal clock was askew from the change in time zones. At least the ship had traveled slowly enough to allow me to somewhat adjust as we progressed through the different time zones. I lay in bed thinking about the previous night—a highlight of my life, thanks to Ray. My adoring husband was back. He'd never really left, but he'd certainly been sidetracked. And now he was even helping the US Army. I was comforted knowing he'd found peace in his heart.

I slipped to the bathroom, grabbed fresh clothes from my bag, and quietly dressed. I slipped on a heavy sweater, opened the door, and scooted to Sue's, where I tapped lightly on the door. She quickly opened it. Norman was still asleep. I was glad I'd be there when he woke, just in case his new surroundings startled him. He woke when the door closed and smiled when he saw me.

I quickly rushed him back to our room and bathroom. He was still dry, which amazed me. Ray was awake; I placed Norman in bed with his dad. Ray looked up at me and said, "Happy birthday." I smiled and thanked him again. What a birthday celebration it was; I felt spoiled again.

I'd thought Norman and his father would cuddle, but instead they rolled and goofed around, and then Ray held Norman up in the air. Norman giggled at his father's antics. We were ready for the day.

After breakfast, I sat down to write Mom and Pop and tell them
we'd arrived and reunited with Ray and about how glorious the day
had been. She would enjoy reading that. I also needed to mail a couple of letters I'd written while on the ship; I put them together in an
envelope destined for St. Charles, Missouri, Ray took it to the office.
Soon it would be on its long journey back to the United States.

Ray found out where Will was stationed in Tokyo. It was quite a
distance, but we could find our way by taking several different buses.
I was thrilled at the prospect of seeing my brother, now twenty-one
years old. Ray didn't know exactly when he could get away but promised he would figure it out before I left Tokyo. He was occupied all
day with his translating, for which he received a small stipend for
his service. I wanted to help out too, but I needed to take care of
Norman.

I walked outside the base with Norman, taking in what I could
of Tokyo and returning for lunch with Ray. Someone told me where
to find a playground, so we visited that in the afternoon. Soon Ray
was done for the day, and we ate dinner together. Norman was back
asleep at Mrs. Johnson's by seven thirty, so Ray and I were left to
enjoy the evening once more in the colonel's room.

Ray could never match the evening before, but he said now was
my real birthday night, so we needed to celebrate again. He relit the
candles and the incense. We sat on the bed with our backs to the wall
and just talked for a long time. He held my hand tightly, like he never
wanted to let it go. I had many stories from my ocean-going cruise,
and Ray laughed hard as I told them. I started laughing too, and we
just couldn't stop. Then I thought of something else that happened,
and it started again. He thought the funniest part was the men on
their hammocks snoring, one louder than the next.

Ray's trip had been on a much smaller vessel with beds—nothing like mine. I asked him to share stories from Santa Fe, since he
hadn't dared reveal many details about his fourth internment camp
in his letters. I don't know if he felt embarrassed, wanted to forget the
experience, or just didn't have much more to tell, but he didn't share
much about this time. Maybe it had been painful to be away from his
son and wife; he did tell me how upset he'd been when he'd learned
he would be deported immediately after the war. None of the Santa

Fe men were allowed to see their families. All were no longer citizens and considered personae non gratae in the United States.

After we'd both shared many stories, our conversation turned more serious. He'd only been home briefly, but it was long enough to learn his sister was angry he was bringing his American wife to Japan. I knew he and Kaito had never really gotten along—probably a result of having no mother to keep order when they were growing up. She had lived alone in the mansion since their father died. However, with the laws such as they were in Japan, nothing belonged to her. All inheritance belonged to Ray, the only surviving son. Ray wasn't greedy in any way, so I guessed the fighting wasn't about money. He warned me to expect her to be rude to us.

He also cautioned me about the utter destruction from the atomic bomb. While his home still stood, the windows were blown out. Many of the homes—especially the ones built with timber—in Hatsukaichi were just gone, or were tilting and ready to fall. All were damaged to some degree by the atomic blast in Hiroshima. He wanted to see what downtown Hiroshima looked like, even though he knew it was horrific. He'd only seen some of it from the train window when he'd arrived, so he said once we were together again in a few weeks, we should take the bus into the heart of Hiroshima to see firsthand for ourselves. I agreed and told him I would do my best to get along with Kaito. Maybe seeing her nephew would soften her disdain for us.

Our adrenalin from our reunion gave way to tiredness; Ray was exhausted from helping with translations all over the base. He leaned into me and rested his head on my shoulder. When his eyes shut, I gently pushed his head back to the pillow and climbed out of the bed. I took my time bathing myself, thinking how glad I was to have these days together as a family and that Ray and I could reconnect as husband and wife in complete privacy, which our lives had lacked for so long. I felt loved and safe; we were a family together again, contented and relaxed. I put on my new silk lingerie, and Ray awakened from his short nap as I stepped out of the bathroom. I could see the delight on his face as I moved slowly to the bed. He jumped up and adjusted the covers for us both to enter. The gentle touch of his hands was soothing. I savored these comfortable and loving moments together. Ray wrapped his arms around me, and we both drifted to sleep while he told me how nice my silk felt against him.

The following afternoon, we began our journey to find Will. We navigated different bus lines, often standing and waiting a long time. Sometimes Norman walked, and other times Ray carried him. Finally, we reached our destination, and Ray spoke with the man at the gate. We entered, and Ray went into the first building while Norman and I waited outside. He returned and said Will was out in the community and would return at five for dinner, so we could walk around and take in the sights till then.

That evening, we were waiting near the gate as Will came riding in with three other soldiers in their jeep. We waved, and he almost jumped out before the jeep stopped. I knew I'd remember that moment forever—Will looked grand in his military uniform, so official. It was hard to believe this was my little brother. He picked up his nephew for the first time and admired him.

We joined Will for dinner in the mess hall and never stopped talking. He shared the whole story of being drafted and trained for this mission. He said that when he was first drafted, he was quite angry, but it hadn't been as bad as he'd feared. He'd known he would be hated as an American soldier, but he was working on community outreach to change those feelings and help bring healing. Thinking about the long return journey back to Ray's base, we didn't dare stay too late, so we promised to write each other and hopefully, in time, to call when we were able. Will didn't think he'd be working in the Hiroshima area, but we promised to visit when we were back in Tokyo. I was sad to tell Will goodbye but glad to know we were together in Japan. Mom would be excited to learn about our visit. Ray, Norman, and I navigated our way back to the base.

My arrival in Tokyo couldn't have gone any better. Ray and I had reconnected in every way. We'd both written endless letters over the many months we were apart, but they were nothing compared to finally getting to be together. With these happy times, I felt relieved I'd made the decision to come to Japan. The journey had been unpleasant because of the seasickness but worth it to reunite with my husband and bring his son to him.

Soon it was time for Norman and me to depart for Hatsukaichi with Ray's friend. Ray told me to leave my new silk lingerie and kimono, since my bag was already full; he would bring them with him later. Ray secured some fresh linens, so I could put them on the bed and in the bathroom for the colonel. I wrote the colonel a note, thanking him for his kindly sharing his private room and restroom, and left it on the pillow.

Chuji arrived as he had promised, and we were all introduced. Ray hated to see us leave, but I think knowing he would return home in ten days made it much easier. We were quickly on our way. In the four days since we'd arrived, the smile never seemed to leave Ray's face, and though we didn't know what was ahead for us, we knew we were finally together, and that was all that mattered as Norman and I departed Tokyo.

Chapter 24
Family Mansion

Our journey to Ray's home involved a four-and-a-half-hour train trip and a walk to the house. Ray had told Kaito to expect us around four in the afternoon.

When we arrived at the train station, it was a complete madhouse. People were everywhere, some sitting on bags, some standing in groups, others leaning on walls, and the noise of the cavernous room was deafening.

Chuji was kind; he carried our bags and asked me about our journey across the Pacific. I knew my Japanese was understandable, and I understood him, but also I knew my Japanese was different. I held Norman tightly in my arms as I followed Chuji through the throng. When we found our track, we learned our train was delayed, so we found a vacant spot against the wall and sat down for a long, uncomfortable wait.

By early afternoon, we still hadn't departed. We took turns finding the restrooms and waiting in long lines to use the facilities. The restrooms were Japanese style: there was no toilet seat but rather an indentation in the floor. You simply squatted down and placed your feet on each side of the toilet, such that you touched nothing. I had no trouble adjusting to this style, having started my life on a farm with only a hole in the ground of our outhouse, but I did realize my knees would need to grow stronger.

The station housed a central kiosk selling prepackaged food; hundreds of people waited in lines, and three clerks worked frantically to serve them. I opened my bag and pulled out some food—several pieces of sliced bread and several bananas—I'd brought from the mess hall wrapped in paper napkins. Chuji thanked me as we ate.

Finally, our train's departure was announced. We traveled with two tickets, because I was planning to hold Norman. Chuji and I were nearly separated as masses rushed to the entrance gate. It was almost hard to breathe in the surging crowd. Slowly we advanced, and as we neared the track, the conductor hollered that all seats were taken. We could get on the train if we wanted, but we would be sitting on the floor. Chuji told me he needed to get home, so he must go; I told him Norman and I could sit on the floor as well. The trip was just four and a half hours long. It would have been impossible for me to figure out how to get back to Ray's base, especially while lugging along my bags and carrying Norman, with only some yen Ray had given me and no idea which bus to take. Chuji was my guardian, and I was not going to separate from him.

We each found a spot on the floor and leaned against the side of a seat. Chuji crammed our bags above with the others. Norman sat still on my lap, looking around at everything; I thought again how lucky I was to have such a good boy. Then the train chugged out of the station.

We were finally off.

We hadn't traveled far when the door at the front of our car slid open and two men appeared. They hollered in broken Japanese, but I still understood.

"They are Korean," Chuji whispered.

Koreans despised their Japanese occupiers, understandably. They were carrying a big gunnysack filled with one-pound bags of rice to sell. While food, especially rice, had been scarce since the end of the war, the men were asking for five times the normal cost. Japanese travelers began to holler back they couldn't possibly afford those prices. Some began calling them names. I pulled my knees up and shielded Norman, holding him tightly to my side, afraid a fight would ensue. No rice was sold in our car. The men began to move toward the next car to continue their attempt to exploit hungry travelers.

As a result of the delayed trains and too many people trying to board, every square inch of the floor and aisle was occupied. Without any hesitation, the first Korean man stepped on the head of a man sitting on the floor, holding the top of the seat for balance. Then the next man did the same. People started screaming. Then I realized I was directly in their path. There was no time to think—only react. I shielded Norman with my body and braced myself as the first man drew nearer, almost jumping from one head to the next. Then he stepped directly on my head, grasping the seat above me, and it felt like a boulder had dropped on me. The second man followed directly behind him. I didn't scream, but I did wonder if my neck was broken: my head started throbbing, and my neck felt stiff and tight. I moved my arms and fingers—I wasn't paralyzed, but I began to shake from the trauma. The men disappeared into the next car, leaving many passengers crying. Chuji asked if I was okay; I told him I thought so. I clung to Norman, terrified of what else might happen. It took all my strength to remain calm and collected. I'd thought the war was over—this sure didn't feel like peace.

The railcar's floor was hard and cold. When the line didn't appear too long and we could navigate through people, we stood to use the bathroom. By the time we arrived at our destination, we were four hours late, and I felt like my body had been assaulted—I hurt everywhere. My neck, shoulders, and head felt injured; my back ached from the long journey with little support and from clinging to Norman. It was the worst train trip of my life.

It felt good to get outside, despite the cold winter air. I pulled out our heavy sweaters and hats for the walk to Ray's home. When we arrived, Chuji rang the bell, and Kaito answered the door. Before we could be introduced, she harped at us for being late. "The soup is cold now." Chuji politely excused himself, and I thanked him for getting us to our new home safely.

I tried to greet Kaito properly and introduce her to Ray's son. As Ray had warned, she wanted no part of any friendly discourse with me. At least she'd made a pot of miso soup, which sat on the stove. "You can heat it up, if you like," she grumbled. At the same time, Norman was getting fussy; I knew he was tired and hungry, since we'd only eaten the meager items I'd stowed away in my bag during our long travel day. I warmed the soup on the stove I would use to cook in the future, looking around to find where everything was stored.

But it was an odd feeling: Kaito made me feel as though I were intruding on her, but I knew the property belonged to Ray. I tried to be as polite as possible. After we ate, I found Kaito in another room and asked her if she could show us our bedroom and bathroom. Kaito gave me a dark stare.

"Typical of my brother—sending you along when he isn't even here," she complained. "He has always been a spoiled brat who only thinks about himself and what he wants. I can't believe how totally irresponsible he is. I don't know what you and your boy are going to eat, because there is no food around here. Here is your room, and here is your bathroom. You are going to wish, sooner or later, you'd stayed in America with all your Yankee friends, instead of coming to live here in Japan with your worthless husband."

With that, she turned and walked away. Her words were stinging and hurtful—from a sister-in-law I had just met. There was nothing I could do but make the best of the situation and wait for Ray.

I felt filthy from the train station and the ride, so I wiped Norman and myself down with only a washrag and water, since there was no soap in the bathroom. Despite Kaito's most unwelcome "welcoming," it felt good to have finally arrived. Norman and I climbed into bed.

When we woke in the morning, I felt the effects of the men using my head as a stepping-stone. I was just grateful I didn't have any broken bones. As I walked around the house, I saw the damage from the bomb, which had fallen six to eight miles from the house. There was broken glass on the floor that hadn't been cleaned up, which Ray had told me to expect, because he hadn't yet been able to find anyone to repair the windows. Luckily, the porch overhang protected the interior from the rain. But the winter breeze blew in—a chilling reminder of what had occurred the previous August—and the big coal-burning hibachi that heated the house couldn't keep up. We wore heavy sweaters inside the house, and I kept Norman with me so he wouldn't get into the glass. In the kitchen was a beautiful refrigerator, but when I opened it, the shelves were bare. I found a little something for breakfast.

After we ate, I gave myself a longer tour of this home where I was not welcome. I could tell this had been a grand place, though it wasn't so grand now. There were six bedrooms, four on the main level and two upstairs, and also four bathrooms, two of the Japanese style with no toilet seat and two of the Western style with a toilet seat. The kitchen, living room, and dining room were big and contained many beautiful collectibles, some of which were shattered from the bomb, their remnants still sitting on the shelf. How spectacular the house must have been before the war! Mrs. Arakawa hadn't been kidding when she'd described Ray's home to me while in the internment camp.

I decided to take Norman for a short walk. I could see why Ray was considered wealthy—as far as I could see, there were no other homes of the same grandeur nearby. The gardens had been neglected, but I could imagine how lovely they once must have been. It also felt eerie: I saw people, yet no one smiled or said a word. Five months after the first atomic bomb in the history of mankind had been dropped, everything seemed frozen in time.

Finally, a man bowed toward me. Had he seen us leave the house? I acknowledged him and spoke a greeting, and Norman and I walked into the village. I saw a shop, and we went inside. The shelves were almost bare. Speaking as sweetly as I could, I asked the clerk if I could please purchase some rice.

Her glare was intense. "Get out of this store, damn Yankee, and don't ever come back," she growled.

I grabbed Norman and quickly turned without saying another word. How did she know I was an American? It must have been the accent—or was it just that she hadn't seen me before? I didn't know, but it hurt just the same. I tried to tell myself to be tough; after all, I'd endured the visceral feelings for the Japanese in Stockton. I was now an outcast in both countries. Was there any place that would accept me? Weren't refugees supposed to be welcome when the war ended? I was hungry, and Norman would be soon, too. We walked back to Ray's, where we weren't welcome either—though it was now my home, too.

When I asked Kaito if there was anything else to eat, she just shrugged and walked away. I scrounged around and found something to feed Norman for lunch, but little for me. Afterward, we went to our room, where Norman and I napped. I wanted badly to talk to Ray, but I knew it would be over a week before he returned.

I will be okay, I told myself.

After Norman woke, I tried to play a little with him in our room. Soon, we walked down to the kitchen for dinner. Kaito was sipping some soup and eating a baked sweet potato. I asked her what Norman and I could eat, and she said we could have the rest of the soup. The miso soup was tasty, but as a broth, it didn't have a lot of calories. That was our dinner. We three sat together, and I served the soup to Norman. Kaito didn't say anything or even glance over at us.

My stomach had growled all day and growled louder as Norman and I went to bed. It seemed Kaito was not going to feed us; I would have to muster the courage to venture out and see if I could find food of any kind. Ray had given me some money, so surely I could find a food shop somewhere in the vicinity where I wouldn't be thrown out. The next morning, there was nothing in the kitchen to eat for breakfast, and I was starting to get desperate. I pulled open the garbage and found the sweet potato skin from Kaito's dinner. I pulled every scrap out of it, dropped it into a pan, and cooked it to soften it as much as possible. That was breakfast for Norman and me. At least it was something. I made sure he ate enough to be full, and then I ate the few leftovers.

Kaito was getting ready to leave. She came into our room and told me there was a trap door in the dining room under the carpet. That was her private storage area. She looked stern as she told me I was not allowed to look into that area under any circumstance. I said I understood, and she spun around and flew out the door to wherever she was going. The situation was getting more bizarre each day.

We left the house again, and Norman held my hand as we walked down the street. I saw the man from the day before. When he bowed this time, I asked if I could speak with him. He said that would be fine.

"But we must move away from the street," he said, "around back, where no one will see me conversing with you." He told me his name was Susumu and that he'd known my deceased father-in-law, Mr. Konishi, who he said had been a fine man. He also knew my husband, but not as well.

When I asked him about finding food, he said that since the war ended, all food had been scarce. There was no rice around. Rationing was ongoing. Promised aid hadn't arrived. Susumu explained he and his wife were living on the little food he was able to purchase. "I received a large bag of sweet potatoes from a charity truck, though." Susumu told me he understood I needed food for the little boy. "I will help the grandson of Mr. Konishi and also his daughter-in-law.

I will wrap up a sweet potato each day for you and leave it on the side of your house."

I was near tears as I thanked him, and I told him my husband would reimburse him for his kindness. He said it was no problem, but I insisted and knew Ray would be grateful to hear that this kind neighbor had helped his wife and son. One sweet potato a day was not much, but it was something I could count on. I would keep looking. Hopefully, when Ray returned, he would be able to find more food.

I put the sweet potato down my dress so no one would see it. We returned home; Kaito had not yet returned. Curiosity got the best of me, so I moved a couple of chairs and slid the dining-room rug over. There was the trap door. I wondered if it was a war bunker; it was in an odd place. I pulled up the lever and lifted the door open.

The area beneath the floor was not huge, likely able to fit several people for a short while. Sitting right in the middle was a huge gunnysack full of sweet potatoes. Kaito and the neighbor seemed to have the same type of sweet potatoes. This crop must have survived the bomb and been delivered to residents by an agency. My sister-in-law would not share one bite with us, but the neighbor had. I would never forget Susumu's kindness; at that moment, he was an angel on earth to me.

I prepared the sweet potato and gave Norman half for dinner. He ate it all. He was just eighteen months old and needed his nutrition. Luckily, sweet potatoes were fairly nutritious.

Ray's home also had two wells, making drinking water plentiful. Chuji and Ray had talked about radiation from the bomb and what the radioactive fallout had contaminated. Had it dissipated by then? They had wondered together about this hidden danger posed by the atomic explosion, knowing many were suffering from radiation sickness. It made no difference to me. I would sacrifice any amount of food for myself to feed my son, and we would drink the water, contaminated or not. There were no alternatives.

The sweet potatoes arrived each day as promised, and I continued to share them with Norman. We ate the peel, and I checked the garbage for Kaito's peels too; sometimes I also found other things in the garbage. However, with each passing day, I felt myself getting weaker, which was predictable, considering the lack of food and nutrition. My stomach felt like it was eating itself. We stayed in our room—I lacked the energy to do anything more than retrieve the sweet potato, cook it, and serve it. All I cared about was taking care of Norman. Somehow, he understood the situation. He didn't complain about eating sweet potato every day or playing with nothing to speak of all day long in the bedroom. With our routine, I seldom saw Kaito, which I'm sure we both preferred.

Finally, the day came for Ray's arrival. I couldn't wait to see him.

Chapter 25

Famine

Ray's train was late, as ours had been. When he finally arrived and saw us, the expression on his face turned to panic, the perpetual smile he'd worn in Tokyo replaced with terror. I couldn't fake how weak I was. He hugged me; I'm sure he could see the agony on my face, because he told me how sorry he was for all we'd gone through. I told him about the kindest neighbor imaginable, Susumu, who kept us alive by dropping off a sweet potato each day. Ray asked about his sister, and I told him she'd only given us some miso soup. He started looking for her, furious. I stayed in the bedroom—I wanted no part of that confrontation.

Soon, I heard them arguing, getting louder and louder. She screamed that she would never help a Yankee. "How much nerve you had to bring her to Japan!"

Ray was clearly shocked that she was so indignant she'd given us almost nothing to eat. He screamed, "If Father were alive, he would disown you as his daughter for treating his daughter-in-law and grandson in this manner." Now I understood firsthand *why* Ray and his sister never got along.

For a second, I wondered what the future would hold, but quickly reality set in, and I wondered what I was going to eat tomorrow. At least Ray was home—but what could he do? I was filled with real fear for our survival. We were trapped now in this desolate place with little life left and no help anywhere. I'd never experienced such utter desperation. Living in three internment camps for years was offensive, but I'd never actually feared for my life.

When Ray returned to our bedroom, he said how deeply he regretted bringing us into this horrible situation. He'd known about the food shortages but thought they would be over soon. He'd never dreamed this would happen when he sent us to his home. "I will go to my uncle's home tomorrow and ask for food," he said. "I will ask some friends from my school days, too."

Ray and I weren't provided ration cards, either because we'd just arrived or because I wasn't a citizen. I didn't know. However, the food was scarce even for those possessing cards.

Ray looked at me. "I will do whatever it takes to look after us," he said.

He would swallow all his pride. The son of the rich man would beg for food.

I gave Ray instructions, and he got Norman ready for bed. Ray thought Norman was big enough to sleep in the twin bed in the bedroom next to ours. Norman hadn't slept in a regular bed yet, but this twin was low. Ray decided he'd be safe sleeping there, and he was. Ray returned to our room, and we both readied ourselves for bed. He held me tight; I knew he felt my pain. How could this have happened? He couldn't believe it. He whispered in my ear, "I am so sorry. I love you."

The next day, Ray took a bus and walked to his uncle's home. Ray's Uncle Zenichi helped as much as he could; he also was low on stored food but was able to give Ray some vegetables, mainly sweet potatoes. It didn't matter. It was food. When Ray returned, I cooked some of the vegetables in water and pretended we were eating soup. We didn't dare eat everything he'd brought at once. We all ate what was cooked. As always, I made sure Norman ate what he needed. He was a growing boy, and he came first. I felt a little better, but not a lot.

The effect of so little food for so long caught up to me. I was starting to feel dizzy and thought I might fall. I told Ray I could no longer walk, and I started crawling—I had no choice. I told him to leave Norman in the room with me with the door shut. I could manage with the two of us together while he was gone. I knew Ray felt like a failure as a husband, even though I didn't blame him for any of this. If he'd known what we would face, he wouldn't have expected us to come. Ray headed out to call on old friends he hadn't seen in years, not as a visitor but as a beggar. Some who were jealous of the rich man's son gave him the cold shoulder, but one family took pity on him and helped him out. He came back with several plates of food. We shared the food, making sure, of course, Norman ate all he wanted.

Our routine didn't change much for days. By that time, February of 1946, famine had engulfed Japan and Europe; war had destroyed much of the world's food supply and the means of delivery. I still crawled, since I thought I would fall if I tried to stand up and maybe hurt myself. Ray's whole purpose in life was to feed his family, and when he brought food home, I was so grateful, but the pains of hunger never subsided.

One day, the postman delivered a letter as Norman and I sat together on the floor. I scooted over to pick it up and read the news from Mom and Pop. They had settled in nicely in the St. Louis area. It took Pop a while to commute to work on two different buses, but at least he was working. Ed and Tom were going to school, and Mom was looking forward to an upcoming event.

> *On Saturday, March 2, one of the* Nisei *has organized a huge picnic in St. Louis for anyone in the area who came from Camp Rohwer. We are going to meet at Forest Park, a giant city park where the 1904 World's Fair was held. Pop has already figured out the buses to take. We are thrilled at the prospect of seeing many of our friends from camp at the picnic. After the picnic, we are going to take Ed and Tom for a visit to the zoo, which is free and is in the same park. We are hoping for an early spring day for our activities. I know you remember the days were warm by early March in southern Arkansas, but we are farther north now in St. Louis. We will enjoy the day no matter the weather.*

This news made me smile—my family seemed content and were getting on with their lives. As much as they'd anticipated the day of deliverance, I knew they'd been anxious about what would become of them. Mom closed by asking about how we were doing:

> *Dearest Janet, I haven't heard from you since your successful arrival in Japan. It made us happy to think about you, Ray, and Norman meeting up with Will in Tokyo. He writes of long days, since there is much to do. I think of you all day long. How anxiously I wait to hear from you. Please hug my precious grandson.*

*I cannot wait for the time I get to hug him myself. All my love—
Mom*

I needed to write back, but my news was all horrible. I didn't
want to worry them. They'd already worried about me before I'd even
arrived in Japan. Finally, I decided I couldn't wait any longer. Mom
would be beside herself if she didn't hear from me soon. I needed to
write and tell them the truth.

After we ate a little soup for lunch, I pulled out a piece of paper
and pencil and spent an hour or more writing. As weak as I was,
writing was not easy. I did not deceive them in any way.

*In case I don't survive, I want you to know how much I have
appreciated having the best parents any daughter could have. You
put us kids first, and you taught us what was important in life. I
was the luckiest girl to grow up with such a loving family. I don't
know if I have ever told you how grateful I am for all you did
for me. When we were facing being locked up by the government,
you kept us calm. Ray feels terrible for bringing Norman and me
over to Japan. He didn't expect the entire country would fall into
a famine. Whatever food we have each day, I make sure Norman
gets what he needs. You know I am strong—you made me that
way. I hope help comes soon. Your loving daughter—Janet*

I folded it up and put it in an envelope; Ray would mail it the
next day. I was sad to send this letter, but it wasn't right to hide what
was really happening from my family. I then wrote a letter to Will in
Tokyo, also explaining that we were struggling to find food. I didn't
want Will to feel bad for us; after all, what could he do? Maybe we
could return to an army base to live where there was food. I knew it
was a silly thought, but survival instincts were taking over.

When Ray and I went to bed that night, I started talking about
Norman—he was my top priority. He'd drunk a little milk when we
arrived in Tokyo, but not any since. I asked Ray if he could possibly
find milk. Ray said he would ask around. We both knew our young
son needed milk for growing bones at his tender age.

The next day, Ray returned with a whole bag of food. I quit asking where he found it to spare him further humiliation; he already

had to beg, though he'd grown up with servants, gardeners, and anything money could buy. We ate well that evening, and for the first time in a while, I stood up and walked around. I was feeling a bit of strength. Ray had found a woman down the road who owned a cow and had stopped and asked her if she would sell any milk. She'd said possibly. Ray and I agreed to walk over there with Norman the next day if I felt up to it.

I wasn't feeling normal, to be sure, but I thought I could make the walk when Ray described how far it was. The woman spoke primarily to him. When I asked a simple question, I felt the look of disdain. She looked down at my hands.

"I'll give you a small container—this size—of milk every day for a year. I want her diamond ring for payment."

Maybe it was the way she said it, or the way she looked at me: it was obvious she did not like me. My ring was precious, but it was just a ring. Milk for Norman was all I cared about. I whispered to Ray she could have my ring, if that's what it took. Ray told her we would accept her offer, and I slid off my wedding ring. We looked at each other as he took my ring and handed it over. It was a moment we would never forget.

Ray told her he would be back in the morning to get the first container of milk. As we walked away, the woman didn't muster a smile or any pleasantry—she just scowled at me. Immediately, Ray told me he would replace the ring when he got back on his feet, and I knew he would. Losing my wedding ring was tough, not because of the value of the ring but because of the demeaning way the lady had treated me. Otherwise, it didn't matter what Ray had paid for the ring; Norman's health was worth any price. Ray picked up Norman for the rest of the walk home down the dirt road.

Ray was up early and left before I was awake to retrieve our first round of milk. He greeted me with a smile: the milk ready and waiting. I got out a pan to heat up the milk for Norman.

"Oh no—Ray, something is wrong. Look at this milk!" I exclaimed, alarmed. It was not the white color of milk; it was watery looking with a yellowish tint. I put my nose in the pan. The milk smelled bad, too. Ray's short-lived pleasure was quickly dashed. We poured it back into the container.

Out the door he went to question the lady who had tricked him into giving up his wife's wedding ring. He was gone for a while and dismayed upon his return. He told me what had happened.

"The milk is bad, and I cannot feed it to my son," he'd said.

"That milk came from my cow this morning," she'd replied. "I gave you the same milk I drank." With that, she'd turned and walked away.

Ray had no choice but to walk away with his container of bad milk. He wanted to return, tell the lady our agreement was cancelled, and demand my ring back, but we were both too weak to do this.

I looked at Ray and swallowed. "What if she put poison in the milk and that's why it looks and smells bad?"

We looked at each other and our baby and pondered something horrible and unthinkable. We would not risk drinking any of the woman's milk and especially wouldn't feed it to Norman; we didn't trust the woman or her product. The ring was just gone.

Ray ate a sweet potato and left on his daily journey of food scrounging. He passed Kaito on his way out the door; neither spoke. We lived together, but we may as well have been in two separate homes. Norman and I went to the bedroom, where we spent most of our time. Ray returned with more food, enough that we could start to store a little extra. Had we turned a corner? We weren't sure. Ray was wearing himself out, eating little food despite making daily trips. And he seemed to have a persistent cough. He was the thinnest I'd ever seen him. He did muster enough energy to put paper over the broken windows and clean up the glass pieces still lying around. As soon as businesses opened up, he would find someone to replace the windows. Of course, the paper wasn't insulation, but at least it limited the stiff breeze.

When we went to bed that evening, I told Ray I needed his help with something. After the incident with the lady and her cow, I'd given up hope of finding milk locally, at least for now. I wanted to see if there was any way to resurrect nursing Norman again myself.

"Is that possible?" he asked quizzically.

It had been eight months since my milk production dried up, and there was no doctor or nurse to consult. I explained how Nurse Gladys had massaged my breasts to get the mammary glands stimulated in the hospital. She'd worked tirelessly, and her patience with the process had brought success. I needed Ray to help me; I was determined to give it my best shot. I wanted Ray to vigorously massage me several times, and then I would see if Norman would latch on again. Ray thought this would be more fun than work, and maybe it was for him. I was still weak, so I wondered if my broken body was capable of reviving milk production.

Twice a day, Ray diligently massaged me. After a couple of days, I picked up Norman and put him to my breast. He recognized and understood where I'd placed his mouth, and he latched on. But sadly, there was nothing. Ray and I were both discouraged but not defeated. We remained hopeful. I knew to drink and eat well from my days in the hospital, so I drank lots of water and tried to eat more. Ray said it didn't matter if we used up the little bit of food we'd stored; I needed to eat. We continued the routine for several more days, and each time Norman tried to nurse, there was nothing—until, one day, I picked him up, held him to me, and couldn't believe my eyes: he was sucking and swallowing! Ray's eyes lit up, too. I pulled Norman off temporarily and saw milk droplets sitting on my nipple. What an exhilarating moment! Heaven had answered my prayers. I wanted to scream for joy—I was feeding my son again.

Once my breasts started producing again, I was able to build up the supply so Norman could nurse three times a day. He seemed satisfied, so I hoped he was getting what he needed. As happy as I was, though, nursing was a drain on my weak body. I moved around only when needed; I had no energy and at times crawled again.

One day, Ray came into the room with a package in his hands. The return address was one he didn't know. He opened it, and out fell five containers of Spam, along with a short note from Will: "Thought you could use these, even though I know you never wanted to see this after leaving camp. I used a false address on the package to disguise mail from a US serviceman. Your brother—Will."

Ray and I hugged each other and couldn't believe our good fortune. We hadn't eaten any meat for weeks. I wished I could hug and thank my brother. Those five cans of Spam were such a relief, like finding water in the desert.

After eating some Spam and vegetables we'd stored for later use, I felt much stronger. I also knew we could run out of food again at any time. Despite this, Ray wanted to take a bus into Hiroshima to walk around the city where the bomb had dropped. The day of our outing was pleasantly sunny. The closer the bus drew to Hiroshima, the worse the landscape became. Some homes lacked roofs. Many homes were just piles of timbers, and others were tilted and ready to fall over at any second. There was rubble and desolation as far as I could see.

What I saw next, I will never forget: dead bodies still lying on the side of the street. These people had evidently been walking or running when they were killed instantly by the blast of the nuclear bomb. Likely, all their family also perished, so there was no one to retrieve their remains; Hiroshima had no functioning local government or national soldiers to remove the dead. Most were partially incinerated by the explosion. I heard one man on the bus say that, in the months since the mushroom cloud of destruction had befallen Hiroshima, those bodies had turned to dust.

This left a permanent imprint on my soul. I'd just seen the horror of war myself and lived through it in the Japanese internment camps. Would mankind ever learn a lesson, so this would never happen again? Would there ever be a world without fighting to seize control? America was the savior of world order but had also crossed a line into destruction capable of ending mankind. The aftermath of war in Hatsukaichi was impactful for me, but ground zero of nuclear warfare was more than I'd preferred to see. I would never forget that day or those sights.

When we arrived in downtown Hiroshima, I saw the Genbaku Dome of the Hiroshima Prefectural Industrial Promotion Hall, which had survived the blast. The bomb had exploded almost directly above the dome, but earthquake reinforcements had supported it. The obvious extent of the bomb was stunning—complete annihilation as far as I could see. We were lucky to live in a home that merely had blown-out windows. The city was rubble. Ray was emotional, remembering what the city had been; I was overwhelmed by the totality of destruction and visible death. Ray shielded Norman's eyes. He didn't want to linger, so we returned to the bus stop to ride back to our home, seven or eight miles away.

As we returned, Ray was emotionally drained by the horror we'd seen. I was weak and weary myself, but he didn't look well; his mental and physical fatigue was evident. He continued to have a chronic cough. I begged him to get more rest. He assured me he would.

One day after Ray departed for his daily food search, I decided to go for a short walk in a different direction. Holding Norman's hand, I set off down the dirt-packed road. Most of the homes we passed were still in various stages of destruction. It almost felt like a spring day, and the air was fresh after a big rain the previous night. I'd dressed Norman in a heavy sweater and draped my overcoat over my shoulders, as it wasn't as cold as I'd thought. A passing woman ignored me. I understood this treatment and how I was evaluated by the local people of Ray's hometown. My clothes, shoes, and overcoat were not Japanese, and when I spoke Japanese, I sounded different, using the Japanese of the lower class. I was not acceptable in any way.

Several men stood conversing on the corner, and I paid little attention to them. I thought one of the men smiled, so I smiled back. Without any warning, one of the other men turned toward me, grabbed my overcoat off my shoulders, and tossed it in the mud puddle on the side of the lane. The other men laughed. I lunged toward the puddle, releasing Norman from my hand, and lifted my coat. It dripped muddy water. All I could do was drop my head, take Norman's hand, reverse direction, and move as quickly as possible toward home. I dared not say anything. Would these men continue to harass me? I wanted to cry but did not. Mom had been right: everyone in Japan hated me because I was an American.

When we got home, I put my coat in the bathtub, but there was no soap; it didn't seem vital when we didn't have food to eat. I scrubbed my coat several times using a sponge, but still I couldn't get some of the mud out of it. I didn't have the energy to keep scrubbing, so finally, I gave up and hung my coat to dry, although it was still covered with mud stains.

Everything hit me all at once. I took Norman into the bedroom, shut the door, and fell down on the bed. I felt myself unraveling in every way. The physical and mental strain was affecting my ability to function. Through my trials of the war, I'd considered myself strong of mind and body, but right now, I felt woefully weak. Maybe I was losing hope for my future. I was nursing my son, giving up precious energy, and barely keeping myself going. Would the famine continue indefinitely? Would I ever get home to America again? Would I spend the rest of my life in a town where all the people despised me?

I felt alone. I missed my family. I needed to summon some adrenalin to keep functioning. All I could do was pray for strength to keep going and keep myself sane.

Ray was upset when he heard about the incident on the street. He wanted to know who had violated his wife and thrown her coat in the mud. I heard him outside talking with two ladies and asking one about the men hanging around the corner. The lady told Ray she had no idea who they were. And then she became rude.

"Every girl in our community would have married you," his neighbor, Mrs. Ishakawa, nearly screamed at him. "You could have had your pick of any of them. And you turn around and marry an American girl and bring her back here. She does not deserve to live in this mansion. You should be ashamed of yourself for disgracing your father in this way. He would never have allowed her to be the mistress of his home."

Ray knew better than to get into a heated argument. "She is my wife, and I love her," he said.

When he came in the house, I told him I'd heard it all through the paper over the windows.

He paused, then smiled. "I was absolutely not interested in any of the girls in this town at all. Sorry, Mrs. Ishakawa."

"It's not important to me to find the man who grabbed my coat and threw it in the mud," I said. "What's done is done. What can you do now besides get in an argument, or worse?" He finally agreed to just let it go.

When Ray returned from food searching the next day, he carried the Tokyo newspaper from the prior week. He was intrigued by a story from America. Churchill had been at Westminster College in Missouri giving a speech about a new war—a "cold war" between the United States and the Soviet Union. We wondered if Mom and Pop lived close to where Churchill spoke. His stirring speech was alarming: he warned of a world in a new form of conflict. After just seven months of peace, the seeds of war were already being planted again in Europe, although the United States prevailed in keeping the Soviet Union out of Japan. Ray and I concluded that Churchill understood world affairs better than anyone, since he expressed concern for the common people who were now experiencing the war's aftermath: famine. We were living this misery personally.

For so many weeks, all Ray had thought about was finding food for us, and we were surviving, although we were still hungry often. It had become a way of life: if Ray brought home some food, we hesitated to eat it all, because we didn't know if we would have enough the next day. He was overwhelmed by the prospect of rebuilding his family's property. The home, gardens, and farm were all in ruin, and his father's cash had been depleted in the years since his death. Spring was coming soon, and Ray had no knowledge of farming. His father's five hectares—about twelve and a half acres or so—was a huge parcel by Japanese standards. He was going to ask his father's brother for assistance, since his uncle had farmed for his dad in the past. Ray knew some of the land was for vegetables, but most was for rice, which required two adjacent parcels. Farming the land and harvesting a crop would hopefully mean the end of our food struggles.

The mail arrived with another package for us, this one from Mom in America. Out fell hard candy and a package of rice. We hadn't eaten any rice for what seemed like years, and we were both excited to eat it for dinner; it seemed a feast for a king. I was thrilled to read Mom's letter—a lifeline to my family, my home, and my country. I knew she must have been overwrought with emotion when she read my letter. Her return letter said she prayed for our situation to improve and asked me to keep writing as often as possible, as she could hardly bear worrying about us without being able to help more than sending a package. Like Will's, Mom's package meant more than she could imagine. It was another gift dropped from heaven.

Also in the mail was a letter addressed to Mr. Konishi that said it was official business. Ray opened the letter, which was written in both Japanese and English. As he read the letter, his face changed from curiosity to shock. The letter was from General Douglas MacArthur, the Supreme Commander for the Allied Powers, or SCAP for short. Ray looked grim as he turned and walked away.

"Oh no—I may lose everything."

He started coughing again. I could tell he wanted to be alone as he walked out the back door and sat on the step. He put his head down between his legs; I think he was crying. A rice dinner now meant nothing. What could possibly have been so upsetting in the letter from General MacArthur? It wasn't as if the general knew Ray personally; plus, Ray had helped the military with translating after arriving in Japan, so he couldn't possibly have done something to offend anyone.

I left him alone to ponder the contents of the letter. He would tell me in time. I prepared the precious rice.

Chapter 26

Rice Returns

Norman and I went for a walk after Ray left to visit his uncle and ask about food. We went a new way—I wasn't going to venture near the corner where the men accosted me. I saw a lady sitting by herself on her porch. It seemed her home hadn't been damaged as severely as some, but part of the roof was missing. I smiled at her.

She replied sweetly, "Hello. How are you?"

This was most unexpected, as I didn't receive a friendly greeting anywhere else in Hatsukaichi. I stopped Norman. "We're getting a bit of fresh air," I said.

She smiled. "Are you an American?"

Oh no, I thought. *Here we go again. No sense in deceiving her.* "Yes, I am. I have only been in Japan for a few months."

Amazingly, she didn't snarl or even glare at me. Instead, she paused before saying, "My name is Hiroko, and I was born in America, but I have lived all my life in Japan. I have married a *Nisei* man who came to Japan before the war. I dream of learning to speak English and going to America someday."

I smiled back at her. "I have been a translator for quite a few years, and I would be happy to teach you English when I get back on my feet. Right now, I'm too weak to help you; we never have enough food to eat."

Hiroko replied, "I know it's a problem everywhere. But my husband has been able to find us food from family elsewhere in Japan, and he brings back big bags of vegetables. However, we have not eaten rice in months. Where do you live?"

When I told her, she knew the home. Of course—everyone knew the Konishi mansion. "The lady in the store ordered me to leave," I explained, "and you are the first person I've spoken to who doesn't hate me for being American."

Hiroko's face seemed gentle. "I am very sorry for you. I know this hatred for Americans will not change. Tonight after ten o'clock, I will bring a bag of vegetables and leave them by your door when no one is around. I want to help you, but I know I would be ridiculed for calling on you in the daytime. We have plenty of vegetables now—some beets and potatoes and daikon, I am sure. I don't mean to be rude to you by coming at that hour."

I quickly interjected. "Oh, that is kind of you, and thank you with all my heart. I understand and appreciate that you would go to the trouble to help me. I will come again when I'm stronger, and we will find time together for you to learn English. It has been such a pleasure to meet you, Hiroko."

She had brightened my outlook and my day. Maybe I'd made my first friend in Japan—even if we were forced to be secret friends.

Ray returned and told me we were all invited to meet many members of his family the following Sunday. They would serve us dinner. Ray said he was looking forward to showing off his wife and son to his uncles, cousins and other extended family. That made me smile, but I wasn't feeling at all attractive. "We will do our best to look as presentable as possible to meet your family," I said. With no soap in the house, I never felt quite clean. But I was looking forward to this family gathering.

As I was getting ready for bed, I slipped outside, found the bag of vegetables, and showed them to Ray. He wasn't a big fan of beets, but they looked like gold—their shoots were still attached, so it was obvious they'd been picked recently. We decided to have beets for breakfast—why not? It was food and energy for the day.

The night before our Sunday dinner visit, I took over an hour to wrap little ringlets of hair around my finger and secure them with bobby pins. I wanted to do my best to look impressive for Ray, since he was excited to introduce me to his extended family. However, my best dress no longer fit me smartly; it just hung on me after the months of uncontrollable weight loss. I asked if Kaito was going, and Ray said no; she'd visited with the relatives a month before we arrived. I guessed the uncle probably understood that brother and sister didn't get along and didn't invite her anyway.

Sunday afternoon, we all dressed as best we could and prepared to leave. Ray smiled at me and said, "They're all going to love you." I wasn't sure, but they were family, and I was hoping for the best.

Ray's uncle's home was typical of the area—not of the size of Ray's home. When we arrived, the kitchen and dining room were crowded. Norman and I were introduced to each person, and all were polite and welcomed us. Dinner was simple; this was not a time of plenty, and I knew the uncle had already helped us with food many times.

Ray told his uncle and the other men he wanted to speak with them after we finished the meal. The men were all served by the women first, and the women and children ate the leftovers—no rice remained from the small amount served. After eating, the men went to another room for their discussions, and I concentrated on learning everyone's name. All were cordial and spoke to me with deference, since I was Ray's wife; it was nice to be treated with respect for the first time since arriving at Ray's home.

The evening was informative for me, and I learned much by observing and listening to the conversations. It was obvious the ladies took note of my shoes, as I didn't have the traditional Japanese slippers; I could feel them staring at my feet. I learned much about how Ray's family lived and more about Japanese culture and complex ancient customs. Traditions ran deep; things were done a certain way because they had been that way for hundreds or thousands of years. The tradition of bowing, the cuisine, the dialect, the clothes, the different forms of Buddhism, the way people entered a home, the way people were matched for marriage—I needed to learn these details as best as I could if I ever hoped to fit in.

Observing the real Japanese culture that evening also helped me understand Ray. I imagined he'd surely been a subject of conversation when he'd goofed off and failed at the university and then was sent by his father to America to grow up. But I also understood he'd grown up in a highly male-centered world. Mom and the other women in America kept traditional matronly roles of raising the children, cooking, and caring for the home, but the women of Japan, with their correctness about everything they did, with so much structure and so little independence—all of this was strikingly different from my American upbringing. It seemed so much of a person's future in Japan depended on that person's sex and family of birth. If two women had the same name, the way each name was spelled was determined by whether the woman came from a wealthy family or not. It was even the law in Japan that all inheritance passed only to the eldest male heir. For centuries, Japanese customs had changed little. America was more relaxed about everything. When I later told Ray I was learning about the ways of Japan, he smiled and said he thought there was a lot of silliness about many of their ways. But I knew if I wanted to fit in, I would have to understand the culture. I also told Ray that when we could afford to go shopping, I needed to purchase a pair of Japanese slipper shoes—all the women at the gathering were wearing these, and I noticed them looking at my leather button-down shoes. Ray said he would be sure to get me to a store for these as soon as possible.

I truly enjoyed the evening meeting his family, and at the end of it, his uncle sent us home with another bag of six sweet potatoes. We both thanked everyone for the lovely evening and for the bag of food. On the way home, Ray told me it had been a constructive evening with his relatives. He'd firmed up their commitments to help him farm his land, since it was time to begin preparing for the upcoming crop, and then he'd told them he planned to give each some of his land; he didn't know if it would be before or after the season.

As part of the occupation of Japan, MacArthur had the final decision on everything. Many of MacArthur's reforms were much needed, and probably the most important change was setting up a democratic government and a new constitution, in which the emperor's status was reduced to only that of a figure head, with no authority over the people. But there was one thing MacArthur did that I felt was terribly wrong: he "stole" the farmland from the landowners and distributed it to the tenant farmers. This was something communists would do, not America. I read the news with my own eyes when Ray let me the read the letter from MacArthur. He would only be allowed to keep a small parcel and the home, and the government would pay almost no compensation. Shocking! As I would learn later, angry common people needed someone to blame for the war. Many were resentful of the rich landowners, who they believed supported the Japanese government's intention to wage war to seize more land in other Asian countries. MacArthur was told the landowners had taken advantage of the tenant farmers, which wasn't true—the farmers were paid 50 percent of the crop, which was and is the typical arrangement. Also, the communists told MacArthur that the redistribution would improve productivity. In the end, 66 percent of the land rented out (over four million acres) of tiny Japan's land was expropriated, and production declined. Had Ray not given away his land, the government would have seized his as well.

To Ray, it was important to keep the land in the family, so he decided to share it with his uncles. His family was delighted to know they would receive some of Ray's inheritance, and they promised to oversee Ray's rice paddies, which required much skill. Ray was pleased with his decision; he always seemed to find a way to share with others, especially family. I admired this quality, which I'd seen back in the early days, when we'd been just friends at camp.

By the time we got home, we were all tired, but I needed to nurse Norman before he went to bed. As I held him in my lap and leaned against the big wooden headboard, we both fell sound asleep. When I woke, I cautiously pulled him away from me under the covers and let him stay the night in bed with us. We were all touching each other, and I felt our close family bond. For once, Ray and I didn't go to bed hungry.

As the weeks wore on, we weren't as hungry, although we ate little meat or protein of any kind and had little starch to give us energy, since Susumu had stopped leaving sweet potatoes after Ray returned from the base. We primarily consumed vegetables; we'd learned to eat anything edible and be grateful for it. Hiroko continued to drop off bags of vegetables periodically, and I would walk by and tell her how much I appreciated her help. Hiroko and I also planned an evening together to start working on her English. Some nights I still went to bed hungry, but others not as much. Despite our sparse diet, I continued nursing Norman.

When spring hit, the farm bustled with activity, primarily in the rice paddies. Kaito kept to herself as much as ever, but Ray decided to discuss hiring a marriage broker for her. As head of the family, he was responsible for arranging a marriage for his sister. She agreed and looked forward to finding a husband appropriate for her. She said little to me; we simply coexisted.

The house was also being repaired. A construction contractor from Hiroshima was back in business. A friend of Ray's father, he showed up at the house one warm, sunny spring day and installed new windows in our home. He told Ray there would be no charge; that was the least he could do to help his friend's family. It was obvious how much Ray's dad had helped many people over the years; I heard people speak of his kindness toward others in need.

With the windows in place, it seemed time to get the house back in order. In the earlier years when Ray's father was alive, a full-time maid and gardener had looked after the house; now, we had no money to hire help. I was determined to get rid of the dirt and despair apparent all over the once-grand mansion. But how would I go about bringing the sparkle back to Ray's home? The thought overwhelmed me. I wasn't sure what to do with the floors, which were made of luxurious tatami wood—I was used to tile; I didn't think I should take a mop and water to the floors, since that might harm the wood. For my first sweep of the house, I collected the broken items from the shelves, dusted everything else, and swept the floors with a broom. I was exhausted; it was a big house, and I wasn't long on energy.

Ray found a used Singer sewing machine in town, which was a welcome addition to our home. He also found a store with material and sewing supplies, so I was able to purchase some fabrics. Norman needed some new clothes; he was outgrowing everything. I created my own patterns and started making clothes for all three of us.

Soon it was July, and Norman was two years old. He was a typical busy boy, investigating everything in his world. Through the summer months, I tried to reach out to women I saw in the neighborhood, hoping to find another two-year-old to invite for playtime. But no matter how hard I tried to fit in, somehow the neighbors knew I was an American—or they knew I was the woman Ray Konishi had married. They typically weren't rude to my face, though that happened, too. Sometimes, I would slip and say an English word; all conversation would stop, and the women would give me cold stares. Their message was clear: they weren't interested in being friends. I did meet with Hiroko when possible, and she enjoyed learning English; helping her made me feel useful.

Mom's letters and boxes were always a highlight when they arrived. She told me Marian was being courted by a *Nisei* man she'd met at a picnic. I was happy for Marian; maybe she would be getting married soon. Mom sent coffee in her box with the letter. Ray and I didn't care that much for coffee, but it was quite scarce in Japan, so it gave me an idea. I took the bag of coffee to the grocery store that had thrown me out in earlier months. When I showed it to the lady and asked her if she would like to swap the coffee for other items, she was eager to trade. This opened up a new world for me; I got some flour and chestnuts in exchange for the coffee. I immediately wrote Mom to thank her once more and tell her how well the coffee had worked out; I asked her to please send more if she could.

Will continued sending anonymous boxes as often as he could. In August, he sent a bag of sugar. That was like sending gold; there had been no sugar anywhere for as long as I could remember. He also sent a letter telling us he'd met a local girl from Tokyo who, it seemed, had started waiting for him to drive through her neighborhood as part of his community outreach routine. He told me about when he first saw her; they'd smiled at each other. And then he'd noticed she seemed to be waiting for him each day, so he finally stopped his jeep to say hello. She was too shy to speak with him and blushed when he spoke to her, but he told us of her gorgeous, innocent beauty. After this had continued for some time, he'd asked her to go to a movie. I smiled when I read his letter; Will was falling in love. I sat down the same day to write Will and thank him for sending along the sugar and other treasures.

Two neighbor ladies mentioned they'd seen the boxes delivered to us. These ladies were not especially friendly and seemed like typical nosy neighbors. To be polite, I told them about my family in America sending us food, and I offered to share some with them. We were all in the same food-shortage boat, so I wanted to be a good neighbor and share. I gave both of them some hard candies and part of my bag of sugar. They were delighted and scurried off. Soon others also showed up when they saw boxes delivered; I was sharing food with women who did not want to befriend me.

Ray still made trips in search of food, but he was also learning from his family and others about how to grow rice. It was a complicated process. But more than farming, Ray was keenly interested in restoring his Japanese garden. He read books and talked with friends and relatives about gardening techniques and tricks and the symbolism each part of the garden represented. Slowly but surely, the garden came back to life as Ray worked meticulously on each component.

Finally, it was time to harvest the rice crop. Ray shared the rice with his relatives who farmed the land and who would soon own some of it as well. He also took a big bag of rice to Susumu to thank him for helping feed his wife and son. He put the rest into storage in a shed by our home. This was a moment of glory for Ray and me: our languishing existence we'd suffered over the last eight months was almost behind us. Rice was more than something to eat; it was sacred nutrition to the Japanese. It was the sustenance for our bodies and souls.

We prepared a wonderful rice dinner for Ray's relatives with pickled daikon I made to celebrate the harvest. We no longer feared for our lives. Once the rice crop was harvested, the men planted sweet potatoes in the fields. They would also harvest other vegetables, such as carrots, onions, and daikon.

From that day forward, we ate rice every day. The tables soon turned between us and our neighbors as others asked us for handouts. Ray never turned anyone away, even those who had previously been rude to me. If people came, he gave them a pound or so of rice. There was plenty in storage for our family until the next year's crop, so he was happy to share his bounty.

Rice was being harvested all over the area, bringing needed food and hope to the people. Soon after the rice crop was complete, rice wine, or sake, became available. Ray enjoyed getting together with the men, drinking sake, and gambling, particularly the game of mahjong. They gathered at the home of one of the men, a bachelor, for their evenings of merriment. I understood it was a common practice in Japan. Pop had played a few card games and enjoyed some sake when I was growing up, but that was a special occasion, maybe once a year, and he'd gambled only pennies. For Ray and the other men of Hatsukaichi, it became a weekly gathering. Sometimes they played more often.

Ray also met some Australian men who were in Hiroshima as part of the clean-up work. They swapped cigarettes for rice—which meant Ray started smoking again. He already coughed often, and smoking surely made it worse. However, he enjoyed talking to these men, and they soon all became comrades.

Thus, the rice crop, which had been so anticipated and so vital to our future, also gave rise to Ray's new vices of smoking, drinking, and gambling. I didn't complain about his new activities, but I was concerned about his health, particularly his chronic cough. I also knew he didn't have a lot of cash; his dad had been clever to only allow a certain number of cash withdrawals over certain times, hoping his estate would remain intact. I wasn't sure what remained, but I was alarmed when Ray told me it was becoming depleted.

Soon, it was fall. One night, there was a chill in the air; Ray and I snuggled together and put a blanket on the bed. Ray told me how much he appreciated how hard I worked to keep the house clean, bringing the majesty back to his once-grand mansion. He knew, as large as the house was, how many hours of toil it took to clean it, and I was still both making our clothes and washing them by hand. Then he told me he had an idea he thought I would enjoy. He suggested we contact my mom's family and pop's family and plan an outing to meet them. I had also thought about meeting my cousins and aunts and uncles—my extended family. Wrapped tightly in his arms, I thanked him for his efforts to make me happy in our difficult situation and told him I would get to work collecting names and addresses from Mom as soon as possible.

During the winter months, I mainly stayed inside, working on sewing projects and playing with Norman. The weather wasn't severe, since Hatsukaichi was in southern Japan, close to the bay. People still asked us for rice, but now it was available in the stores. Many still waited for their homes to be repaired, due to lack of money and of carpenters and other installers. People also asked us for wood to heat their homes from the large stockpile we'd accumulated. We never turned anyone away empty handed. Will told us he was getting married, but he said it would be a small gathering in Tokyo; he looked forward to the day we could meet his new wife. I could tell from Will's letters he'd found his life's love.

The marriage broker told Ray he'd found a suitable match for Kaito—a successful man, a sake maker, who could give her a lifestyle to which she was accustomed. He was twelve years older than she was—also a good omen; this was also the same age difference as my parents'. Kaito met the prospective husband, and agreed to the match. Ray was delighted to find a husband for Kaito and even more excited knowing she would soon leave our home. He spoke with Kaito, who was obviously pleased with her future husband, and Ray wasn't needed for all the wedding planning now underway. Thankfully, her new husband paid for the entire affair. Ray was also relieved to learn that we were most assuredly not invited guests. He looked forward to their springtime wedding, since he would no longer have to deal with his sister. Even at this transitional moment, there was no familial bond between them.

One day, Ray met a young doctor from northern Japan who had just finished his schooling. He was coming to work in the Hiroshima area, where thousands still suffered from effects of the atomic bomb, especially radiation disease. Ray told Dr. Yamaguchi about his cough, and the doctor thought he should investigate. I knew Ray hadn't returned to vitality, even after our diet had improved with the rice harvest. Dr. Yamaguchi ran tests on Ray and stopped by our house to discuss them with him, as he was walking down our road anyway. The doctor looked at Ray and said, "I am sorry to tell you this, but you have tuberculosis. With the poor sanitation after the war, many people have this disease and other diseases, too."

We froze. The doctor added he could get some medicine for Ray, but likely he would live only to his early forties. I started peppering the doctor with questions, most of which he couldn't answer. Dr. Yamaguchi also said he didn't know how long he would be staying in the area, since he hadn't been able to find a relatively permanent place to live. Immediately, Ray said, "You can come live with us; we have plenty of room."

"That's a kind offer," the doctor said. "But aren't there rules prohibiting people who aren't family from moving in with you?"

"Of course," Ray said. "There are rules for everything in Japan. I'm not concerned. How about this: you may live in our home upstairs, where you will have complete privacy, and dine with us, and all I'll ask in return is that you take care of me."

"That would be very kind of you—thank you," Dr. Yamaguchi replied. "I have one immediate request of you: quit smoking."

"I understand," Ray said.

I could tell Ray was close to breaking down, so I asked the doctor to follow me upstairs and showed him his private bedroom and bathroom. When I returned downstairs, Ray was in the bedroom, trying to conceal he was crying. I hugged him and began to cry with him. We were already emotionally weak, which made it all the harder to absorb the diagnosis of tuberculosis. I summoned the strength to take Ray's hand and tell him he was going to survive—I was sure of it. He looked into my eyes, and I could tell he wanted to believe me but didn't share my confidence. Over the next few months, he demonstrated determination to follow the doctor's orders, forcing himself to quit smoking and taking every pill the doctor ordered for him.

Then it was time to visit Pop's relatives, with whom I'd been in touch on a couple of occasions. We hopped on the bus for Nagoya. It was a marvelous visit; I was thrilled to meet Pop's eldest sister and her family. Pop's family business had been quite prosperous through the years; he no doubt would have joined it himself if he hadn't left Japan to avoid the war and the upcoming draft. Interestingly, none of the wealth of Pop's family business ever made its way to America.

Pop's brother, my uncle, ran the family rental business, which he showed us. He explained that some seasons were extremely busy and others were slow, and by the end of the conversation, Ray had offered to assist my uncle when he needed help and Ray was free. My uncle said he would find accommodations for us, and so it was settled; we would visit at a future date and Ray would help with the business while we were there. Ray was all smiles; I knew we could use the cash, too.

We also made a journey to meet some of Mom's family; they had mainly scattered, so we weren't able to meet many on her side. Those we met were polite and seemed happy we'd come to visit them. It was quite evident Mom's family were victims of the war; they'd been poor before the war, so they struggled even more facing food and clothing shortages afterward. We made note to bring bags of rice when next we visited.

Since we weren't invited to Kaito's wedding, Ray suggested we take a sightseeing trip to Tokyo for a few days and clear out of the way of the wedding preparations. Maybe we would be lucky enough to see the cherry blossom trees in full bloom. Ray also wanted to show me the beautiful Meiji Jingu Shrine. He made a hotel reservation for two nights and bought train tickets for the three of us. We enjoyed a lovely trip and saw some of the breathtaking vistas with hundreds of blooming cherry-blossom trees lining the riverbanks.

Upon our return, we found the house drastically different. It was as if we'd been robbed—but the robber was family. Kaito had taken the ornate statues and all the silk pieces, fine linens, and anything impermanent in nature. Ray was furious with her for not asking, not sharing any of it with us, and not caring how she offended him. As awful as it felt at that moment, I encouraged Ray not to pursue his sister and stir up the hatred between them. She was gone, and the barren house felt peaceful, so we carried on with the house stripped of its finery.

In July 1947, Norman turned three. I took him to a pediatrician for the first time since leaving America. The doctor thought he was doing well, but he told me it was time to stop nursing him. Milk was now available in the store, he said, and the cow's milk would be best for Norman at this stage of his growth. He complimented me for my fortitude but said it would also be good for my health to give up milk production. It only took a week to transition Norman to drinking milk from a cup, and I dried up quickly. I didn't feel as emotional giving up nursing for the second time. I knew it was time.

Over the next couple of years, Ray took Norman and me to see many sights. Ray's tuberculosis had thankfully moved into remission, and his health, while not great, seemed to have stabilized; nevertheless, he managed to carry on with all activities. And we really enjoyed traveling together. One of my favorite sights was a giant statue of Great Buddha in the Kōtoku-in Temple, which dated to 1252. We also visited my relatives with the leasing business, and Ray enjoyed working there several times. Once he mistakenly recorded a plow as the rental, though it was a horse; luckily, my uncle wasn't angry, and my family thoroughly enjoyed teasing Ray for his error.

We now ate all the rice we wanted, but still we didn't have much protein in our diet. Ray got a telephone installed in the house—the first telephone in the mansion. Most people didn't have a phone. When ours was ready, I wished I could call Mom and Pop; I missed hearing their voices.

One day, as I was leaving to go shopping, I told Norman and Ray I would return in a few hours. Four-year-old Norman looked up and said, "Mom, could you bring me home a brother or a sister?"

Ray and I both laughed, but it was a difficult moment. We had resumed our intimacy when we finally felt up to it, and secretly I hoped I would conceive another child—a miracle baby—despite what I'd been told when Norman was born. Although I still dreamed of having a daughter, somehow I knew I would never fall pregnant again. Ray and I were content with and grateful for our son, and we carried on with our lives, neither of us putting pressure on the other; however, though we understood it would probably never happen, we both dreamed of another child.

Since Norman didn't have a brother or sister, I made sure we owned pets. We got a dog and a cat, both of which Norman adored. Somehow a goat adopted us, too—one more friend for Norman. Every morning, the goat showed up and baaed at me, so I fed it; then later in the day, it would be back and baaing again, so I would feed it again. Sometimes, it climbed on our shed and couldn't get down, so it baaed because it was stuck. Norman was much more amused with the goat than I was. The goat found a soft spot with me, though, and soon it was a frequent visitor.

I wrote often to Mom and Pop in Missouri, Will in Tokyo, Christine in California, Loretta in Hawaii, and now Marian, who was newly married and living in St. Louis. Fran, Ed, and Tom were still living with Mom and Pop. They moved from St. Charles to the city of St. Louis, where they rented a larger row house. They said it was easier to get around, and they enjoyed living in the city. Pop's day was much shorter now that he lived closer to his landscaping employment. Mom still sent coffee, and I still used it for swapping.

Mom learned through an old Stockton friend that a classmate of mine, Charlotte Kuranishi, was now living in Hiroshima. Mom passed along Charlotte's address. I put a letter in the mail the following day, and soon we set a date to get together. I was thrilled to see an American friend from my childhood. We laughed about old stories from our school days and shared experiences from our years during and after camp life. After our visit, we promised to get together again.

For our sixth wedding anniversary on September 12, 1949, Ray presented me with a little package. He made sure to give me a gift every year, some bigger and grander than others, and I always gave him a gift, too. This year, the package was tiny. I opened it up and found a sparkling diamond ring. Ray looked at me and said, "Will you marry me?"

I burst out laughing—and almost crying, too. "You mean I haven't been married all this time? Of course, I am now and will forever belong to you."

Since trading my diamond ring for the bad milk, I'd been wearing a simple band—maybe gold or maybe not—that Ray had found in an old antique store. I wondered whether the woman with the cow wore my previous wedding ring or if she'd sold it for cash. The new diamond was more smashing than my first one. I told Ray I would wear it proudly, and he never stopped smiling all evening. Ray's thoughtfulness touched me. He also promised to get me a perfect strand of Japanese pearls. All I could do was smile and once again enjoy my doting husband.

In the fall of 1949, it was time for Norman to start school. I had taught him colors and numbers, and he was even reading—all in Japanese, of course. I was a typical mother taking her son to school on the first day: I hid my emotion, but it was a milestone, and I walked home thinking of the day he was born. Norman was wearing a new sweater his grandma had made him, which looked smart with his shorts. It didn't occur to me the sweater could look somehow "foreign" and draw attention to Norman.

A week later, he came home extremely upset. Some of the boys had grabbed his sweater and thrown it into a shallow river. They'd also teased him about being an American, saying he shouldn't be in *their* school. Norman had turned and run home. I went to the river, retrieved the sweater, and worked as hard as I could to get the stains washed out; I was only partially successful.

After this, Norman was scared of the bullies. I thought it coincidental that we'd both encountered bullies in our early school years. I went to speak with his teacher, who was sympathetic and said she would assist in any way she could. However, she told me that Norman shouldn't wear nice clothes and sweaters to school, because it drew attention to him and made him look somehow American. Still, the teasing continued to some degree, and Norman endured it. I hurt for my son when he walked in the door with mud spots all over the back of his clothes where the bullies had thrown mud at him. There was no other school to take him to. I was helpless to do any more for him, and I worried each day how he would be treated.

We received another package from Mom with a dozen large Hershey bars in it. Norman took them to school and gave everyone half of a Hershey bar—sweet bribery that seemed to help temporarily decrease the badgering. Also, I often made rice cakes, and sent them to school for Norman to share; these were a hit, too.

As I explained these developments to Ray, he was quite concerned about Norman. His son, who arrived in Japan at just eighteen months old, was being picked on at school for being an American. Ray was not happy. As we lay in bed together, Ray pulled me over to him and said, "Will it ever stop?"

I looked at him. "Do you think there's any way we could go back to America?"

He only said he hoped someday we could. How I dreamed to go home.

PART 6

BACK TO THE AMERICAN DREAM

Chapter 27
Homeward Bound for the United States

The next couple of years were filled with hard work. The mansion was a monster to take care of by myself; it was not appropriate to give housekeeping chores to my son. I cooked all our meals and enjoyed learning to prepare new Japanese dishes, and I still sewed new clothes for us and washed our clothes by hand.

Ray worked hard on the farm and in the garden. He studied gardening on his own, learned techniques, and returned the garden to its former splendor with hours of prepping and grooming. He took great pride in our showcase garden, which was hardly seen by many, since we almost never entertained. Ray still coughed some, but he looked much better. He continued to enjoy his evenings of drinking sake and gambling with the local men. The social life that my mom envisioned I would encounter never developed. The old order of Japan had now changed. After the war, nothing was as it had been before, according to Ray. But also, the stigma of Ray marrying an American woman never subsided.

Dr. Yamaguchi still lived with us, and after he got married in his hometown far north in Japan, he brought his lovely young wife to live with us also. The big addition to our household was a new television. Ray watched it much more than I did, since I was usually busy with my never-ending chores.

Despite owning the Konishi mansion, we weren't living as millionaires. I found myself teaching Ray about managing money and trying to explain tactfully how important it was to save it; from an early age, I'd learned how to do without, but Ray hadn't learned that lesson. Money had been handed to him ever since he was a young child. Now he was worried his health could fail and he could run out of money. We hired no help, and we certainly did not live a lavish lifestyle. I knew Ray lost money on occasion with his gambling, though I never knew how much, and I never asked.

Life in Japan was different in every way from what he'd expected. The Konishi mansion wasn't bustling with hired help and activity, as it had been in his youth. I only wore the gorgeous kimono he'd bought for me a handful of times to family events, with our modest lifestyle. Maybe others thought of us as millionaires, and this was how Ray wanted us to be viewed. He wasn't phony, pretentious, or trying to impress—neither of us were interested in behaving as aristocrats—but he feared looking like a failure and didn't want to be the subject of gossip for losing his father's fortune. The local people probably knew little about the forced land redistribution other than what the news reported since it didn't affect them. He worked as hard as the farmhands who had tilled the land when he was a child, and I in turn accepted the tall task of keeping the mansion tidy and clean; truly, we shared more in common with the working poor than the wealthy. I never lived the elegant life of wife to the rich man's son, which many of the girls at camp had envied, and Mom had feared would be my undoing.

After the initial years of American occupation of Japan, communism was infiltrating the Asian region. In 1949, the communists took over China, and civil war broke out in Korea in 1950. So it wasn't surprising when in 1952 Ray and I learned of a new treaty between the United States and Japan—they had become allies. This was welcome news for citizens of both countries. The occupation was over, and the former enemies were at peace. I dreamed every day of going home to America and to my family, although I didn't tell Ray how badly I wanted this. With this news, I wondered if we could regain our US citizenship.

Ray made a trip into Tokyo to see about something regarding his father's estate; while he was there, he stopped at the American embassy. He learned of rumors that President Eisenhower might send a ship to Japan to pick up the *Nisei* who wanted to return to America, but no one knew for sure. The only certainty was that anyone who wanted to return to America would need a passport. Ray didn't know if he and I could obtain them, since we'd both renounced our citizenship—and, of course, he'd been sent off to Santa Fe. The man at the embassy said many people came to him asking the same questions, but he had no answers.

The man at the embassy gave Ray a copy of an article about some women in the camp with us at Tule Lake who had renounced and were trying to regain their citizenship. The court said these women renounced "not as a result of their free and intelligent choice but rather because of mental fear, intimidation, and coercions depriving them of the free exercise of their will. . . . the conditions at Tule Lake amounted to unnecessarily cruel and inhuman treatment of these citizens." Reading about this case brought back a rash of memories and also gave me hope that maybe I could regain my citizenship too.

By then, life was much better than when I'd first arrived, but I still dealt with prejudice—subtler now, but still prevalent. We found no feeling of acceptance in our community; Norman encountered resentment at school, and even Ray was chastised for going to America, returning to take over his father's estate, and bringing along an American wife. Beyond facing prejudice, I was wearing myself out with cleaning, cooking, and caring for the family. Thinking about America made me more homesick than ever. Traveling around Japan had given me a fondness for its history, beauty, and culture, but I was an American and always would be.

After reading about the court case in America, I convinced Ray to contact an attorney to attempt the application process for reinstatement of our citizenship and passports. Ray emphasized that I shouldn't get my hopes up; he figured the odds were probably still quite remote. The attorney, Mr. Sakurai, was in Tokyo. It took Ray all day to navigate buses, trains, and sidewalks to get to Mr. Sakurai's office and then to return home.

Ray decided after the hassle of getting to his destination on this trip that it was time to learn to drive and get his own car. He found a driving class in Hiroshima, and when he got his license, he was excited. He bought a used car that made a lot of noise but putted along. Meanwhile, we waited to hear from Mr. Sakurai, who was checking all the channels and connections he had, searching for news of a possible return to America for the renouncers. He confirmed it would only be a formality to get Norman's passport, as he'd been only a child when he came to Japan and was therefore still a US citizen.

We carried on with our routines until a letter arrived. Mr. Sakurai had arranged for us to be interviewed at the American embassy as part of our application for reinstatement of our US citizenship. There would also be a physical exam. I could hardly wait for the date to arrive. I wanted to write to Mom and Pop about our appointment with the embassy, but if it didn't work out, they would be crushed, so I decided it was best to wait and write once I knew the outcome. My heart raced with the news.

Ray didn't trust his jalopy to make the drive to Tokyo, so we again took the train for the excursion. We arrived an hour early, just to be sure. During our appointment, we were questioned individually by the American official. My interview took much longer than Ray's. The interviewer told me how excellent my Japanese and English skills were and how much they needed translators with my competence. I smiled and explained to him about my years as the block manager, now an asterisk on my file. He offered me a job, which of course, I wasn't interested; I was only looking for a passport to go home. I wondered if he was kidding, but he did seem quite genuine, and it made me hope that he would surely recommend that my passport should be reinstated. Ray thought his interview was fine, as far as he could tell. Our physical took only a few minutes with a nurse and proceeded without incident, but Ray did tell her he'd been diagnosed some years back with tuberculosis. We both knew it was important to be honest about everything we were asked.

We returned home for the waiting game, but at least we'd started the process. Hope filled my thoughts. I so desperately wanted to go home.

In about six weeks' time, an envelope arrived stamped "Official Business." The return address was Embassy of the United States of America, Tokyo, Japan. My heart nearly jumped out of my chest. I was terrified to break the seal and peek into the envelope, so I waited for Ray to return from the farm. When I saw him, I called to him to come quickly. He raced into the house, and I handed him the envelope. We looked into each other's eyes and said nothing. Ray tore open the seal and dumped out the contents. First he picked up and opened a US passport for Norman Konishi; then he picked up another one for Janet Konishi.

"Really? Really?" I said. "Hooray, hooray!" I was overjoyed. Then it hit me: "Where is yours?"

All that remained was a folded piece of paper. Ray read the short letter, and his expression said it all as he handed it over: "Mr. Ray Konishi, we are sorry, but your request to restore your citizenship in the United States of America has been rejected."

That was it—rejection without explanation. My mood instantly changed from euphoria to despair. Ray put everything back in the envelope. "I will contact Mr. Sakurai to see if he can find out why I was rejected," he said. That was that, at least for now.

It was a gut-wrenching moment—Norman and I could go home, but Ray could not. We decided it would be best not to mention anything just now, to Norman or anyone else, about the passports until we learned the reasons for Ray's rejection. Thankfully, Norman was at school, so he missed the intensity of the moment.

Neither of us said any more about it until we were alone in our bedroom. "Why do you think you were rejected?" I asked. "Is it the tuberculosis? Could it be your pro-Japanese antics at Tule Lake? Being sent to Santa Fe—was that unforgivable? Did you say something you shouldn't have in the interview?" I thought to myself it was cruel of the authorities to allow me to return and not my husband.

We were both struggling to process the news. Ray was clueless as to the reason, but we both feared his radical behavior in the camps had doomed him to never become an American again. We hoped his lawyer could get some answers.

Mr. Sakurai followed up right away, which we appreciated; we learned the decision had been made by the US Department of State in Washington, DC. The local embassy in Japan had been informed of the decision, and they had no details to share. But they suspected it was the tuberculosis, as it was considered highly transmittable. The only shred of good news from the attorney was that Ray could reapply at a future date—not right away, but after some time—and request that the government change its mind. Mr. Sakurai also informed us that President Eisenhower was going to send a US Navy vessel to return US citizens to America at no charge. It was expected in the next six months.

Ray departed for our bedroom early in the evening. Norman, now eight, cleaned up and got to bed by eight, since it was a school night and he would be up quite early in the morning. I joined Ray, who was lying on the bed with his eyes closed.

"Are you okay?" I asked.

He sat up quickly. "Janet, I have been such a failure as your husband," he muttered. "I got sent off to Santa Fe and left you with a newborn. Then I expected you to come join me in Japan, and I should have known I was bringing you and Norman into a dangerous, even deadly situation. I was being selfish, because I love you and couldn't imagine living without you. Then I sent you back to the house with Kaito for those days of hell she brought on you. Then we endured months upon months of scrounging for food and worrying day to day about our own survival. I dreamed of the day when you would live like a queen in Japan with everything my father left me, but the reality is you have worked endlessly keeping up with this home. And you have been hated as an American, just as your mom warned you. You are the kindest person I have ever known—how could anyone not see that? How could anyone be rude to you? And you have never complained. You have always been at my side. You don't even complain about my gambling and drinking nights. I don't know how lucky I was to find you," shaking his head in disbelief. "I love you."

He paused, and then he broke down crying. "I just know I'm not worthy. I want you and Norman to get on the ship for America and, when you get there, find a lawyer and file for a divorce from me. You are still young, and you will make another man the happiest man in the world, like you have done for me. I may not live long with the TB; there's no reason for you to stay here any longer. I have already put you through too much."

All I could do was reach over and hold him close in my arms. After a minute, I pulled back and looked him in the eye. "Ray, no one ever told me it would be easy. I didn't marry you for your millions, although I know many others would have. You never intended for me to be hurt by anything you did—it just happened. You are my husband. I love you, and I will not divorce you. But I *am* going to go home to America—now that Norman is eight years old, I know it's important to get him started in American schools; an American education is his hope for the future. And I miss my family; it's been almost nine years since I saw them. It's time for all of us to leave Japan. The lawyer told you to reapply; surely, in time, when you tell them your wife and son are in America waiting for you, they will take pity on you. I will wait for you—you have my word on that."

Ray's eyes glazed over. "Thank you darling. I don't deserve you. I love you with all my heart. I agree we must get Norman in American schools as soon as possible, but I'm worried about how you will survive once you get to America. I know you can live with your family, but how will you support yourself? What if you can only find work as a housekeeper? What if you can't find work?"

I shook my head. "Please don't worry yourself about me finding work. Maybe they'll need translators in St. Louis. Or maybe I can teach classes in sewing. We'll be safe and fed with my family. Don't worry about me having money—I don't need much."

"Of course, I have no doubt. I just feel like such a failure. You were supposed to live like royalty with me, and you'll be going to America with nothing. It makes me sad. How long will we be apart? The last time was over a year, and I could hardly bear it."

"It will all work out in time—we have to count on that. Norman and I will be fine, and we will wait for you."

As I finished, we hugged even tighter and slid onto the bed together. Neither of us wanted to let go. I wrestled with so much raw emotion contemplating our future lives with many uncertainties. I told Ray to recall *gaman*—we needed to have patience and carry on with dignity again.

When I slipped into bed that evening, I could be alone with my thoughts. I knew I wasn't the same person I'd been when I married Ray. At that time, I wouldn't have had the will to leave Ray and return to America; I would have stayed with him, even if it meant I might never return to America. Through everything I'd experienced, I had gained courage to do the right thing: I needed to leave the place that didn't want me, and I needed to get Norman home to an American education. I knew the women of this village, immersed in the traditional male-dominated Japanese culture, would never leave their husbands for a trip across the world. For that matter, many American women, friends from my youth, would have been too overwhelmed to take a trip across the world without their husbands. But I did not hesitate—I needed and wanted to go.

I thought about Ray, who had also changed through the years. On top of growing up in Japan's male-centered culture, he was a rich man's once-proud son, so his confession was startling; he had already apologized for his activities that sent him to Santa Fe, and now he'd mustered the courage to understand his own failings through the years and apologize for acting selfishly rather than trying to protect me. Further, he hadn't begged me to stay, as much as I knew he wanted to. Ray, as the head of our household, for the first time was putting my feelings ahead of his. He supported my decision to leave.

Mr. Sakurai notified us he'd reserved two places for Norman and me to depart Tokyo Harbor for the United States on the SS *President Wilson* in March 1953. We used new suitcases to pack for the long voyage across the Pacific; I left my handmade duffel bag—empty but full of memories—behind. I wrote letters to my jubilant family with as much as I knew of the details. Norman and I would have a day layover in Honolulu, so Loretta would meet us at the dock there; then Christine and her husband would pick us up when we docked in San Francisco, and we would visit with them for a couple of weeks before taking the long train trip to St. Louis, Missouri, and our new home.

Loretta was a mother to two sons now, and Christine had four daughters. I would even get to see Will and maybe his wife, now expecting their second child, in Tokyo. Will was still serving in the US Army.

I couldn't wait for the day of our departure. Norman was also excited to be going to America, the country of his birth; however, it was excruciating for him to leave his pets behind—he adored his dog and kitty cat. Ray promised to take excellent care of them, and he promised that when he came to America, he would first find them a good home. I understood how hard this was for Norman, and I remembered the days before we'd been forced into the Stockton Assembly Center, when so many of my friends had to abandon their pets. They'd endured the double horror of saying goodbye and desperately searching for a home for their beloveds. Maybe Norman would return to Japan in time to see his pets again; if not, he understood his pets would have a good home.

A week before our scheduled departure, Ray, wanting to give Norman and me a proper send-off, invited the extended family and a couple of friends for a party at the mansion. None of the guests were Americans, but they were gracious and wished me well. They probably didn't understand the deep feeling of joy in my soul that

I was going home. I could hardly wait. Everyone seemed to enjoy themselves at the party, and I appreciated this loving gesture from Ray; I knew he felt the same gut-wrenching uncertainty that I felt over not knowing when or if he would be allowed to reinstate his US citizenship.

Finally, my wait was over: we would leave the next day for the United States. That evening, we ate our last meal together as a family for who knew how long. At bedtime, I put on the silk lingerie Ray had purchased for me upon my arrival in Tokyo. I'd also found some incense in the market, and I lit it. As hard as it was to say goodbye, I was hoping to make our last night memorable for Ray. He hadn't smiled once all day, but now he did. During this last time together in Japan, he was filled with passion; his hands and fingers touched every inch of my silken attire. I knew he wanted the moment and the feelings—the night—to never end. He kept asking, "How long do you think I'll have to wait to join you in America?" He knew there was no answer—and no guarantee he would ever be allowed to return to America. We both finally fell asleep contemplating living apart once more.

Morning came quickly. As I prepared to leave the house, I thought about the past few years. During my time in Japan, I'd met some Japanese who were kind to me—though these were few and far between—and I'd enjoyed meeting my parents' and Ray's extended family members. Overall, however, my years in Japan had been extraordinarily difficult, to say the least—but they'd been hard for the Japanese, too. We'd all faced the end of World War II together. I'd endured days, weeks, and months when I'd wondered whether I would survive the famine, and I'd lost almost all energy to carry on, to find reason for hope. But I'd refused to internalize the hatred directed toward me and my family by those who despised us (me) for being Americans, and instead, I'd learned to respect the beauty, history, and culture of my ancestors. Maybe in the future, I would return as a visitor; maybe then I could truly enjoy Japan.

We would catch the first train of the day from Hiroshima to Tokyo, followed by the bus to the harbor. I clutched our two passports and put them safely in my purse. Our connections went smoothly; only Will waited for us at the ship's dock, since his wife wasn't feeling well. It was great to see him. Ray's camera was ready to record our departure, and we took pictures on the dock. We'd previously discussed that we wouldn't show a big display of emotion when we separated—it was the Japanese way. Ray told his son to be the number-one student in his new school, just as he'd been the last two years. Norman gave his dad a big hug, and then Ray turned to me, told me he loved me, and hugged me, clearly not wanting to let go. I could feel his grief as he embraced me with all his might.

Sadness set in as I turned and walked away; I had to trust everything would work out in time. On the ship's deck, I looked down at Ray before we departed; he looked so alone, standing there and waving at us. We hadn't cast off yet, but it seemed we were already thousands of miles apart. Ray took photos of us climbing the gangway, which he would send to us later; I also sent Ray a picture of us on the deck taken by a friendly man before we departed. We were given streamers to throw, and the scene was quite festive. I waved until we were out of sight—waving goodbye to both Ray and Japan after seven long years. I was overjoyed to think I would soon see Mom and Pop, whom I hadn't seen since I'd left Camp Rohwer over nine years earlier.

Thankfully, our accommodations on the naval vessel were better than on our last voyage. The room of hammocks and snoring men was gone. Now there were rooms with two or three double beds; Norman and I shared one. There was a community bathroom in the hallway, though, again, it had no shower. For our first meal, they served a green salad and beef stroganoff with mashed sweet potatoes and rolls. I looked at the sweet potatoes and couldn't eat one bite; I doubted I would ever eat a sweet potato again—my memories of eating them were just too painful. But everything else was tasty. The sea was calmer this time of year, so I wasn't seasick. I was jubilant to be going home; I knew each hour that passed was an hour closer to arriving home to my America.

During our layover in Hawaii, we enjoyed a fabulous visit with Loretta; she and I were thrilled to meet each other's sons. In San Francisco, John met us at the pier, and we spent several wonderful days with Christine and her daughters. She said she wished she had a son, and I told her how lucky she was to have her daughters. We had some good laughs and reminisced about our days sleeping together in Stockton. Norman enjoyed meeting his cousins, aunts, and uncles, though he didn't speak English terribly well and they didn't speak Japanese well. Finally, we boarded the train bound for St. Louis. I didn't know what to expect in our new city; all I knew was I would soon see my siblings and beloved parents.

When the whistle blew and the conductor hollered for Union Station St. Louis, we gathered our bags and waited patiently at the top of the stairs between the entrances to the railcars. After the train screeched to a halt, the conductor opened the door and put down a stepstool to assist everyone.

There they were on the platform: Mom, Pop, Marian and her new husband, Fran, Ed, and Tom. My tears gushed forth. I hugged everyone and then hugged them all again, and everyone hugged Norman, who looked like he didn't know what hit him. I felt immeasurable relief, joy, and peace. Every part of me came from Mom and Pop; they'd even helped save my life in Japan. I thought I must pinch myself to believe this reunion was finally happening. After seven long years of separation, I was rejoined with my family and once again a proud citizen and resident of the United States of America.

Chapter 28
World War II Finale

We climbed on the bus, still talking. Our letters over the years couldn't compare to being together and hearing everyone's stories in person.

As I looked at each member of my family, I could tell how many years had passed since I'd seen them last. Pop was almost sixty-eight and still landscaping full time; he still appeared strong and durable. Mom had just turned fifty-six and clearly put on weight as she passed through menopause. They were both older in face and body, but their spirits soared, just as I remembered. Fran was now twenty-five, and she told me of a sweetheart, another *Nisei*, her honey. "Great news!" I replied happily. My two little brothers were both teenagers, Tom sixteen and Ed fourteen. I couldn't believe how much of their lives I'd missed. Ed even confessed he didn't remember me well, since he'd been just five when Ray and I had departed for Tule Lake. Norman didn't say much at first; it was probably too much to take in.

We arrived at the Hayashi family home on Semple Street. It was like the other houses on the block, with about eight stairs leading to the front door. On the main floor, it had a living room, dining room, kitchen, and partial bath; upstairs housed a full bath and three bedrooms. There was also an unfinished cellar. My family all offered their rooms for Norman and me; I was touched by their joy to be living together again. Fran turned over her bedroom and double bed to us.

"It's no problem to sleep on the pull-out couch, especially when I don't have to share it with anyone," she said. We laughed, remembering our old days of sleeping together.

Mom prepared a feast for our homecoming, complete with many of my favorites. When Mom brought out the dishes, she also put two letters from Ray on my plate. He'd written the first before we left Japan, to be sure it would be waiting for us. In that letter, he wrote how much he missed me—then confessed he was looking at me as he wrote it. I smiled. He'd written the other letter after we left, telling me how quiet it was living alone in the Konishi mansion. He also said he dreaded doing his own cooking and cleaning.

I felt spoiled living with Mom and Pop again. Mom prepared dishes from my childhood, and they seemed to taste even better now. I wanted to help out any way I could, but all my family wanted me to do was relax and visit as much as possible. From my letters home, Mom and Pop knew how desperate our situation had been when there was precious little food—that when I'd been so gaunt and weak, I'd had to crawl on the floor; if I'd perished without telling them how difficult things were, it would have hurt them terribly. Mom also knew how I'd been treated by the Japanese in Hatsukaichi, which she'd fully anticipated and desperately tried to warn me about. But she'd never dwelled on my poor decision to go to Japan after the war; she'd just tried to help by sending boxes with rice, chocolate, hard candies, and coffee. I did tell Mom I didn't think I could ever face eating another sweet potato, and she fully understood: none of the Hayashis had eaten any pork and beans or Spam since leaving camp. Mom was exuberant about our safe return, and she couldn't get enough of Norman. She'd finally met her first grandson.

After dinner, we walked to the school Norman would be attending. My family showed me the bus stop, which wasn't too far from my new home. Before I went to bed, I wrote Ray about our arrival; I'd already sent him a letter from Christine's home.

On Norman's first day of school, he and I arrived early and met with the assistant principal. Norman's language skills consisted of spoken and written Japanese and limited oral English, so he would need to start out in kindergarten. We both understood, but I knew it was hard to be an eight-year-old and walk into class with the five-year-olds. No one was rude, and Norman caught on quickly, also working on English at home. In a short time, he moved to first grade, then to second grade. By the summer recess, he'd made it all the way back to third grade. He was years ahead in math skills, and his English was progressing quickly.

Once I knew Norman could walk back and forth to school by himself, I started looking for a job. Fran knew of an employment agency, so I set out. Friendly people greeted me when I walked in the door. After a brief wait, I was asked to take an exam. I didn't know shorthand, but I told them I was good with figures. After I'd completed the exam and waited for the lady to review it, she asked me to step into her office. She said I hadn't missed any of the math questions, so she thought I might be a good candidate for a bookkeeping position. I told her I'd taken bookkeeping in high school, so I would be a good fit. She escorted me to the door and said she would contact me when she found a placement for me.

I returned home and told Mom. Soon, Norman walked in the door for lunch; of course, his grandma was waiting with lunch prepared for him. They both enjoyed hearing about my trip to the employment agency.

Within two days, the lady offered me a position at the N. O. Nelson Manufacturing Company, an industrial supplier. I would be paid twice a month. "They will expect you in the morning," she said. She gave me directions and their address, and I realized I could get there using two buses. I couldn't believe it had happened that fast—I was starting a new job in my new city!

That evening, I wrote Ray a letter with the details. I told him I would write again after my first day on the job, but then I would probably be able to write only once a week, since I would have long days working from eight to five and commuting both ways.

My first day went fabulously. I met everyone in the small office and learned about my job. I was in charge of preparing the deposit for the bank and taking it every day—a task well suited for me. In a few weeks' time, I would be given the accounts-payable responsibility. I knew right away I'd found a job to my liking, and I couldn't believe my good fortune to be working so quickly. Plus, Mom was at home to take care of Norman's lunches and be with him after school; it was a relief to know Mom was home if Norman became ill.

We settled into our new lives quickly. Norman looked up to his Uncle Tom and Uncle Ed and was interested in anything they were doing, although they were teenagers and busy with plenty of activities at their school and hours of homework every week. Whenever the family was all together, I answered many questions about Japan. Pop and Mom were especially pleased we'd visited their extended families, and I'd brought some pictures to share. I knew Ray would be visiting the Hayashi business again to help them out.

Soon it was Easter. Though we weren't Christian, we still celebrated. We dressed up and went to Forest Park, where there was a free zoo and an Easter egg hunt. Norman thought it great fun to run all over Art Hill looking for the treats. I was impressed with my new home; St. Louis was beautiful as spring erupted with daffodils dotting the landscape, and blooming trees everywhere.

The next letter from Ray contained bad news. I knew he was concerned about our finances, but now he said we were almost broke. With little income from the farm and so many expenses and taxes for the mansion, he was running out of cash. His plan was to sell all his property once he knew he could return to America. If he sold his father's estate now, it would be a huge humiliation for him; everyone would guess he'd run out of money, and to suffer that embarrassment would be crushing. The doctor living with us never paid anything aside from taking care of Ray, as Ray and I both thought it was important to help him out. I knew Ray lost money gambling, but I didn't think it was significant. When he'd given away most of the land, he'd lost the benefit of selling the crop to generate cash for maintenance of the property and paying the taxes. I wrote him back and told him I would send him a little money out of my paycheck. Since starting my new job, I was helping Mom and Pop with expenses, but I could do without, and maybe sending him a little would help him. This certainly wasn't the financial situation in which any of us had expected Ray to end up.

I awoke one chilly morning to a horrible toothache. I couldn't remember how many years it had been since I'd gone to a dentist, but I was planning on finding a new one in St. Louis for myself and Norman. When I walked into work and told the general manager how I felt, he sent me home to find a dentist. He couldn't believe I'd come to work in that kind of pain, but I'd never taken a sick day and didn't want to break that record.

Luckily, I found a dentist nearby who could see me right away. After an x-ray and a look at my teeth, he told me he was sorry to give me the news, but my teeth were all rotting. One by one, I would lose them all eventually. Surprised about how degenerated my teeth were at my young age, he asked about the last five to ten years of my life. I explained about my years in Japan, surviving a famine and nursing Norman through the many long months while enduring poor nutrition. The only solution was to pull all my teeth. I was just thirty-five years old, now destined to wear dentures.

The next few years fell into a comfortable routine for us. My job went well; I was complimented on the accuracy of everything I did. Norman made straight As. Tom graduated from Soldan High School in 1955 and was drafted into the army. Ed graduated in 1956. Fran was married and living close by. I sent money every month to Ray from my paychecks. He was appreciative of this little bit which he easily converted to yen, and said it made all the difference to him. He was proud that Norman was doing so well in school. Meanwhile, Mr. Sakurai continued to tell Ray it wasn't yet the right time to apply for reinstatement of his US citizenship.

How special it was to see old friends from Stockton and camp days; I became acquainted with many other *Nisei* who settled in the St. Louis area. There was a Japanese Women's Club that met every month, and I tried to make the meetings if possible with my work schedule. Sometimes, there were picnics in the park for the Japanese. I felt a real sense of community I hadn't felt since before the war. Not once did I feel any resentment for being Japanese—what a sense of relief it was to just fit in the world again. St. Louis welcomed me by paying no particular attention to me, which meant treating me and my family like regular members of society. I just blended in with the world, a comfortable anonymity I hadn't felt since before Pearl Harbor, when I was selling movie tickets at Mrs. Arakawa's theater. It seemed those years of my youth were a lifetime ago.

Meanwhile, Ray's letters arrived like clockwork. I knew he missed me terribly. "It's so hard for me to function in every way," he wrote, "because I have lost half of myself. How I ache for you day and night. I never dreamed we would be apart for so long."

Our smooth lives in St. Louis suffered a terrible jolt in 1956 when Mom had a stroke. She survived but was quite limited afterward. Now Norman came home for lunch and fed Grandma. I tried to keep watermelon in the house when it was in season, and I would slice it up before leaving in the morning so that after school, Norman and Grandma could eat their watermelon together. It was difficult for everyone to see Mom so debilitated. I bathed her and tried to help any way I could. She was just fifty-nine years old; we could see her slipping away.

In 1958, we lost Mom. For her, it was for the best, as her life had become unbearable without the ability to do anything for herself. Pop was heartbroken to lose her but relieved she no longer suffered. I loved Mom, who always put her children first; she'd taught me patience and tolerance and made me strong in her image. I'd often needed that strength to persevere when I thought I couldn't carry on. I respected Mom's keen intellect and trusted her completely; I knew it would be hard for me now when I needed advice. During her last few years, I was grateful to be there to help her when she needed it. As the eldest daughter, I was now the matriarch of the Hayashi family, and I felt the responsibility for Pop and for my own son. I never would have imagined when Ray said goodbye to Mom as we left Camp Rohwer in 1944, he would never see her again—after all, she was the reason I'd told Ray no and then yes to getting married. I hoped Ray could return to America soon.

We decided to move, because we all missed Mom terribly and felt her all over our home. We rented a ranch-style home in a neighboring community called Pine Lawn for ten dollars per month and found friends to help with our move. Pop, at seventy-three, was still working, though not as many hours. He could cover the rent, and I told him I could cover the household expenses with my paychecks. Norman would finish his junior and senior years of high school at Normandy High, one of the finest in the state. My boss was a good man, and most days he drove me to work, since I wasn't too far out of his way.

The decade changed, and 1960 arrived. It was hard to believe almost seven years had elapsed since I'd left Japan. One day, a letter arrived from Ray—this time with thrilling and hopeful news: Mr. Sakurai had heard the United States was softening its reluctance to regrant citizenship to the remaining renouncers. By 1959, a total of 5,409 renouncers had applied for reinstatement, and 4,987 requests were granted. Of course, Ray was one of the 422 who were rejected. Ray was leaving in two days for another appointment with the US embassy. I knew by the time I got the letter, he'd already been, so I couldn't wait for the next letter.

Three days later, another letter arrived. "Fingers crossed," Ray wrote. He thought everything had gone well and that the nurse wasn't concerned about the TB, which hadn't been active in years. Although no one ever confirmed this, we always believed his tuberculosis was the reason his initial passport request had been rejected and his attorney had advised him to wait so long to reapply. I received many more letters from Ray, but none mentioned the passport issue—it was the waiting game all over again. Then I opened yet another one-page letter, and a few lines leapt right off the page: "My passport has arrived! Hooray! I have to make my own arrangements and pay for my passage to America. I've put the home and remaining pieces of my estate up for sale. It won't be long now, my love."

We were all excited. I could hardly believe Ray was really coming soon.

Japan's economy began to take off in the 1960s, so the sale of Ray's property was a matter of perfect timing. He put all the money from the transaction in the bank in Japan and purchased his ticket for the next ship to San Francisco. By then, Kaito had four children, and though she kept only necessary minimal contact with Ray, he told me he wanted to help her children—they were his father's grand-children, along with Norman. When they came of age, he planned to use the cash from the sale to buy each one of them a home. The rest would be for our travel when we visited Japan, and then whatever was left would belong to Norman. All that made sense to me, too.

Beyond excitement over the news, I felt a sense of apprehension about the years elapsed since we'd lived together. What if Ray arrived in St. Louis, decided he didn't like it, and wanted me to go back to Japan with him? What if he couldn't find work in St. Louis? Would he get frustrated? Would he feel resentful toward America for all the years he'd waited to be reinstated as a citizen? What if he didn't feel the same about me now? What if I didn't feel the same about him? Would he be comfortable living with Pop and Ed? Would Ray annoy them? Who would be the alpha male in our home? Was he healthy? Would he be happy? Would everyone get along? How could it not be somewhat strained after so long?

I had time to think about all these things, but I said nothing to anyone about my worries; I probably would have talked to Mom about it, but she was gone. All I could do was be the same old Janet and hope for the best. With my family around, I didn't plan a big romantic homecoming. By then, Norman was sleeping in a twin bed in Ed's bedroom, so Ray would join me in the double bed in my room. I knew Ray would be floored that his son, now a teenager, was taller than he was.

Ray visited with Loretta and her family in Hawaii and with Christine and John in California for a couple of days before heading to St. Louis. Ed, Pop, Norman, and I all stood on the concrete train platform when his train arrived. As Ray departed the carriage, he looked like the happiest man in America—a US citizen once more, reunited with his family. He hugged everyone, the smile I knew only too well plastered on his face. We embraced, and he touched my cheek and looked into my eyes as he whispered, "I love you." The men helped Ray with his bags, and we took the bus home to Pine Lawn.

World War II was finally over for Ray and me; it had lasted almost twenty years. Finally, we could be a family again, living peacefully in America. Ray and I were forty-one years old. Our twenties and thirties had been anything but youthful, carefree times, and although we'd been married for over seventeen years, we hadn't lived together for even half that time. Luckily, neither of us was bitter or angry at anyone or any country. Mom and Pop deserved the credit for teaching me to hold no grudges or resentment; I think I helped Ray to also accept life that way. *Gaman* was in our hearts through all those years.

As we walked into our cozy little rented home, Ray grabbed my hand and squeezed it tightly. "I will never let go of you again," he said.

I smiled at my admiring husband; his love for me hadn't changed since that first time he'd asked me to marry him. We had faced bumps in the road, and I knew we would face more—that was part of life. But now, it was 1961, and finally we could live our own happily ever after.

Epilogue

My job with N. O. Nelson Company—which eventually became Dapsco—lasted until I retired at sixty-five in 1985, after working there for thirty-two years. In 1975, Dapsco hired an intern named Judy. We became lifelong friends. She is the one who has put words to my story.

After arriving in St. Louis, Ray worked for a landscape designer for several years. With my encouragement, he eventually opened his own landscape business specializing in Japanese gardens. Over the years, Ray gained many loyal customers who treasured his expertise. In one more ironic twist, the son of a rich man who had grown up with gardeners working tirelessly at his family estate became the gardener to members of the August Busch family of Anheuser-Busch fame.

Eventually, Ray and I bought our own home in the suburb of Manchester, where he enjoyed planting his garden every year. Based on the laws of the 1920s, Mom and Pop were never allowed to own property in America or officially become American citizens. But this was never of concern to them. Pop was able to take two sentimental trips back to Japan to visit his extended family. He lived the rest of his nearly ninety years with Ray and me.

Norman earned a full scholarship to Washington University in St. Louis, where he majored in physics and philosophy, and then he went on to earn master's degrees in both computer science and particle physics.

Eventually, government hearings were held on the internment of Japanese Americans in World War II to investigate all phases of this action and how we'd been treated. President Reagan signed a law that entitled every former living internee to be compensated twenty thousand dollars each; each also received a letter of apology from President Reagan. Even Norman, only an infant at the time of internment, received his wartime remuneration.

Ray had insisted I retire so we could travel more, and we took an extended trip to Europe and many others to Japan. We enjoyed the Japanese clubs in St. Louis and volunteered extensively in the Japanese Garden at the Missouri Botanical Garden. This masterpiece, still considered one of the most beautiful Japanese gardens outside Japan, was a gift to St. Louis for welcoming the tired and dejected Japanese at the end of WWII. Ray's love for me never changed: all he ever wanted was to be with me. If I wasn't going somewhere, my doting husband wasn't, either. That was my Ray.

Sadly, my beloved Ray passed away in 1993, close to our fiftieth wedding anniversary. The doctor was baffled about what had taken his life; it wasn't the tuberculosis he had feared for so long. In the autopsy, the doctors discovered Ray's organs were child sized; they hadn't matured properly in his youth. Despite his father's riches, Ray's poor diet in his early years had impacted his life. We had encountered many ironies together; this was a final sad irony in Ray's life.

Often, I have been asked to tell my internment camp story. I have been interviewed by grade schoolers, middle schoolers, high schoolers, university students, university faculty, and book clubs, and I have always tried to give my time freely when asked. It has never been hard for me to share, because these memories are not something I try to forget or deny; I am not angry about or ashamed of them. Over the years, through all the interviews, I've shared many stories and answered many questions, but I knew it was not the whole story.

Now it is all here—my American story.

Bibliography

Blakemore, Erin. "The Brutal History of Japan's 'Comfort Women.'" History.com, February 20, 2018. https://www.history.com/news/comfort-women-japan-military-brothels-korea.

DeWitt, J. L. *Civilian Exclusion Order No. 1*. San Francisco: Western Defense Command and Fourth Army, 1942. http://digitalassets.lib.berkeley.edu/jarda/ucb/text/cubanc6714_b016b01_0001_1.pdf.

———. *Civilian Exclusion Order No. 53*. San Francisco: Western Defense Command and Fourth Army, 1942. Accessed online through javadc.org. http://www.javadc.org/java/docs/1942-05-07%3B%20WDC%20%20Civilian%20Exclusion%20Order%20No.53,p4_dg%3Bay.pdf.

———. *Western Defense Command Public Proclamation No. 1*. San Francisco: Western Defense Command and Fourth Army, 1942. Accessed online through the University of Washington digital collection. http://cdm16786.contentdm.oclc.org/cdm/ref/collection/pioneerlife/id/15329.

Gutierrez, Lisa. "'A rain of ruin': Watch Truman announce the Hiroshima atomic bomb." *Kansas City Star*, updated August 8, 2017. https://www.kansascity.com/news/nation-world/article30215037.html.

Kashima, Tetsuden. "Custodial detention / A-B-C list." Densho Encyclopedia, 2018. http://encyclopedia.densho.org/Custodial_detention_/_A-B-C_list/#Custodial_Detention_Program.

Kennedy, Ellen Clare. "The Japanese-American Renunciants: Due Process and the Danger of Making Laws During Times of Fear." JPRI working papers, Japan Policy Research Institute, October 2006. http://www.jpri.org/publications/workingpapers/wp110.html.

"Renunciation Act of 1944." Infogalactic.com. Updated June 1, 2016. https://infogalactic.com/info/Renunciation_Act_of_1944.

Retonel, Mark Erick A. "Hayashi Ichizo: Inspiring Kamikaze, a Suicide Bomber." *Just Typical M.E.* (blog). March 26, 2015. https://premear111.wordpress.com/tag/hayashi-ichizo/.

Roosevelt, Franklin D. "A date which will live in infamy" speech. December 8, 1941. Accessed online through George Mason University's *History Matters: The US Survey Course on the Web*. http://historymatters.gmu.edu/d/5166.

————. "Executive Order 9066—Authorizing the Secretary of War to Prescribe Military Areas." 1942. Accessed online through *The American Presidency Project*. http://www.presidency.ucsb.edu/ws/index.php?pid=61698.

————. "Regulations Pertaining to Alien Enemies, Proclamation 2537." *Federal Register* 7, no. 12 (1942): 329. Accessed online through the Library of Congress digital collection. http://cdn.loc.gov/service/ll/fedreg/fr007/fr007012/fr007012.pdf.

Slavin, Erik. "Would Japan have surrendered without the atomic bombings?" *Stars and Stripes*, August 5, 2015. https://www.stripes.com/news/special-reports/world-war-ii-the-final-chapter/wwii-victory-in-japan/would-japan-have-surrendered-without-the-atomic-bombings-1.360300.

At home in Stockton before the war

Senior high school photo

My scrapbook; the government called it *relocation* so I did too.

Photo from Camp Rohwer

The block manager leaving the office

At Camp Rohwer, wearing a sweater I'd knitted for myself

Precious Mom & Pop

New clothes I made for Mom and myself

Our wedding day

I had just finished making this pink-and-white polka dotted dress. Ray and I as newlyweds.

Ray the fireman

Ray's ID Card from the Sante Fe Internment Camp

Baby Norman & me

Visiting my brother Will in Japan

Traveling in Japan

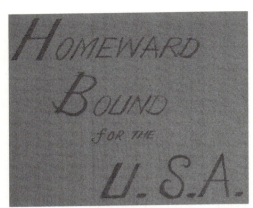

My scrapbook—the cover says it all.

Boarding the ship for the US—an excruciating goodbye

Happily ever after as middle-aged Americans

Made in the USA
Monee, IL
22 July 2023

39708802R00171